The Gen X Series

ENGLISH OLYMPIAD 8

Useful for English Olympiads Conducted at School, National & International Levels

Author
Sahil Gupta

Peer Reviewer
P. Shyamla

Strictly According to the Latest Syllabus of English Olympiad

Published by:

F-2/16, Ansari road, Daryaganj, New Delhi-110002
☎ 23240026, 23240027 • *Fax:* 011-23240028
✉ info@vspublishers.com • 🌐 www.vspublishers.com

  Online Brandstore: amazon.in/vspublishers

Regional Office : Hyderabad
5-1-707/1, Brij Bhawan (Beside Central Bank of India Lane)
Bank Street, Koti, Hyderabad - 500 095
☎ 040-24737290
✉ vspublishershyd@gmail.com

Follow us on:

BUY OUR BOOKS FROM: | AMAZON | FLIPKART |

© Copyright: *V&S PUBLISHERS*
ISBN 978-93-579407-6-4
New Edition

DISCLAIMER

While every attempt has been made to provide accurate and timely information in this book, neither the author nor the publisher assumes any responsibility for errors, unintended omissions or commissions detected therein. The author and publisher makes no representation or warranty with respect to the comprehensiveness or completeness of the contents provided.

All matters included have been simplified under professional guidance for general information only, without any warranty for applicability on an individual. Any mention of an organization or a website in the book, by way of citation or as a source of additional information, doesn't imply the endorsement of the content either by the author or the publisher. It is possible that websites cited may have changed or removed between the time of editing and publishing the book.

Results from using the expert opinion in this book will be totally dependent on individual circumstances and factors beyond the control of the author and the publisher.

It makes sense to elicit advice from well informed sources before implementing the ideas given in the book. The reader assumes full responsibility for the consequences arising out from reading this book.

For proper guidance, it is advisable to read the book under the watchful eyes of parents/guardian. The buyer of this book assumes all responsibility for the use of given materials and information.

The copyright of the entire content of this book rests with the author/publisher. Any infringement/transmission of the cover design, text or illustrations, in any form, by any means, by any entity will invite legal action and be responsible for consequences thereon.

Publisher's Note

General Trade and Mass Appeal books across various genres have helped **V&S Publishers** to gain widespread popularity. In a short span of 10 years, we have successfully published more than 1000 titles across 9 languages in our 50 subject categories. Being into the publishing business for about 40 years, we have always been a dynamic publishing house, with a massive distribution network, across India; including E-commerce platforms.

Understanding the need of inculcating knowledge and developing a spirit of healthy competition amongst students to make them ready for the world outside schools and colleges; we created Olympiad Series under the **GEN X SERIES Imprint** which, owning to its rich content and unique representation became popular amongst students, in no time. The motivation is not to improve marks in terms of numbers, but is to make sure that the students are already prepared to face competitive environment with respect to college admissions and cracking various entrance examinations, while ensuring their conceptual clarity.

Published for classes 1-10 across subjects English, Mathematics, Science, Computers, General Knowledge, the books are unlike any other in the market and are written in a guidebook pattern and exhaustively include examples and Multiple-Choice Questions.

Here, we present the latest Edition of **ENGLISH OLYMPIAD CLASS 8.**

Unique Features of the book are as follows:

- Authored by Subject Matter Experts' and Peer reviewed by School Principals and HOD's for the respective subjects
- Books based on principles of Applied Psychology and Bloom's Taxonomy
- Suited for Olympiad Examinations held at School level, National level & International Level irrespective of organizing body.
- The only Olympiad Book in India written in Guidebook Pattern with Concise Theory, images and illustrations.
- Exhaustively include Examples, MCQs, Subjective Questions, and HOTS with Answer Keys & Solutions.
- Multiple Model Papers for thorough practice also given inside the book with solutions.
- OMR sheets appended at the end of the book for simulating exam environment.

Besides, we are also planning to launch an App very soon for the Olympiad preparation which further testifies our constant endeavor to keep up with student demands. We have made sure to closely follow syllabus patterns of not only Olympiad conducting bodies but also education boards & organizations like CBSE and NCERT, to make sure that our books prove useful to students; helping them to boost their academic performance in schools as well.

P.S. While every care has been taken to ensure the correctness of the content, if you come across any error, howsoever minor, do not hesitate to discuss with teachers while pointing that out to us in no uncertain terms.

We wish you All the Best!

DISTINCTIVE

WHY OLYMPIADS?
Olympiads are just like competitive exams; conducted by various bodies at national and international levels. The aim is to experience a competitive examination at the school level and also to help students to discover their interest acrss subjects like English, Mathematics, Science and General Knowledge.

WHY V&S OLYMPIADS?
We at V&S Publishers aim to build an avid-reading student audience. Hence, our resolve is to follow an innovative pedagogic pattern which would help students to navigate through the book with utmost ease and comfort. Crisp theory practical examples and illustrations keep our book interactive and comprehensive.

01 LEARNING OBJECTIVES
They list the whole chapter as subtopics, helping the teachers to guide children in a step-by-step manner.

02 DID YOU KNOW
Enhance your knowledge by getting acquainted with some amazing facts across various subjects like science, Mathematics and English.

03 MULTIPLE CHOICE QUESTIONS
MCQs act as an excellent learning aid, helping you to understand and work on your mistakes.

04 THINGS TO REMEMBER
A quick recap of the chapter in a summarized format helps in faster revision along with conceptual clarity.

05 HOTS
The High Order Thinking Questions aim to help the student to solve Application-based questions and gain practical understanding of the subject.

FEATURES

06 SUBJECTIVE QUESTIONS
Help to place the knowledge gained in orderly fashion by using "WH" questions, mostly in the form of bullet points.

07 ACHIEVER'S SECTION
Offers a quick revision of the book along with some new facts for the students to discover.

08 A SET OF OMR SHEETS
To allow the student to practice question in an exam-like format which would help them to get the "feel" of how Olympiad exams take place.

09 MODEL TEST PAPERS
Two model test papers are provided at the end of each book, which help the student to test the knowledge which they have gained after thorough reading of all chapters.

10 ANSWER KEY & SOLUTIONS
Detailed Answer Key along with explanations aid the pupil to indentify, understand the mistakes they make during the course of Olympiad preparation.

COMPLEMENT SCHOOL SYLLABI
The syllabi across all Olympiad examination closely follow the pattern of academic books. Hence, they not only provide a competitive examination experience, but also help to revise topics for school examinations as well, while strengthening conceptual precision.

ENHANCEMENT OF ANALYTICAL & LOGICAL REASONING
Practicing analytical ability questions, not only helps in developing intellectual ability but also plays a vital role in building critical thinking ability which helps an individual to think about a question or a crisis like situation in day to day life; from all aspects and directions.

Note to Parents

Dear Parents,

Olympiad examinations come with a plethora of advantages. First and foremost among such advantages is the application of knowledge studied, in the form of multiple-choice questions. It helps the child not only to step away from rote learning, but also helps them to exhibit their competencies across various subjects.

In addition to this, Olympiads help the student to understand the importance of revision and practice, and to imbibe upon these practices; which also prove useful in academic performance of the child.

The Olympiads are conducted across multiple subjects, and help the child to recognize their field of interest, thereby encouraging the students to make a career in the field where they can excel the most.

However, cognitive development of a child is not just limited to the four walls of classroom. Following steps can be encouraged by you, to ensure their ward is able to grasp various concepts with ease or lesser difficulty:

- **Eat a balanced diet:** Ensure intake of vitamins and minerals to keep you active. Include fruits and super foods like millet in your diet to ensure healthy functioning of organs. Huge intake of junk food should be avoided.
- **Indulge in outdoor activities:** Outdoor games break the monotony of life. Play your heart out in greenery to keep yourself alert, active and fit.
- **Sleep well:** A sound sleep of 7-8 hours refreshes the brain and makes it ready to understand new topics with more clarity. A sleep derived person faces difficulty in doing even the simplest tasks of day to day life.
- **Reduce your Screen time:** More screen time leads to not only weakening of eyesight but decreases concentration span. Regulated Screen time should be encouraged
- **Do not hesitate to raise a hand:** Having a doubt in class? Do not hesitate to ask your parents or teachers. This ensures more Conceptual Clarity and hence leads to Application based understanding of various subjects and topics.
- **Teach and Learn:** No need to do rote-learning. Once you understand a topic teach or explain it to your friends, siblings and parents. It brings clarity and ensures the child does his revision this way.
- **Keep smiling:** A positive attitude promotes a growth mindset and encourages the child to be more inquisitive and try to learn something new, everyday!

HAPPY LEARNING!

Contents

SECTION 1: WORD AND STRUCTURE KNOWLEDGE

1. Spellings and Collocations — 9
2. Synonyms, Antonyms, Homonyms and Homophones — 20
3. Analogies and One Word — 48
4. Phrasal Verbs, Idioms and Proverbs — 65
5. Nouns and Pronouns — 92
6. Verbs and Adverbs — 101
7. Adjectives — 107
8. Articles and Prepositions — 112
9. Conjunctions and Punctuations — 125
10. Question Tags — 137
11. Tenses — 142
12. Voices and Narration — 154

SECTION 2: READING COMPREHENSION

Reading Comprehension — 179

SECTION 3: SPOKEN AND WRITTEN EXPRESSIONS

Spoken and Written Expression — 192

SECTION 4: ACHIEVERS' SECTION

Some Thoughtful Questions — 197
Subjective Section — 200
Model Test Paper-1 — 210
Model Test Paper-2 — 214

ANSWER KEYS (Access Content online on Dropbox) — 219
Appendix — 230

SECTION 1
WORD AND STRUCTURE KNOWLEDGE

Spellings and Collocations   1

Learning Objectives : In this chapter, students will learn about:
- ✓ Rules of Spelling
- ✓ Collocations and its different types

CHAPTER SUMMARY

Some people think if they learn a spelling rule, they'll be able to spell. Unfortunately, the trouble with rules is you have to remember the rule along with which words work with the rule and the words that don't.

But some people like learning rules, get a buzz out of finding out how to use them. It's always good to know why spelling is the way it is, and knowing spelling rules is one of many strategies to help you spell well. So even if you forget the rule, maybe you'll remember the spelling pattern, and at least you hopefully will know why a spelling is the way it is.

Rules of Spellings

- The 'i before e except after c' rule
  'believe'–'receive'

  As a basic rule this is great, but there are exceptions, such as, 'ancient,' 'leisure,' 'neighbour/neighbor'

  We have a longer version of the rule:

  i before e except after a long c but not when c is a "sh" sound and not when sounded like 'a' as in 'neighbour' or 'weigh.'

  Example: (i before e rule) 'believe,' 'achieve,' (except after c), 'receive,' 'ceiling' (but not when c is sounded like sh) 'ancient,' 'proficient' (not when sounded like 'a') 'eight,' 'beige'

  But there are always exceptions so watch out for them.

- Changing 'y' to 'ies'
  If the word has a consonant before the 'y', take off the 'y' and add 'ies':

Example:

baby — babies
company — companies
difficulty — difficulties

You might not know the spelling rule but you might know the spelling pattern.

When the word ends in a vowel + y just add 's'

Example:

key — keys
delay — delays
trolley — trolleys

(because we can't have three vowels in a row, such as, 'delaies')

> **TRIVIA**
>
> Can you believe that there is a word in the English language for "Day after tomorrow"? It was "Overmorrow" and was never used.

- Adding -es to words ending in -s, -ss, -z -ch -sh –x

  This was added centuries ago to stop the plural 's' clashing with these letters and it softens the 's' sound to a 'z' sound.

Example:

bus — buses
business — businesses

watch — watches
box — boxes
quiz — quizzes

- Doubling up rule:

Example:

put — putting
big — bigger
quiz — quizzes
swim — swimming

When a word has one syllable + 1 vowel next to 1 consonant, we double up the final consonant with a vowel suffix:

Example:

sit — sitter
big — biggest
tap — tapping
shop — shopper/shopping
fat — fatten, fattening, fatter, fattest

This happens in longer words when the stress is on the final syllable:

begin (beGIN) — beginner, beginning
refer (reFER) — referring, referred
occur (ocCUR) — occurring, occurred, occurrence

- Drop the 'e' rule

We usually drop the final silent "e" when we add vowel suffix endings.

Example: write + ing = writing
hope + ed = hoped
excite + able = excitable
arge - largish
close - closing
sense + ible = sensible
opposite + ion = opposition
imagine + ation = imagination

We keep the 'e' if the word ends in –ce or –ge to keep a soft sound, with able/ous

Example: courage + ous = courageous
outrage + ous = outrageous
notice + able = noticeable
manage + able = manageable

- Changing the 'y' to 'i' when adding suffix endings.

If a word ends in a consonant + y, the y changes to i (unless adding endings with "i" -ing -ish, which already begins with an i)

Example: beauty + ful > beauti + ful = beautiful, beautify, beautician
happy + ness = happiness, happily, happier, happiest
angry + er = angrier, angriest, angrily
pretty: prettier, prettiest but prettyish
ready: readily, readiness
dry: dried, but drying, dryish
defy: defies, defied, but defying
apply: applies, applied but applying

- Changing '-f' to '-ves' or '-s'

Most words ending in '-f' or '-fe' change their plurals to '-ves'

Example:

calf — calves
half — halves
knife — knives
leaf — leaves
loaf — loaves
life — lives
wife — wives
shelf — shelves
thief — thieves
yourself — yourselves

Some words can have both endings -ves or -s:

Example:

scarf — scarfs/scarves
dwarf — dwarfs/dwarves
wharf — wharfs/wharves
handkerchief — handkerchiefs/handkerchieves

For words ending in –ff, you just add -s to make the plural.

Example:

cliff — cliffs
toff — toffs
scuff — scuffs
sniff — sniffs

For some words ending in –f, add -s:

Nouns, which end in two vowels plus –f, usually form plurals in the normal way, with just an -s

Example:

chief	–	chiefs
spoof	–	spoofs
roof	–	roofs
chief	–	chiefs
oaf	–	afs

Exceptions:

thief	–	thieves
leaf	–	leaves

- Words ending in -ful

The suffix –ful is always spelt with one L.

Example: grate + ful = grateful; faith + ful = faithful; hope + ful = hopeful; careful, helpful, useful; beautiful (notice the "y" becomes "i")

- Adding -ly

When we add -ly to words ending in –ful, then we have double letters:

Example: gratefully, faithfully, hopefully

We also add -ly to words ending in 'e'

Example: love + ly = lovely

like + ly = likely

live + ly = lively

complete + ly = completely

definite + ly = definitely

but not truly (true + ly). This is a common misspelled word.

The 'e' at the end changes to 'y' in these -le words

Example: gentle > gently; idle > idly; subtle > subtly

- When we add "all" to the beginning of words we drop the l:

Example: all + so = also; all + most = almost; although, always, almighty, already

alright ('all right' as two words is used in more formal English)

altogether (Note that 'altogether' and 'all together' do not mean the same thing. 'Altogether' means 'in total', whereas 'all together' means 'all in one place' or 'all at once'.

Example: There are six bedrooms altogether, It was good to have a group of friends all together; they came in all together.)

Collocations

The meaning of "collocation," according to Cambridge dictionary, is:

1. "A word or phrase that is often used with another word or phrase, in a way that sounds correct to people who have spoken the language all their lives, but might not be expected from the meaning."
2. "The combination of words formed when two or more words are often used together in a way that sound correct."

Importance of Collocation

Knowing collocation will improve your English speaking and writing skill because:

- Using wrong collocation is an error.
- Using correct collocation will show the level of your English; the better you use collocation, the better your English will be.
- Using correct collocation makes your English more like a native speaker.

Tips to Learn Collocation

- Read newspaper, magazine or even story in English.
- As you read, connect the keywords and make a line between them.
- Use different highlighters for every type of collocation.
- Write down the example which you find from the article onto your notebook.
- Organize your collocation list into its pattern.

Types of Collocation

There are six main types of collocation.

Adjective + noun

There are many adjectives, which can gather with noun, but I will write some adjectives to give you obvious example.

Example: He has been a 'heavy smoker' and drinker all his adult life.

She speaks English quite well but with strong 'French accent.'

They have a 'hard life' and worked through a 'hard time.' We don't have 'hard evidence' that they had used 'hard drugs.'

The doctor ordered him to take 'regular exercise.'

The Titanic sank on its 'maiden voyage.'

Noun + noun (such as collective noun)
Example: I would like to buy two 'bars of soaps.'

There is a 'glass of water' on the table.

Would you like to have a 'cup of coffee'?

He will give a 'bar of chocolate' to his girlfriend on Valentine's Day.

Her 'bouquet of flower' is the best of all.

Verb + noun
Example: I always try to 'do my homework' in the morning after 'making my bed.'

Do you think the bank would 'forgive a debt'?

We are going to 'have lunch' together, would you like to join?

Every day, I 'take a shower' at 6 o'clock.

Adverb + adjective
Example: This test is 'ridiculously easy'! I didn't even study, but I will get high score.

Janet is a 'highly successful' businesswoman. She owns several restaurants and hotels around the country.

That is 'utterly ridiculous.' She didn't steal your favorite book. She wasn't even in the office yesterday.

Roger is 'strongly opposed' to anything bad for health. He doesn't eat junk food at all.

Are you okay? I am 'deeply concerned' about you. You have been desperate since you lost your job.

Verbs + prepositional phrase (phrasal verb)
Example: Their behavior was enough to 'drive anybody to crime.'

We had to return home because we had 'run out of money.'

I am going to 'look up the meaning' in the dictionary

She is going to 'dress up for her first date' with him.

You have to 'make up your mind' before doing something.

Verb + adverb
Example: Mary 'whispered softly' in John's ear.

The boy 'speaks politely,' and is very well-behaved.

The accident happened because he was 'driving dangerously.'

After 2 years in London, he 'speaks English fluently.'

I 'waited patiently,' but she never came.

General Collocations

Many good learner's dictionaries show collocations associated with specific words. There are also dictionaries of collocations, though they are more difficult to find.

Verb collocations
have a bath
have a drink
have a good time
have a haircut
have a holiday
have a problem
have a relationship
have a rest
have lunch
have sympathy
do business
do nothing
do someone a favour
do the cooking
do the housework
do the shopping
do the washing up
do your best
do your hair
do your homework
make a difference
make a mess
make a mistake
make a noise
make an effort
make furniture
make money
make progress

make room
make trouble
take a break
take a chance
take a look
take a rest
take a seat
take a taxi
take an exam
take notes
take someone's place
take someone's temperature
break a habit
break a leg
break a promise
break a record
break a window
break someone's heart
break the ice
break the law
break the news to someone
break the rules
catch a ball
catch a bus
catch a chill
catch a cold
catch a thief
catch fire
catch sight of
catch someone's attention
catch someone's eye
catch the flu
pay a fine
pay attention
pay by credit card
pay cash
pay interest
pay someone a compliment
pay someone a visit
pay the bill
pay the price
pay your respects
save electricity

save energy
save money
save one's strength
save someone a seat
save someone's life
save something to a disk
save space
save time
save yourself from the trouble
keep a diary
keep a promise
keep a secret
keep an appointment
keep calm
keep control
keep in touch
keep quiet
keep someone's place
keep the change
come close
come complete with
come direct
come early
come first
come into view
come last
come late
come on time
come prepared
come right back
come second
come to a compromise
come to a decision
come to an agreement
come to an end
come to a standstill
come to terms with
come to a total of
come under attack
go abroad
go astray
go bald
go bankrupt

go blind
go crazy
go dark
go deaf
go fishing
go mad
go missing
go on foot
go online
go out of business
go overseas
go quiet
go sailing
go to war
go yellow
get a job
get a shock
get angry
get divorced
get drunk
get frightened
get home
get lost
get married
get nowhere
get permission
get pregnant
get ready
get started
get the impression
get the message
get upset
get wet
get worried

Miscellaneous collocations
bang on time
dead on time
early 12th century
free time
from dawn till dusk

great deal of time
late 20th century
make time for
next few days
past few weeks
right on time
run out of time
save time
spare time
spend some time
take your time
tell someone the time
time goes by
time passes
waste time
annual turnover
bear in mind
break off negotiations
cease trading
chair a meeting
close a deal
close a meeting
come to the point
dismiss an offer
draw a conclusion
draw your attention to
launch a new product
lay off staff
go bankrupt
go into partnership
make a loss
make a profit
market forces
sales figures
take on staff
a ball of string
a bar of chocolate
a bottle of water
a bunch of carrots
a cube of sugar
a pack of cards
a pad of pap

MUST REMEMBER

- When a word has one syllable + 1 vowel next to 1 consonant, we double up the final consonant with a vowel suffix.
- "A word or phrase that is often used with another word or phrase, in a way that sounds correct to people who have spoken the language all their lives, but might not be expected from the meaning."
- "The combination of words formed when two or more words are often used together in a way that sound correct."

PRACTICE EXERCISE

I. Choose the word which is correctly spelled.

1. (a) Adulation (b) Adlation (c) Aduletion (d) Addulation
2. (a) Adulterate (b) Adeldurate (c) Adulterat (d) Adultarate
3. (a) Adventitious (b) Adventitous (c) Adventitus (d) Adventituous
4. (a) Advercity (b) Advercety (c) Adversity (d) Advercity
5. (a) Affedevit (b) Afidevit (c) Affidevit (d) Affidavit
6. (a) Agglomeration (b) Aglomeration (c) Agglomaration (d) Aglomaration
7. (a) Agrandize (b) Aggrandize (c) Aggranndice (d) Aggradise
8. (a) Aberant (b) Abbarant (c) Aberrant (d) Abberant
9. (a) Abeyense (b) Abayance (c) Abeyence (d) Abeyance
10. (a) Abstemius (b) Abstemaus (c) Abstemious (d) Abstemous
11. (a) Cacophone (b) Cacophoney (c) Cacophoni (d) Cacophony
12. (a) Capricious (b) Cappricious (c) Caprisious (d) Carisuous
13. (a) Centrefuge (b) Centrifuse (c) Centifuse (d) Centrifuge
14. (a) Chauvinist (b) Chaubinist (c) Chauviniste (d) Chaubenist
15. (a) Compendioum (b) Compendium (c) Compandium (d) Commppendium
16. (a) Connillatory (b) Concilletry (c) Conciliatory (d) Concilletry
17. (a) Deference (b) Defferance (c) Defference (d) Defference
18. (a) Delineate (b) Deleneat (c) Dileneate (d) Deleneate
19. (a) Deppricate (b) Dapricate (c) Depricate (d) Deprecate
20. (a) Desiccate (b) Desicate (c) Descicate (d) Deccicate
21. (a) Dicotomy (b) Dicotemy (c) Dichotomy (d) Dechotomy
22. (a) Embelis (b) Embelesh (c) Embellish (d) Embelish
23. (a) livelihood (b) livelyhood (c) livlihood (d) livelyhud
24. (a) foyere (b) foayer (c) foyer (d) fouyer
25. (a) Entrepreneur (b) Entrapreneur (c) Entrepraneur (d) Enterprenuer
26. (a) Itinarery (b) Itinerary (c) Itenary (d) Itinarary
27. (a) Survaillance (b) Surveillance (c) Survellance (d) Surveilance
28. (a) Sepulchral (b) Sepilchrle (c) Sepalchrul (d) Sepalchrl
29. (a) Acommodation (b) Accomodaton (c) Accommodation (d) Acomodation
30. (a) Faithfuly (b) Sincerely (c) Truely (d) Affectionatly
31. (a) Klaptomania (b) Klepptomania (c) Kleptemania (d) Kleptomania
32. (a) Schedulle (b) Schedeule (c) Schdule (d) Schedule
33. (a) Skillful (b) Skillfull (c) Skilfull (d) Skilpull
34. (a) Judicious (b) Cancious (c) Dilicous (d) Gracous
35. (a) Gaurantee (b) Guarantee (c) Garuntee (d) Guaruntee
36. (a) Friming (b) Burnning (c) Running (d) Fryng
37. (a) Dammage (b) Damaige (c) Dammege (d) Damage
38. (a) Accomplish (b) Acomplush (c) Ackmplesh (d) Accompalish
39. (a) Puerrile (b) Puerrille (c) Purrile (d) Puerile

16

International English Olympiad - 8

40. (a) Satelite (b) Sattelite (c) Satellite (d) Sattellite
41. (a) Inoculation (b) Innoculation (c) Inocculation (d) Inocullation
42. (a) Velnerable (b) Vulnarable (c) Vulnerable (d) Valnerable
43. (a) Simpal (b) Bannar (c) Pattren (d) Modern
44. (a) Scripher (b) Scripture (c) Skripture (d) Scriptur
45. (a) Comitte (b) Commitee (c) Committee (d) Comiittee
46. (a) Exaggerate (b) Exeggrate (c) Exagerate (d) Exadgerate
47. (a) Asspersion (b) Voluptuous (c) Voguei (d) Equestrain
48. (a) Hindrance (b) Hinderrance (c) Hindrence (d) Hinderence
49. (a) Parallelled (b) Parralleled (c) Paralleled (d) Paraleled
50. (a) Lckadaisicle (b) Lackdaisical (c) Lackadisical (d) Lackadaisical
51. (a) Equanimity (b) Equannimity (c) Equanimmity (d) Equinimity
52. (a) Occured (b) Occurad (c) Ocurred (d) Occurred
53. (a) Occasion (b) Occassion (c) Ocasion (d) Ocassion
54. (a) Grief (b) Breif (c) Recieve (d) Diceive
55. (a) Furnituer (b) Exampel (c) Medicine (d) Sampal

II. Choose the correct collocation to fill in the blanks.

1. I hope to _____ my own business one day.
   (a) do (b) have (c) make (d) has
2. I don't _____ many hobbies.
   (a) do (b) have (c) make (d) has
3. My wife usually _____ the bed, rather than me.
   (a) does (b) has (c) makes (d) have
4. Many countries _____ problems with obesity.
   (a) do (b) have (c) make (d) has
5. I _____ a mistake in my IELTS reading the last time I took the test.
   (a) did (b) had (c) made (d) has
6. I _____ my break at work at 3.15.
   (a) do (b) have (c) make (d) has
7. Reading a lot _____ a real difference to your IELTS score.
   (a) does (b) has (c) makes (d) have
8. I'm planning to _____ a holiday in June or July.
   (a) do (b) have (c) make (d) has
9. I _____ my shopping at the weekends.
   (a) do (b) make (c) has (d) made
10. I don't _____ much sympathy with students who fail because they did not study.
    (a) do (b) have (c) make (d) did

III. Fill in the blanks with the correct option:

1. I'm an _____ admirer of your work.
   (a) ardent (b) triumphant (c) stale (d) considerable
2. This new process is a _____ advance in technology.
   (a) ardent (b) significant (c) stale (d) considerable
3. He knows the interviewer already and that will give him an _____ advantage over me.
   (a) ardent (b) significant (c) unfair (d) considerable

4. I wouldn't upset him. He can be a _____ adversary.
   (a) ardent (b) significant
   (c) unfair (d) dangerous

5. He gave me some _____ advice and I took it.
   (a) ardent (b) significant
   (c) unfair (d) blunt

6. We know very little about this. We need to bring in an _____ adviser to help us.
   (a) outside (b) significant
   (c) unfair (d) dangerous

7. I don't like this at all. It's a really _____ affair.
   (a) outside (b) ugly
   (c) unfair (d) dangerous

8. It's not a very challenging job. I only have to deal with _____ affairs.
   (a) outside (b) ugly
   (c) everyday (d) dangerous

9. They don't always agree but I think there is a bond of _____ affection between them.
   (a) outside (b) ugly
   (c) everyday (d) deep

10. It seems no time at all since I started work and here I am at _____ age.
    (a) outside (b) ugly
    (c) everyday (d) retirement

11. That type of behaviour was possible in a _____ age but we are more tightly regulated these days.
    (a) bygone (b) ugly
    (c) everyday (d) deep

12. I don't trust him. I think he has a _____ agenda.
    (a) bygone (b) hidden
    (c) everyday (d) deep

13. We cannot tolerate this sort of _____ aggression from a competitor in one of our key markets.
    (a) bygone (b) hidden
    (c) naked (d) deep

14. We have a _____ agreement with them and we must respect it.
    (a) bygone (b) hidden
    (c) naked (d) binding

15. I think they must be providing them with some kind of _____ aid. But I don't know what.
    (a) bygone (b) hidden
    (c) naked (d) covert

16. I agree with the _____ aims of what you are trying to do but not with some of the details.
    (a) broad (b) hidden
    (c) naked (d) binding

17. I'm sure he's got the job. He's walking around with a _____ air.
    (a) broad (b) triumphant
    (c) naked (d) binding

18. You need to open the windows and get rid of the _____ air in here.
    (a) broad (b) triumphant
    (c) stale (d) binding

19. The problems in Tokyo have caused _____ alarm on Wall Street.
    (a) broad (b) triumphant
    (c) stale (d) considerable

20. He definitely wasn't there. He has a _____ alibi.
    (a) broad (b) triumphant
    (c) stale (d) cast-iron

HOTS

In sentence below, one word has been printed in bold type which is wrongly spelt. Choose the correctly spelt word.

1. His life is so hectic that he is prepared to be tolerant of trivial **pecadillos**.
    (a) pecedillos (b) pecedilos
    (c) peccadillos (d) peccadillos
2. The weather is so hot that I am feeling full of **longour**.
    (a) languor (b) langur
    (c) langoor (d) languor
3. It was an unexpected **denuement** in the play performed by the artists.
    (a) denoument (b) denuemant
    (c) denuement (d) denouement
4. I am reading various **hiroglyphics** of ancient Egypt.
    (a) hyroglyphics (b) hieroglyphics
    (c) hyrographics (d) hieroglyphics
5. Everyone has a few **idiosyncracies**.
    (a) idiosyncrasies (b) idiosyncrasies
    (c) idosyncracies (d) idiosincracies

Spellings and Collocations

Synonyms, Antonyms, Homonyms and Homophones

Learning Objectives : In this chapter, students will learn about:
- ✓ Synonyms and Antonyms
- ✓ Homophones and Homonyms

CHAPTER SUMMARY

Synonym
Synonym is a word or phrase that means exactly or nearly the same as another word or phrase in the same language, for example,'shut' is a synonym of 'close.'

Words with Synonyms
The following is a list of synonyms, arranged alphbetically, that can help you build your vocabulary and add variety to your writing.

Word	Synonyms
A	
Abandon	desert, forsake
Abase	debase, degrade, humble, humiliate, disgrace
Abettor	accessory, accomplice, confederate, conspirator
Abolish	repeal, rescind, revoke, abrogate, annul, nullify, cancel
Acknowledge	admit, confess, own, avow
Acquit	exculpate, exonerate, absolve
Active	agile, nimble, brisk, sprightly, spry, bustling
Advise	counsel, admonish, caution, warn
Affecting	moving, touching, pathetic
Affront	insult, indignity
Afraid	fearful, frightened, alarmed, scared, aghast, terrified, timid
Agitate	abash, mortify, chagrin, humiliate
Agnostic	skeptic, infidel, unbeliever, disbeliever
Allay	alleviate, mitigate, assuage, mollify, relieve
Allow	permit, suffer, tolerate

Amuse	entertain, divert
Announce	proclaim, promulgate, report, advertise, publish, bruit, blazon, trumpet, herald
Answer	reply, response, rejoinder, retort, repartee
Antipathy	aversion, repugnance, disgust, loathing
Artifice	ruse, trick, dodge, maneuver, wile, stratagem, subterfuge, finesse
Ascend	mount, climb, scale
Ascribe	attribute, impute
Ask	inquire, question, interrogate, interpolate, query, quiz, catechize, request, beg, solicit, entreat, beseech, crave, implore
Assault	onslaught, brawl, melee, tournament, battle, conflict, strife
Asseverate	allege, assert, avouch, avow, maintain, claim, depose, augur, prognosticate
Associate	colleague, partner, helper, collaborator, coadjutor, companion, helpmate, mate, teammate, comrade: chum, crony, consort, accomplice, confederate
Attach	affix, annex, append, subjoin
Attack	assail, assault, invade, beset, besiege, bombard, cannonade, storm
Awkward	clumsy, ungainly, gawky, lanky
B	
Begin	commence, inaugurate, initiate, institute, originate, start, found
Belief	faith, persuasion, conviction, tenet, creed
Belittle	decry, depreciate, disparage
Benevolent	charitable, gracious, humane, sympathetic
Bind	secure, fetter, shackle
Bit	jot, mite, particle, grain, atom, speck, mote, whit, iota, tittle, scintilla
Bite	nibble, gnaw, chew, masticate, champ
Blemish	stain, discoloration, speck, mark, smudge, flaw, defect, blot
Bluff	blunt, outspoken, downright, brusque, curt, crusty
Boast	brag, vaunt, vapour, gasconade
Body	corpse, remains, relics, carcass, cadaver, corpus
Bombastic	sophomoric, turgid, tumid, grandiose, grandiloquent, magniloquent
Boorish	churlish, loutish, clownish, rustic, ill-bred
Booty	plunder, loot, spoil
Break	crack, fracture, sever, rend, burst, smash, shatter, shiver

Synonyms, Antonyms, Homonyms and Homophones

Brittle	frangible, friable, fragile, crisp
Building	edifice, structure, house
Burly	pudgy, chubby
Burn	scorch, singe, sear, parch, char, incinerate, cremate
Busy	industrious, diligent, assiduous, sedulous
C	
Call	clamour, roar, scream, shout, shriek, vociferate, yell, halloo, whoop
Calm	still, motionless, tranquil, serene, placid
Care	concern, solicitude, anxiety
Careful	cautious, wary, circumspect, canny
Celebrate	commemorate, observe
Charm	amulet, talisman
Charm	enchant, fascinate, captivate, enrapture, bewitch, infatuate, enamour
Cheat	defraud, swindle, dupe
Chirrup	trill, pipe, quaver, peep, cheep, twitter
Choke	strangle, suffocate, stifle, throttle
Choose	pick, select, cull, elect
Clash	collision, contest, skirmish, encounter, brush, bout, set-to
Cleft	chasm, fissure, gap, opening, interstice, burrow, crater, eyelet
Coax	wheedle, cajole, tweedle, persuade, inveigle
Color	hue, shade, tint, tinge, tincture
Combine	unite, consolidate, merge, amalgamate, weld, incorporate, confederate
Comfort	console, solace
Complain	grumble, growl, murmur, repine, whine, croak
Complaint	disorder, distemper, infirmity, malady
Concise	terse, succinct, compendious, compact, sententious, pithy
Condescend	deign, vouchsafe
Confirm	corroborate, substantiate, verify
Confirmed	habitual, inveterate, chronic
Connect	join, link, couple, attach, unite
Consternation	panic, terror, horror, misgiving, anxiety, scare, tremor, coruscate
Continual	continuous, unceasing, incessant, endless, uninterrupted, unremitting, constant, perpetual, perennial
Contract	agreement, bargain, compact, covenant, stipulation

Copy	duplicate, counterpart, likeness, reproduction, replica, facsimile
Corrupt	depraved, perverted, vitiated
Costly	expensive, dear
Coterie	clique, cabal, circle, set, faction, party
Courage	bravery, resolution, dauntlessness, gallantry, boldness
Critical	judicial, impartial, carping, caviling, captious, censorious
Crooked	awry, askew
Cross	fretful, peevish, petulant, pettish, irritable, irascible, angry
Crowd	throng, horde, host, mass, multitude, press, jam, concourse
Cruel	brutal, ferocious, fierce, savage, barbarous, truculent
Crusty	cynical, misanthropic, saturnine, splenetic
Cry	weep, sob, snivel, whimper, blubber, bawl, squall, howl, wail
Curious	inquisitive, prying, meddlesome
Cut	cleave, hack, haggle, notch, slash, gash, split, chop, hew, lop
D	
Dainty	delicate, exquisite, choice, rare
Danger	peril, jeopardy, hazard, risk
Darken	obscure, bedim, obfuscate
Dead	lifeless, inanimate, deceased, defunct, extinct
Deadly	mortal, fatal, lethal
Death	decease, demise
Decay	decompose, putrefy, rot, spoil
Deceit	deception, double-dealing, duplicity, chicanery, guile, treachery
Deceptive	deceitful, misleading, fallacious, fraudulent
Decorate	adorn, ornament, embellish, deck, bedeck, garnish, bedizen, beautify
Decorous	demure, sedate, sober, staid, prim, proper
Deface	disfigure, mar, mutilate
Defeat	subdue, conquer, overcome, vanquish, subjugate, suppress
Defect	fault, imperfection, disfigurement, blemish, flaw
Delay	defer, postpone, procrastinate
Demoralize	deprave, debase, corrupt, vitiate
Deny	contravene, controvert, refute, confute
Deportment	demeanor, bearing, port, mien

Word	Synonyms
Deprive	divest, dispossess, strip, despoil
Despise	contemn, scorn, disdain
Despondency	despair, desperation
Destroy	demolish, raze, annihilate, exterminate, eradicate, extirpate
Detach	separate, sunder, sever, disconnect, disjoin, disunite
Determined	persistent, dogged
Devout	religious, pious, godly, saintly
Die	expire, perish, decease, succumb
Difficulty	hindrance, obstacle, impediment, encumbrance, handicap
Difficulty	predicament, perplexity, plight, quandary, dilemma, strait
Dip	douse, duck, plunge, immerge, immerse, submerge, sink, dive
Dirty	filthy, foul, nasty, squalid
Discernment	perception, penetration, insight, acumen
Disease	sickness, illness, indisposition, ailment, affection
Disgraceful	dishonorable, shameful, disreputable, ignominious
Disgusting	sickening, repulsive, revolting, loathsome, repugnant, abhorrent, noisome, fulsome
Dishonor	disgrace, ignominy, infamy, obloquy, opprobrium
Disloyal	false, unfaithful, faithless, treacherous, treasonable
Dispel	disperse, dissipate, scatter
Dissatisfied	discontented, displeased, malcontent, disgruntled
Divide	distribute, apportion, allot, allocate, partition
Do	perform, execute, accomplish, achieve, effect
Doctrine	dogma, tenet, precept
Dream	reverie, vision, fantasy
Dress	clothes, clothing, garments, apparel, raiment, habiliments
Drink	imbibe, sip, sup, swallow, quaff, tipple, tope, guzzle
Drip	dribble, trickle
Drunk	drunken, intoxicated, inebriated
Dry	arid, parched, desiccated
E	
Early	primitive, primeval, primordial, primal, pristine, aboriginal
Eat	bolt, gulp, gorge, devour
Element	component, constituent, ingredient, share, lot, allotment

Elicit	extract, exact, extort
Embarrass	disconcert, discompose, discomfit, confuse, confound
Enclose	surround, encircle, circumscribe, encompass
Encroach	infringe, entrench, trench, intrude, invade, trespass
Encumber	forestall, suppress, repress, prevent
End	conclude, terminate, finish, discontinue, close
Enemy	foe, adversary, opponent, antagonist, rival
Enough	adequate, sufficient
Entice	inveigle, allure, lure, decoy, seduce
Erase	expunge, cancel, efface, obliterate
Error	mistake, blunder, slip
Estimate	value, appreciate
Eternal	everlasting, endless, deathless, imperishable, immortal
Examination	inquiry, inquisition, investigation, inspection, scrutiny, research, review, audit, inquest, autopsy
Example	sample, specimen, instance
Exceed	excel, surpass, transcend, outdo
Excuse	pardon, forgive, condone
Expand	dilate, distend, inflate
Expel	banish, exile, proscribe, ostracize
Experiment	trial, test
Explain	expound, interpret, elucidate
Explicit	exact, precise, definite
F	
Face	countenance, features, visage, physiognomy
Faculty	gift, endowment, aptitude, attribute, talent, predilection, bent
Failing	shortcoming, defect, fault, foible, infirmity
Fame	honor, renown, glory, distinction, reputation, repute, celebrity
Famous	renowned, celebrated, noted, distinguished, eminent, illustrious
Fashion	mode, style, vogue, rage, fad
Fast	rapid, swift, quick, fleet, speedy, hasty, celeritous, expeditious, instantaneous
Fasten	tie, hitch, moor, tether
Fat	fleshy, stout, plump, buxom, corpulent, obese, portly, pursy

Synonyms, Antonyms, Homonyms and Homophones

Fate	destiny, lot, doom
Fawn	truckle, cringe, crouch
Fear	dread, fright, apprehension, affright, alarm, dismay, timidity
Feign	pretend, dissemble, simulate, counterfeit, affect, assume
Feminine	female, womanly, womanlike, womanish, effeminate
Fertile	fecund, fruitful, prolific
Fiendish	devilish, diabolical, demoniacal, demonic, satanic
Fight	combat, struggle, scuffle, fray, affray, attack, engagement
Financial	monetary, pecuniary, fiscal
Fit	suitable, appropriate, proper
Flame	blaze, flare, glare, glow
Flat	level, even, plane, smooth, horizontal
Flatter	blandish, beguile, compliment, praise
Flee	abscond, decamp
Fleeting	transient, transitory, ephemeral, evanescent
Flexible	pliable, pliant, supple, limber, lithe, lissome
Flit	flutter, flicker, hover
Flock	herd, bevy, covey, drove, pack, brood, litter, school
Flog	maul, drub, switch, spank, bastinado
Flow	pour, stream, gush, spout
Follow	pursue, chase
Follower	adherent, disciple, partisan, henchman
Fond	loving, doting, devoted, amorous, enamored
Force	compulsion, coercion, constraint, restraint
Force	strength, power, energy, vigor, might, potency, cogency, efficacy
Foretell	predict, prophesy, forecast, presage, forebode, portend
Frank	candid, open, artless, guileless, ingenuous, unsophisticated
Free	liberate, emancipate, manumit, release, disengage, disentangle, disembarrass, disencumber, extricate
Freshen	refresh, revive, renovate, renew
Friendly	amicable, companionable, hearty, cordial, neighbourly, sociable
Frighten	affright, alarm, terrify, terrorize, dismay, appall, daunt, scare
Frolicsome	merry, jolly, sportive, jovial, jocular, jocose, jocund
Frown	scowl, glower, lower

Frugal	sparing, saving, economical, chary, thrifty, provident, prudent
Frustrate	foil, thwart, counteract, circumvent, balk, baffle, genial, complaisant, affable

G

Game	play, amusement, pastime, diversion, fun, sport, entertainment
Gather	accumulate, amass, collect, levy, muster, hoard
Get	acquire, obtain, procure, attain, gain, win, earn
Ghost	spirit, specter, phantom, apparition, shade, phantasm
Gift	present, donation, grant, gratuity, bequest, boon, bounty, largess, fee, bribe
Give	bestow, grant, confer, present, furnish, supply
Glad	happy, cheerful, mirthful, joyful, joyous, blithe, gay
Glower	lower, peek, peep, gape, con, pore, ogle, leer, view, survey
Grand	magnificent, gorgeous, splendid, superb, sublime
Greet	hail, salute, address, accost
Grief	sorrow, distress, affliction, trouble, tribulation, woe
Grieve	lament, mourn, bemoan, bewail, deplore, rue
Guard	defend, protect, shield, shelter, screen, preserve

H

Habit	custom, usage, practice, wont
Habitation	abode, dwelling, residence, domicile, home
Hang	electrocute, guillotine, lynch, dispatch, decimate, crucify
Harass	annoy, irritate, vex, fret, worry, plague, torment, molest
Harmful	injurious, detrimental, pernicious, deleterious, baneful, noxious
Haste	celerity, speed, hurry, expedition, dispatch
Hate	detest, abhor, loathe, abominate, despise
Hatred	hate, animosity, ill-will, enmity, hostility, bitterness
Have	possess, own, hold
Headstrong	wayward, willful, perverse, forward
Healthful	wholesome, salutary, salubrious, sanitary, hygienic
Heavy	weighty, burdensome, onerous
Help (noun)	aid, assistance, succour
Help (verb)	assist, aid, succour, abet, second, support, befriend
Hesitate	falter, vacillate, waver

Hide	conceal, secrete
High	tall, lofty, elevated, towering
Hinder	restrain, obstruct, impede, hamper, retard, check, curb, clog
Hint	intimate, insinuate
Hole	cavity, excavation, pit, cache, cave, cavern, hollow, depression
Holy	sacred, hallowed, sanctified, consecrated, godly, pious, saintly, blessed
Hopeful	expectant, sanguine, optimistic, confident
Hopeless	despairing, disconsolate, desperate
I	
Idle	inert, lazy, indolent, sluggish, slothful
Ignorant	illiterate, uninformed, uneducated, untutored, unlettered
Immemorial	elderly, aged, hoary, decrepit, senile, superannuated
Impolite	discourteous, inurbane, uncivil, rude, disrespectful, pert, saucy, impertinent, impudent, insolent
Importance	consequence, moment
Impostor	pretender, charlatan, masquerader, mountebank, deceiver
Imprison	incarcerate, immure
Improper	indecent, indecorous, unseemly, unbecoming, indelicate
Impure	tainted, contaminated, polluted, defiled, vitiated
Inborn	innate, inbred, congenital
Incite	instigate, stimulate, impel, arouse, goad, spur, promote
Incline	tip, lean, cant, slant, slope, tilt, list, careen, dip
Increase	grow, enlarge, magnify, amplify, swell, augment
Indecent	indelicate, immodest, shameless, ribald, lewd, lustful, lascivious, libidinous, obscene
Insane	demented, deranged, crazy, mad
Insanity	dementia, derangement, craziness, madness, lunacy, mania, frenzy, hallucination
Insipid	tasteless, flat, vapid
Insulting	scornful, imperious, contumelious, impudent, impertinent
Intention	intent, purpose, plan, design, aim, object, end
Interpose	intervene, intercede, interfere, mediate
Intrepidity	daring, valour, prowess, fortitude, heroism
Irreligious	ungodly, impious, godless, sacrilegious, blasphemous, profane

Irritate	exasperate, nettle, incense
J	
Join	connect, unite, couple, combine, link, annex, append
Journey	voyage, tour, pilgrimage, trip, jaunt, excursion, junket
K	
Kill	slay, slaughter, massacre, butcher, murder, assassinate, execute
Kind	compassionate, merciful, lenient, benignant, benign, clement
Kindle	ignite, inflame, rouse
L	
Lack	want, need, deficiency, dearth, paucity, scarcity, deficit
Lame	crippled, halt, deformed, maimed, disabled
Large	great, big, huge, immense, colossal, gigantic, extensive, vast, massive, unwieldy, bulky
Laugh	giggle, snicker, titter, chuckle, guffaw, cachinnate, chortle, roar
Laughable	comical, comic, farcical, ludicrous, ridiculous, funny, droll
Lead	guide, conduct, escort, convoy
Lecture	preach, harangue, rant, roar, spout, thunder, declaim, harp
Lengthen	prolong, protract, extend
Lessen	decrease, diminish, reduce, abate, curtail, moderate, mitigate, palliate
Liberal	generous, bountiful, munificent
Lie (noun)	untruth, falsehood, falsity, fiction, fabrication, mendacity, canard, fib, story
Lie (verb)	prevaricate, falsify, equivocate, quibble, shuffle, dodge, fence, fib
Likeness	resemblance, similitude, similarity, semblance, analogy
Limpv	flaccid, flabby, flimsy
List	roll, catalogue, register, roster, schedule, inventory
Look	glance, gaze, stare, peer, scan, scrutinize, gloat, glare
Loud	resonant, clarion, stentorian, sonorous
Love	affection, attachment, fondness, infatuation, devotion
Low	base, abject, servile, slavish, menial
Loyal	faithful, true, constant, staunch, unwavering, steadfast
Lurk	skulk, slink, sneak, prowl

M	
Make	create, frame, fashion, mold, shape, form, forge, fabricate, invent, construct, manufacture, concoct
Malice	malevolence, malignity, rancour, resentment, dudgeon, grudge
Manifest	plain, obvious, clear, apparent, patent, evident, perceptible, noticeable, open, overt, palpable, tangible, indubitable, unmistakable
Many	various, numerous, divers, manifold, multitudinous, myriad, countless, innumerable
Margin	edge, limit, border, boundary, bound, bourn, brim, rim, brink
Masculine	male, manly, manlike, manful, mannish, virile
Matrimonial	conjugal, connubial, nuptial, marital
Meaning	significance, signification, import, purport
Meet	encounter, collide, confront, converge
Meeting	assembly, assemblage, congregation, convention, conference, concourse, gathering, mustering
Melt	thaw, fuse, dissolve, liquefy
Memory	remembrance, recollection, reminiscence, retrospection
Merciless	unmerciful, pitiless, ruthless, fell
Mercy	clemency, lenity, leniency, lenience, forbearance
Misrepresent	misinterpret, falsify, distort, warp
Mix	compound, amalgamate, weld, combine, blend, concoct
Model	pattern, prototype, criterion, standard, exemplar, paragon, archetype, ideal
Motive	incentive, inducement, desire, purpose
Move	actuate, impel, prompt, incite
N	
Name	appellation, designation, denomination, title, alias, cognomen, patronymic, nom
Near	nigh, close, neighboring, adjacent, contiguous
Neat	tidy, orderly, spruce, trim, prim
Needful	necessary, requisite, essential, indispensable
Negligence	neglect, inattention, inattentiveness, inadvertence, remissness, oversight
New	novel, fresh, recent, modern, late, innovative, unprecedented
Nice	fastidious, dainty, finical

Noisy	clamorous, boisterous, turbulent, riotous, obstreperous, uproarious, vociferous, brawling
Noticeable	prominent, conspicuous, salient, signal
O	
Occupation	employment, calling, pursuit, vocation, avocation
Old	ancient, olden, antique, antiquated, archaic, obsolete, venerable
Order (noun)	command, mandate, behest, injunction, decree
Order (verb)	command, enjoin, direct, instruct
Oversight	supervision, direction, superintendence, surveillance
P	
Pacify	appease, placate, propitiate, conciliate, mollify
Pale	pallid, wan, colorless, blanched, ghastly, ashen, cadaverous
Part	piece, portion, section, subdivision, fraction, installment
Patience	forbearance, resignation, longsuffering
Pay	compensate, recompense, remunerate, requite, reimburse, salary, wages, honorarium, hire
Penetrate	pierce, perforate
Perforation	puncture, rent, slit, crack, chink, crevice, cranny, breach
Pirate	corsair, raider, burglar, footpad, highwayman, depredator
Pity	sympathy, compassion, commiseration, condolence
Place	office, post, position, situation, appointment
Plan	design, project, scheme, plot
Playful	mischievous, roguish, prankish, sportive, arch
Plentiful	plenteous, abundant, bounteous, copious, profuse, exuberant, luxuriant
Plunder	rifle, loot, sack, pillage, devastate, despoil
Polite	civil, obliging, courteous, courtly, urbane, affable
Poverty	want, need, destitution, indigence, penury
Pretty	beautiful, comely, handsome, fair
Profitable	remunerative, lucrative, gainful
Promenade	prowl, hobble, limp, perambulate
Prompt	punctual, ready, expeditious
Proudv	arrogant, presumptuous, haughty, supercilious, insolent
Prune	reap, mow, clip, shear, trim, dock, crop, shave, whittle, slice
Pull	draw, drag, haul, tug, tow

Synonyms, Antonyms, Homonyms and Homophones

Punish	chastise, chasten, castigate, scourge
Push	shove, thrust
Puzzle	perplex, mystify, bewilder
Q	
Quarrel	altercation, disagreement, contention, controversy, breach
Queer	odd, curious, quaint, ridiculous, singular, unique, bizarre, fantastic, grotesque
R	
Raise	lift, heave, hoist, erect, rear, elevate, exalt, enhance
Rash	incautious, reckless, foolhardy, adventurous, venturous, venturesome
Rebellion	insurrection, revolt, mutiny, riot, revolution, sedition
Recover	regain, retrieve, recoup, rally, recuperate
Reflect	deliberate, ponder, muse, meditate, ruminate
Relate	recount, recite, narrate, tell
Relinquish	waive, renounce, surrender, forego, resign, abdicate
Renounce	abjure, forswear, recant, retract, repudiate
Replace	supersede, supplant, succeed
Reprove	rebuke, reprimand, admonish, chide, upbraid, reproach, scold
Repulsive	unsightly, loathsome, hideous, gruesome
Requital	retaliation, reprisal, revenge, vengeance, retribution
Responsible	answerable, accountable, amenable, liable
Reveal	disclose, divulge, manifest, show, betray
Reverence	veneration, awe, adoration, worship
Rich	wealthy, affluent, opulent
Ridicule	deride, mock, taunt, flout, twit, tease
Ripe	mature, mellow
Rise	arise, mount, ascend
Robber	bandit, brigand, desperado, buccaneer, freebooter
Rogue	knave, rascal, miscreant, scamp, sharper, villain
Round	circular, rotund, spherical, globular, orbicular
Rub	polish, burnish, furbish, scour
Rumpus	ruction, spat, tiff, fuss, jar, feud
Run	scamper, scurry, scuttle, scud, scour, pace, gallop, trot, lope

Rupture	dispute, dissension, bickering, wrangle, broil, squabble, row
Rural	rustic, pastoral, bucolic

S

Sad	grave, sober, moody, doleful, downcast, dreary, woeful, somber, unhappy, woebegone, mournful, depressed, despondent, gloomy, melancholy, heavy-spirited, sorrowful, dismal, dejected, disconsolate, miserable, lugubrious
Satiate	sate, surfeit, cloy, glut, gorge
Say	utter, pronounce, announce, state, declare, affirm, aver
Scoff	jeer, gibe, fleer, sneer, mock, taunt
Secret	covert, surreptitious, furtive, clandestine, underhand, stealthy
See	perceive, descry, distinguish, espy, discern, note, notice, watch
Seep	ooze, infiltrate, percolate, transude, exude
Sell	barter, vend, trade
Shape	form, figure, outline, conformation, configuration, contour, profile
Share	partake, participate, divide
Sharp	keen, acute, cutting, trenchant, incisive
Shine	beam, gleam, glisten, glister, glitter, glare, flare, flash
Shore	coast, littoral, beach, strand, bank
Shorten	abridge, abbreviate, curtail, truncate, syncopate
Show	exhibit, display, expose, manifest, evince
Shrink	flinch, wince, blench, quail
Shun	avoid, eschew
Shy	bashful, diffident, modest, coy, timid, shrinking
Sign	omen, auspice, portent, prognostic, augury, foretoken, adumbration, presage, indication
Silent	reserved, uncommunicative, reticent, taciturn
Simple	innocent, artless, unsophisticated, naive
Sing	chant, carol, warble, troll, yodel, croon, hum, chirp
Skilful	skilled, expert, adept, apt, proficient, adroit, dexterous, deft, clever, ingenious
Skin	hide, pelt, fell
Slander	defame, asperse, calumniate, traduce, vilify, malign, libel
Sleep	slumber, repose, nap, doze, drowse, lethargy, dormancy, coma

Synonyms, Antonyms, Homonyms and Homophones

Sleepy	drowsy, slumberous, somnolent, sluggish, torpid, dull, lethargic
Slit	score, lance, carve, bisect, dissect, amputate, detruncate
Slovenly	slatternly, dowdy, frowsy, blowzy
Sly	crafty, cunning, subtle, wily, artful, politic, designing
Smell	odour, savour, scent, fragrance, aroma, perfume, redolence, tang
Smile	smirk, grin
Sneak	shamble, amble, wander, stamp, slouch, gad, gallivant, glide, hike
Solitary	lonely, lone, lonesome, desolate, deserted, uninhabited
Song	ballad, ditty, lullaby, hymn, anthem, dirge, chant, paean, lay
Sour	acid, tart, acrid, acidulous, acerbitous, astringent
Sparkle	twinkle, dazzle, glimmer, glow, radiate, scintillate
Speak	discourse, expatiate, descant, comment, argue, persuade, plead
Speech	discourse, oration, address, sermon, declamation, dissertation, exhortation, disquisition, harangue, diatribe, tirade, screed, philippic, invective, rhapsody, plea
Spend	expend, disburse, squander, waste, lavish
Splinter	sunder, rive, crush, batter, demolish, rupture
Spoiler	despoiler, forager, pillager, plunderer, marauder, myrmidon
Spot	blotch, speckle, fleck, dapple, smear, smutch, brand, defacement
Spruce	natty, dapper, smart, chic
Stale	musty, frowzy, mildewed, fetid, rancid, rank
Stay	tarry, linger, stop, sojourn, remain, abide, live, reside, dwell
Steal	abstract, pilfer, filch, purloin, peculate, swindle, plagiarize
Steep	precipitous, abrupt
Stingy	close, miserly, niggardly, parsimonious, penurious, sordid
Storm	tempest, whirlwind, hurricane, tornado, cyclone, typhoon
Straight	perpendicular, vertical, plumb, erect, upright
Strange	singular, peculiar, odd, queer, quaint, outlandish
Strike	hit, smite, thump, beat, cuff, buffet, knock, whack, belabour
Strong	stout, robust, sturdy, stalwart, powerful
Stupid	dull, obtuse, stolid, doltish, sluggish, brainless, bovine
Suave	bland, unctuous, fulsome, smug, complaisant, elegant
Succeed	prosper, thrive, flourish, triumph
Succession	sequence, series

Sullen	surly, sulky, crabbed, cross, gruff, grumpy, glum, morose, dour
Supernatural	preternatural, superhuman, miraculous
Supplicate	importune, petition, plead, pray
Suppose	surmise, conjecture, presume, imagine, fancy, guess, think, believe
Surprise	astonish, amaze, astound
Swearing	cursing, profanity, blasphemy, execration, imprecation
T	
Talk	chat, chatter, prate, prattle, babble, gabble, jabber, tattle
Talkative	loquacious, garrulous, fluent, voluble, glib, chattering, long-winded
Teach	instruct, educate, train, discipline, drill, inculcate, instill, indoctrinate
Tear	rend, rip, lacerate, mangle
Thoughtful	contemplative, meditative, reflective, pensive, wistful
Throw	pitch, hurl, dash, fling, cast, toss, flip, chuck, sling, heave
Tire	weary, fatigue, exhaust, jade, fag
Toddle	waddle, shuffle, mince, stroll, saunter, ramble, meander
Tool	implement, instrument, utensil
Trifle	dally, dawdle, potter
Trim	dapper, spruce, genteel, urbane, well-bred, gracious, affable
Trust	confidence, reliance, assurance, faith
Try	endeavor, essay, attempt
Turn	revolve, rotate, spin, whirl, gyrate
Twaddle	blab, gossip, palaver, parley, converse, mumble, mutter, stammer
U	
Ugly	homely, uncomely, hideous
Unwilling	reluctant, disinclined, loath, averse
V	
Vestments	attire, garb, habit, costume, uniform
W	
Walk	plod, trudge, tread, stride, stalk, strut, tramp, march, pace
Watchful	vigilant, alert
Wave (noun)	billow, breaker, swell, ripple, undulation
Wave (verb)	brandish, flourish, flaunt, wigwag
Weak	debilitated, feeble, infirm, decrepit, impotent, enervated, languid
Weariness	languor, lassitude, enervation, exhaustion

Synonyms, Antonyms, Homonyms and Homophones

Wearisome	tiresome, irksome, tedious, humdrum
Wet (adjective)	humid, moist, damp, dank, sodden, soggy
Wet (verb)	moisten, dampen, soak, imbrue, saturate, drench
Whim	caprice, vagary, fancy, freak, whimsy, crotchet
Whip	chastise, castigate, flagellate, scourge, lash, trounce, thrash
Wicked	sinful, felonious, illegal, immoral, heinous, flagitious
Wind	breeze, gust, blast, flaw, gale, squall, flurry
Wind	coil, twist, twine, wreathe
Winding	tortuous, serpentine, sinuous, meandering
Wise	learned, erudite, sagacious, sapient, sage, judicious, prudent
Wonderful	marvelous, phenomenal, miraculous
Work	labor, toil, drudgery
Workman	labourer, artisan, artificer, mechanic, craftsman
Write	inscribe, scribble, scrawl, scratch
Y	
Young	youthful, boyish, girlish, juvenile, puerile, immature, callow, adolescent

Antonym

An antonym is a word which means the opposite of another word. Antonyms are also called opposites. One way of mastering a language involves learning its vocabulary. Synonyms and opposites are helpful in this sense.

Examples: Two opposites of 'light' are 'dark' and 'heavy'.

A
absent	:	present
abundant	:	scarce
accept	:	decline, refuse
accurate	:	inaccurate
admit	:	deny
advantage	:	disadvantage
against	:	for
agree	:	disagree
alive	:	dead
all	:	none, nothing
ally	:	enemy
always	:	never
ancient	:	modern
answer	:	question
antonym	:	synonym
apart	:	together
appear	:	disappear, vanish
approve	:	disapprove
arrive	:	depart
artificial	:	natural
ascend	:	descend
attic	:	cellar
attractive	:	repulsive
awake	:	asleep

B
backward	:	forward
bad	:	good
beautiful	:	ugly
before	:	after
begin	:	end
below	:	above
bent	:	straight
best	:	worst
better	:	worse, worst

big	:	little, small
black	:	white
blame	:	praise
bless	:	curse
bitter	:	sweet
borrow	:	lend
bottom	:	top
boy	:	girl
brave	:	cowardly
build	:	destroy
bold	:	meek, timid
borrow	:	lend
bound	:	unbound, free
boundless	:	limited
bright	:	dim, dull
brighten	:	fade
broad	:	narrow

C

calm	:	windy, troubled
can	:	cannot, can't
capable	:	incapable
captive	:	free
careful	:	careless
cheap	:	expensive
cheerful	:	sad, discouraged, dreary
clear	:	cloudy, opaque
clever	:	stupid
clockwise	:	counterclockwise
close	:	far, distant
closed	:	ajar, open
clumsy	:	graceful
cold	:	hot
combine	:	separate
come	:	go
comfort	:	discomfort
common	:	rare
conceal	:	reveal
contract	:	expand
cool	:	warm
correct	:	incorrect, wrong
courage	:	cowardice
create	:	destroy
crooked	:	straight
cruel	:	kind
compulsory	:	voluntary
courteous	:	discourteous, rude

D

dangerous	:	safe
dark	:	light
day	:	night
daytime	:	nighttime
dead	:	alive
decline	:	accept, increase
decrease	:	increase
deep	:	shallow
definite	:	indefinite
demand	:	supply
despair	:	hope
dim	:	bright
disappear	:	appear
discourage	:	encourage
diseased	:	healthy
down	:	up
downwards	:	upwards
dreary	:	cheerful
dry	:	moist, wet
dull	:	bright, shiny
dusk	:	dawn

E

early	:	late
east	:	west
easy	:	hard, difficult
empty	:	full
encourage	:	discourage
end	:	begin, start
enter	:	exit
even	:	odd
expand	:	contract
export	:	import
exterior	:	interior
external	:	internal

F

fade	:	brighten
fail	:	succeed
false	:	true
famous	:	unknown

Synonyms, Antonyms, Homonyms and Homophones

far	:	near
fast	:	slow
fat	:	thin
feeble	:	strong, powerful
few	:	many
find	:	lose
first	:	last
float	:	sink
foolish	:	wise
fore	:	aft
free	:	bound, captive
fold	:	unfold
forget	:	remember
found	:	lost
fresh	:	stale
frequent	:	seldom
friend	:	enemy
for	:	against
fortunate	:	unfortunate
full	:	empty

G

generous	:	stingy
gentle	:	rough
get	:	give
giant	:	tiny, small, dwarf
girl	:	boy
give	:	receive, take
glad	:	sad, sorry
gloomy	:	cheerful
go	:	stop
good	:	bad, evil
grant	:	refuse
great	:	tiny, small, unimportant
grow	:	shrink
guest	:	host
guilty	:	innocent

H

happy	:	sad
hard	:	easy
hard	:	soft
harmful	:	harmless
harsh	:	mild
hate	:	love
haves	:	have-nots
healthy	:	diseased, ill, sick
heaven	:	hell
heavy	:	light
help	:	hinder
here	:	there
hero	:	coward
high	:	low
hill	:	valley
hinder	:	help
honest	:	dishonest
horizontal	:	vertical
hot	:	cold
humble	:	proud

I

ill	:	healthy, well
immense	:	tiny, small
important	:	trivial
in	:	out
include	:	exclude
increase	:	decrease
inferior	:	superior
inhale	:	exhale
inner	:	outer
inside	:	outside
intelligent	:	stupid, unintelligent
interesting	:	boring
interior	:	exterior
interesting	:	dull, uninteresting
internal	:	external
intentional	:	accidental

J

join	:	separate
junior	:	senior
just	:	unjust
justice	:	injustice

K

knowledge	:	ignorance
known	:	unknown

L

landlord	:	tenant
large	:	small

last	:	first
laugh	:	cry
lawful	:	unlawful, illegal
lazy	:	industrious
leader	:	follower
left	:	right
lend	:	borrow
lengthen	:	shorten
lenient	:	strict
left	:	right
less	:	more
light	:	dark, heavy
like	:	dislike, hate
likely	:	unlikely
limited	:	boundless
little	:	big
long	:	short
loose	:	tight
lose	:	find
loss	:	win
loud	:	quiet
love	:	hate
low	:	high
loyal	:	disloyal

M

mad	:	happy, sane
major	:	minor
many	:	few
mature	:	immature
maximum	:	minimum
melt	:	freeze
merry	:	sad
messy	:	neat
minor	:	major
minority	:	majority
miser	:	spendthrift
misunderstand	:	understand
more	:	less

N

nadir	:	zenith
narrow	:	wide
near	:	far, distant
neat	:	messy, untidy
never	:	always
new	:	old
night	:	day
nighttime	:	daytime
no	:	yes
noisy	:	quiet
none	:	some
north	:	south

O

obedient	:	disobedient
odd	:	even
offer	:	refuse
old	:	young
old	:	new
on	:	off
open	:	closed, shut
opposite	:	same, similar
optimist	:	pessimist
out	:	in
outer	:	inner
over	:	under

P

past	:	present
patient	:	impatient
peace	:	war
permanent	:	temporary
plentiful	:	scarce
plural	:	singular
poetry	:	prose
polite	:	rude, impolite
possible	:	impossible
poverty	:	wealth, riches
powerful	:	weak
pretty	:	ugly
private	:	public
prudent	:	imprudent
pure	:	impure, contaminated
push	:	pull

Q

qualified	:	unqualified
question	:	answer

quiet	:	loud, noisy
R		
raise	:	lower
rapid	:	slow
rare	:	common
regular	:	irregular
real	:	fake
rich	:	poor
right	:	left, wrong
right	:	side-up - upside-down
rough	:	smooth
rude	:	courteous
S		
safe	:	unsafe
same	:	opposite
satisfactory	:	unsatisfactory
secure	:	insecure
scatter	:	collect
separate	:	join, together
serious	:	trivial
second	:	hand - new
shallow	:	deep
shrink	:	grow
sick	:	healthy, ill
simple	:	complex, hard
singular	:	plural
sink	:	float
slim	:	fat, thick
slow	:	fast
sober	:	drunk
soft	:	hard
some	:	none
sorrow	:	joy
sour	:	sweet
sow	:	reap
straight	:	crooked
start	:	finish
stop	:	go
strict	:	lenient
strong	:	weak
success	:	failure
sunny	:	cloudy
synonym	:	antonym
sweet	:	sour
T		
take	:	give
tall	:	short
tame	:	wild
them	:	us
there	:	here
thick	:	thin
tight	:	loose, slack
tiny	:	big, huge
together	:	apart
top	:	bottom
tough	:	easy, tender
transparent	:	opaque
true	:	false
truth	:	flasehood, lie, untruth
U		
under	:	over
unfold	:	fold
unknown	:	known
unqualified	:	qualified
unsafe	:	safe
up	:	down
upside	:	down - right-side-up
upstairs	:	downstairs
us	:	them
useful	:	useless
V		
vacant	:	occupied
vanish	:	appear
vast	:	tiny
victory	:	defeat
virtue	:	vice
visible	:	invisible
voluntary	:	compulsory
W		
war	:	peace
wax	:	wane
weak	:	strong
wet	:	dry
white	:	black
wide	:	narrow
win	:	lose

wisdom	:	folly, stupidity
within	:	outside
wrong	:	right

Y

yes	:	no
yin	:	yang
young	:	old

Z

zip	:	unzip
zenith	:	nadir

> **TRIVIA**
>
> If you were to write out every number name in full (one, two, three, four…), you wouldn't use a single letter B until you reached one billion.

Homonym

A homonym is one of a group of words that share the same spelling and the same pronunciation but have different meanings. This usually happens as a result of the two words having different origins.

Example: Bear (animal), Bear (to take responsibility for something)

Homophone

A homophone is a word that is pronounced the same as another word but differs in meaning.

Example: The words may be spelled the same, such as rose (flower) and rose (past tense of 'rise'), or differently, such as carat, caret, and carrot, or to, two and too.

Homonyms vs Homophones

All homonyms are homophones because they sound the same. However, not all homophones are homonyms. Homophones with different spellings are not homonyms.

Examples

Aid	:	Aide
Affect	:	Effect
Aisle	:	I'll - Isle
Aloud	:	Allowed
Altar	:	Alter
Ark	:	Arc
Ball	:	Bawl
Base	:	Bass
Beech	:	Beach
Birth	:	Berth
Bore	:	Boar
Byte	:	Bite
Blew	:	Blue
Bow	:	Bough
Boy	:	Buoy
Bread	:	Bred
Browse	:	Brows
Cell	:	Sell
Cereal	:	Serial
Chilly	:	Chili, Chile
Chord	:	Cord
Complement	:	Compliment
Counsel	:	Council
Creak	:	Creek
Crews	:	Cruise
Dual	:	Duel
Fair	:	Fare
Fairy	:	Ferry
Feat	:	Feet
Fir	:	Fur
Flea	:	Flee
Gorilla	:	Guerrilla
Grease	:	Greece
Groan	:	Grown
Hall	:	Haul
Halve	:	Have
Holey	:	Holy - Wholly
Incite	:	Insight
Jeans	:	Genes
Knead	:	Need
Knight	:	Night
Lessen	:	Lesson
Links	:	Lynx
Loan	:	Lone
Oral	:	Aural
Ought	:	Aught
Oar	:	Or - Ore
Overdo	:	Overdue

Synonyms, Antonyms, Homonyms and Homophones

Peak	:	Peek	Soar	:	Sore
Phase	:	Faze	Sole	:	Soul
Pole	:	Poll	Toe	:	Tow
Pray	:	Prey	Vary	:	Very
Principal	:	Principle	Wail	:	Whale
Raze	:	Raise	Wait	:	Weight
Real	:	Reel	We	:	Wee
Ring	:	Wring	Weather	:	Whether
Role	:	Roll	Which	:	Witch
Sew	:	So, Sow	Whose	:	Who's
Site	:	Sight, Cite			

MUST REMEMBER

- Synonym is a word or phrase that means exactly or nearly the same as another word or phrase in the same language.
- An antonym is a word which means the opposite of another word. Antonyms are also called opposites.
- A homonym is one of a group of words that share the same spelling and the same pronunciation but have different meanings.
- A homophone is a word that is pronounced the same as another word but differs in meaning.
- All homonyms are homophones because they sound the same. However, not all homophones are homonyms. Homophones with different spellings are not homonyms.

PRACTICE EXERCISE

I. Choose the option which is synonym of the given words.

1. Abandon
   (a) try (b) join
   (c) keep with (d) forsake
2. Abdicate
   (a) join (b) search
   (c) abandon (d) advance
3. Absolute
   (a) division (b) complete
   (c) small (d) half
4. Abstain
   (a) refrain (b) ingest
   (c) take in (d) consume
5. Accord
   (a) confer (b) refusal
   (c) dissension (d) opposition
6. Acquaint
   (a) withhold (b) conceal
   (c) familiarise (d) risky
7. Aggravate
   (a) decline (b) acquire
   (c) excited (d) irritate
8. Latent
   (a) apparent (b) manifest
   (c) concealed (d) obvious
10. Sporadic
    (a) methodical (b) continuous
    (c) occasional (d) constant
11. Resume
    (a) complete (b) a new start
    (c) halt (d) cease
12. Melange
    (a) mixture of medley (b) optical illusion
    (c) desert (d) household
13. Lethargy
    (a) laxity (b) vivacity
    (c) awakening (d) vitality
14. Ameliorate
    (a) worsen (b) to appease
    (c) aggravate (d) to improve
15. Emulate
    (a) deny (b) imitate
    (c) neglect (d) question
16. Hybrid
    (a) division (b) purebred
    (c) crossbred (d) unmixed
17. Amoral
    (a) unprincipled (b) immoral
    (c) innocent (d) controlled
18. Rectify
    (a) bear (b) correct
    (c) validate (d) destroy
19. Parasite
    (a) a loss of motion (b) blessing
    (c) disease (d) one that clings
20. Eulogistic
    (a) unmannerly (b) wanderer
    (c) praising (d) insulting
21. Nostalgic
    (a) indolent (b) diseased
    (c) homesick (d) soothing
22. Largesse
    (a) hindrance (b) unkindness
    (c) malevolence (d) liberal
23. Consummation
    (a) ultimate completion
    (b) act of forgiveness
    (c) commencement
    (d) unfulfillment
24. Privy
    (a) revealed (b) uncocealed
    (c) secretive (d) unaware
25. Emancipate
    (a) make a solemn declaration
    (b) imprison
    (c) correct morally
    (d) set free
26. Brazen
    (a) melodramatic (b) shamefaced
    (c) modest (d) shameless

Synonyms, Antonyms, Homonyms and Homophones

27. Cajole
    (a) discourage
    (b) persuade
    (c) disenchant
    (d) dissuade
    (e) craze
28. Rigid
    (a) unreliable
    (b) hard
    (c) inexact
    (d) voluminous
29. Acronym
    (a) poem of sorrow
    (b) pen name used by an author
    (c) similar meaning
    (d) word formed from an abbreviation
30. Spew
    (a) take up liquids
    (b) throw in water
    (c) to come forth in a flush
    (d) split
31. Sozzled
    (a) drunk
    (b) moderate
    (c) culturad
    (d) burning
32. Rookie
    (a) expert
    (b) professional
    (c) a new recruit
    (d) an old man
33. Dissolute
    (a) repulsive
    (b) respectful
    (c) virtuous
    (d) immoral
34. Patron
    (a) venerable old man
    (b) one who gives encouragement to others
    (c) antagonist
    (d) detractor
35. Presage
    (a) to foretell
    (b) make ready
    (c) assume
    (d) consider
36. Attrition
    (a) attraction
    (b) happiness
    (c) strengthening
    (d) decline
37. Accolade
    (a) fruit
    (b) balcony
    (c) outer garments
    (d) honour
38. Benign
    (a) injurious
    (b) gentle
    (c) malignant
    (d) unfriendly
39. Candid
    (a) experienced
    (b) frank
    (c) deceitful
    (d) secretive
40. Ingenious
    (a) misleading
    (b) clever at inventing
    (c) alarm
    (d) unresourceful

II. Choose the option which is opposite of the given words.

1. Indiscreet
   (a) reliable
   (b) honest
   (c) discreet
   (d) stupid
2. Familiar
   (a) unpleasant
   (b) dangerous
   (c) friendly
   (d) strange
3. Tangible
   (a) intangible
   (b) concrete
   (c) actual
   (d) solid
4. Love
   (a) villainy
   (b) hatred
   (c) compulsion
   (d) force
5. Famous
   (a) disgraced
   (b) unknown
   (c) evil
   (d) popular
6. Absolute
   (a) deficient
   (b) faulty
   (c) limited
   (d) scarce
7. Frugal
   (a) copious
   (b) extravagant
   (c) generous
   (d) ostentatious
8. Insipid
   (a) tasty
   (b) stupid
   (c) discreet
   (d) feast
9. Able
   (a) disable
   (b) inable
   (c) unable
   (d) misable
10. Hostility
    (a) courtesy
    (b) hospitality
    (c) relationship
    (d) friendliness
11. Crowded
    (a) busy
    (b) congested
    (c) quiet
    (d) deserted

12. Comic
    (a) emotional (b) tragic
    (c) fearful (d) painful
13. Hapless
    (a) cheerful (b) consistent
    (c) fortunate (d) shapely
14. Flimsy
    (a) frail (b) filthy
    (c) firm (d) flippant
15. Equanimity
    (a) resentment (b) dubiousness
    (c) duplicity (d) excitement
16. Addition
    (a) division (b) enumeration
    (c) subtraction (d) multiplication
17. Zenith
    (a) acme (b) top
    (c) nadir (d) pinnacle
18. Doubtful
    (a) famous (b) certain
    (c) fixed (d) important
19. Perennial
    (a) frequent (b) regular
    (c) lasting (d) rare
20. Benign
    (a) malevolent (b) soft
    (c) friendly (d) unwise
21. Hindrance
    (a) aid (b) persuasion
    (c) cooperation (d) agreement
22. Extricate
    (a) manifest (b) palpable
    (c) release (d) entangle
23. Repress
    (a) inhibit (b) liberate
    (c) curb (d) quell
24. Acquitted
    (a) freed (b) burdened
    (c) convicted (d) entrusted
25. Provocation
    (a) vocation (b) pacification
    (c) peace (d) destruction
26. Subservient
    (a) aggressive (b) straightforward
    (c) dignified (d) supercilious
27. Lend
    (a) borrow (b) cheat
    (c) pawn (d) hire
28. Faint-Hearted
    (a) warm-hearted (b) full-blooded
    (c) hot-blooded (d) stout-hearted
29. Remiss
    (a) forgetful (b) watchful
    (c) dutiful (d) harmful
30. Transparent
    (a) semi-transparent (b) muddy
    (c) opaque (d) dark
31. Honorary
    (a) dishonorable (b) reputed
    (c) paid (d) official
32. Meticulous
    (a) mutual (b) shaggy
    (c) meretricious (d) slovenly
33. Loquacious
    (a) reticent (b) talkative
    (c) garrulous (d) verbose
34. Confess
    (a) deny (b) refuse
    (c) contest (d) contend
35. Annoy
    (a) praise (b) rejoice
    (c) please (d) reward
36. Repel
    (a) attend (b) concentrate
    (c) continue (d) attract
37. Suppress
    (a) encourage (b) allow
    (c) praise (d) permit
38. Niggardly
    (a) frugal (b) thrifty
    (c) stingy (d) benerous
39. Impasse
    (a) resurgence (b) breakthrough
    (c) continuation (d) combination

Synonyms, Antonyms, Homonyms and Homophones

40. Haphazard
    (a) fortuitous   (b) indifferent
    (c) methodical   (d) accidental

III. Fill in the blanks with the correct option.

1. I didn't ____ what she said.
   (a) hear   (b) here
   (c) knew   (b) known
2. They forgot to take ____ printouts.
   (a) there   (b) their
   (c) they're   (d) none of these
3. Venison is the meat from a ____.
   (a) dear   (b) deer
   (c) cow   (d) camel
4. The house is by the ____.
   (a) see   (b) sea
   (c) saw   (b) seen
5. She held the ____ in her hand.
   (a) reigns   (b) rains
   (c) reins   (d) none of these
6. They tried to ____ the painting.
   (a) steel   (b) steal
   (c) stole   (b) stolen
7. He had to ____ the button on.
   (a) sow   (b) sew
   (c) either (a) or (b)   (d) none of these
8. I hope the ____ is fine.
   (a) weather   (b) whether
   (c) wether   (d) none of these
9. He was a medieval ____.
   (a) night   (b) knight
   (c) man   (d) person
10. The building ____ is huge.
    (a) site   (b) sight
    (c) scene   (d) view
11. She's as mad as a March ____.
    (a) hair   (b) hare
    (c) fair   (d) fare
12. She gave him a _____ of her mind.
    (a) peace   (b) piece
    (c) lot   (d) none of these
13. He ____ a snowball at the police officer.
    (a) threw   (b) through
    (c) throw   (d) thrown
14. It's a ____ of time.
    (a) waist   (b) waste
    (c) wait   (d) want
15. They didn't ____ us of the danger.
    (a) warn   (b) worn
    (c) wear   (d) wore
16. They read the poems ____.
    (a) allowed   (b) aloud
    (c) allow   (d) allowing
17. It's made from wheat ____.
    (a) flower   (b) flour
    (c) floor   (d) float
18. They've got a ____ at the Ritz.
    (a) suit   (b) suite
    (c) sweet   (d) none of these
19. On the ____, I enjoyed it.
    (a) whole   (b) hole
    (c) total   (d) none of these
20. It's not much ____ to go.
    (a) father   (b) farther
    (c) further   (d) farthest
21. You're no ____ of mine!
    (a) sun   (b) son
    (c) shun   (d) shine
22. He's the ____ to the throne.
    (a) air   (b) heir
    (c) here   (d) none of these
23. The tea's a bit ____.
    (a) weak   (b) week
    (c) weaken   (d) woken
24. She's the ____ owner.
    (a) soul   (b) sole
    (c) whole   (d) total
25. The book is _____ back at the library in two weeks.
    (a) dew   (b) due
    (c) dow   (d) valid
26. You slow a car with the ____.
    (a) brake   (b) break
    (c) broke   (d) broken
27. The negative feeling you get when you do something wrong is ____.
    (a) gilt   (b) guilt
    (c) guilty   (b) none of these

28. The cyclist was ____ very fast.
    (a) peddling
    (b) pedalling\pedaling
    (c) peddled
    (d) peddle
29. It was ____ madness.
    (a) sheer
    (b) shear
    (c) same
    (d) similar
30. The eagle is a bird of ____.
    (a) prey
    (b) pray
    (c) hunter
    (d) hunt
31. Could you ____ the film for a minute?
    (a) paws
    (b) pause
    (c) either (a) or (b)
    (d) none of these
32. After standing for an hour in the heat, he ____.
    (a) feinted
    (b) fainted
    (c) faint
    (d) found
33. Don't tell them anything- they're not very ____.
    (a) discrete
    (b) discreet
    (c) desperate
    (d) none of these
34. He's very old-fashioned and ____.
    (a) stayed
    (b) staid
    (c) stood
    (d) stay
35. Floating ____ are used to help boats navigate.
    (a) boys
    (b) buoys
    (c) bouys
    (d) bought
36. He's very ____ and worries about his appearance all the time.
    (a) vein
    (b) vane
    (c) vain
    (d0 vaned
37. They took blood from my ____.
    (a) vane
    (b) vein
    (c) vain
    (d) vained
38. I am an innocent ____ in all of this.
    (a) pawn
    (b) pon
    (c) pon
    (d) pony
39. That's a ____ tree.
    (a) beach
    (b) beech
    (c) breaches
    (d) none of these
40. We have to make sure the timing's right. We must be in ____.
    (a) sink
    (b) sync
    (c) sank
    (d) sunk

HOTS

Choose the correct synonym from the options below.

1. Beautiful
   (a) Bright
   (b) Pretty
   (c) Mirthful
   (d) Gracious
2. Hardworking
   (a) Content
   (b) Fair
   (c) Sincere
   (d) Diligent
3. Lazy
   (a) Secure
   (b) Lethargic
   (c) Opportunist
   (d) Withdrawn
4. Outgoing
   (a) Extrovert
   (b) Attractive
   (c) Objective
   (d) Trustworthy
5. Amiable
   (a) Determined
   (b) Sharp
   (c) Kind
   (d) Lovely

Synonyms, Antonyms, Homonyms and Homophones

Analogies and One Word

Learning Objectives : In this chapter, students will learn about:
- ✓ Analogy and its types
- ✓ Concept and usage of One Words

CHAPTER SUMMARY

An analogy (dog is to puppy as cat is to kitten, or, as it commonly appears on standardized tests, especially in higher grades: dog : puppy :: cat : kitten) is a comparison between two things that are usually thought to be different from each other, but have some similarities. They help us understand things by making connections and seeing relationships between them based on knowledge we already possess.

Analogies are a ubiquitous staple of standardized tests. This type of comparison plays a significant role not only in improving problem solving and decision making skills, but also in perception and memory, as well as communication and reasoning skills. Learning analogies can help with reading and building vocabulary.

Types of Analogies
- Synonym
  Example: happy : joyful :: sad : depressed
- Antonym
  Example: inflation : deflation :: frail : strong
- Characteristic
  Example: tropical : hot :: polar : cold
- Part/Whole
  Example: finger : hand :: petal : flower
- Degree
  Example: mist : fog :: drizzle : tropical storm
- Type
  Example: golden retriever : dog :: salmon : fish
- Tool/Worker
  Example: pen : writer :: voice : singer
- Action/Object
  Example: fly : airplane :: drive : car
- Item/Purpose
  Example: knife : cut :: ruler : measure
- Product/Worker
  Example: poet : poem :: baker : pie

Analogy vs. Metaphor
An analogy is a parallel comparison between two different things, whereas a metaphor is more of a direct comparison between two things, often with one word being used to symbolically represent another. "All the world's a stage. And all the men and women merely players." is an example of a famous metaphor. William Shakespeare is directly comparing the world to a stage, with the people playing "roles" as they go about their daily lives. A comparable analogy would be "Players are to stage as figure skaters are to ice rink."

Analogies at a glance
- Elementary School Analogy Words
  Example: big, snow, hand, pencil, apple, cat, happy, milk, ruler, eye
- Middle School Analogy Words
  Example: gigantic, anxious, blustery, thermometer, chameleon, barren, staff, drizzle, fiction, digestion
- High School Analogy Words

Example: carnivore, abhor, placid, laceration, adulation, hone, democracy, confederacy, milliliter, philanthropist

TRIVIA

The original story from Tales of 1001 Arabian Nights begins, 'Aladdin was a little Chinese boy.'.

One Word

One word can often express an idea of phrase or clause and can help in writing or communicating precisely.

One Word Substitution – A

Abdurate	Unmouable - stubborn - unyeilding
Aborigines	The original inhabitants of a country
Abridge	To condense
Absolute Zero	It is the lowest temperature possible
Acceterate	Cause to move faster
Accelerate	Speed up
Acerose	Needle-shaped
Acess	Means of approaching
Acoustics	Relating to sound
Acrophobia	Pathological fear of high places
Acumen	Superior mental acuteness
Adhoc	For the purpose
Adolscence	A stage of growth between boyhood and youth.
Adulation	Excessive devotion
Aerial	Living in air
Aeronautics	Science of flight of aeroplanes
Aesthetic	A love of beauty
Affidavit	A written statement given on oath
Affinity	Having a natural attention to
Aggravate	To make worse
Aglophoble	A person who hates England
Agonostic	One who thinks that everything is known through god only
Alimony	Money giving to a woman who divorces his husband
Allegory	Description of a subject with symbolical representation to another
Allusive	Having reference to something
Alluvial	Sandy soil deposited by running water
Alpinism	Mountain climbing
Altimeter	Instrument used for measuring altitudes in aircraft
Altruist	One who works for the good of others
Amateur	One who learns a subject as a hobby
Ammeter	Instrument used for measuring the electrical currents in amperes
Amnesty	General pardon of the offenses against government
Amoyan	Strong and powerful person
Amphibian	Living/Operating on land and water
Amphibious	Animals that can be live on land and water
Ample	Adequate or more than dequate - in extent, size etc
Anachronism	Comparing modern persons with ancient persons
Anachronism	Something out of its proper time
Anachronistic	A word which can be interpreted in any way
Anachronistic	Set in wrong time or period
Anaesthetics	Drugs causing unconsciousness such as chloroform
Anaesthetist	One who gives chloroform to a patient

Analogies and One Word   49

Analogy	Relation - Relationship	Aquantie	Relating to water
Anarchist	One who is out to destroy government	Aquarium	A thing where fishes are kept
Anarchist	One who provokes disorder in a state	Aquatic	Living in water
		Arbitrator	One who is appointed by two parties & decide their difference
Anatomist	One who describes the parts of the human body		
Anatomy	Study of sciences relating to the bodily structure of human	Arboreal	Living in trees
		Arboriculture	Cultivation of trees and vegetables
Anile	Like a weak old woman.	Archaeologist	One who studies human antiquities
Anemometer	Instrument used for measuring the force and velocity of winds		
		Archaism	Using ancient Languages
Annihilate	Destroy utterly	Archeologist	One who make a scientific study of human antiquities
Annuity	Yearly grant - beings - animals and plants by way of disection		
		Archipelago	See which has number of small islands
Annular	Ring shaped	Archive	That what is not in current use
Anodyne	Pain reliever		
Anonymus	That which is written without name	Aristocracy	The rule by nobels
		Arsenal	A place where weapons are manufactured and stored
Antagonist	Enemy - Antagonism		
Anthropologist	One who studies history relating to the development of man from primitive ages	Articulate	To pronounce clearly
		Astronomy	Study of heavenly bodies
		Atheist	One who has no belief in god
Antibiotics	Drugs which completely destroys bacteria	Atmosphere	The air surrounding the earths
Antiquarian	A person who is interested in antiquities	Audible	That which can be heard
		Audiometer	Instrument used for measuring the intensity of sound
Aphelion	The point in a planet's orbit that tis farthest from the sun		
Apiary	a bee house (Contains several hives)	Audiophone	Instrument used for improving imperfect sense of hearing
Apirigee	A point as above that is nearest to earth		
		Aurora Australis	Southern lights
Apologist	One who says sorry (Sorrow) for his mistakes		
		Aurura Borealis	Northern lights
Aporhtegm	Words spoken by great men		
Apostasy	To renounce one's faith or religion	Autocracy	Absolute rule by one person
		Autocrat	Who exercises absolute power
Apostate	One who deserts his religion or principles		

Avairy	A building for keeping - rearing and breeding of birds
Avalanche	A heavy mass of snow falling down a hill with great noise
Avarice	Greed - Inordinate desire to gain and hoard wealth

One Word Substitution – B

Ballad	A short narrative poem - adopted for writing and sighning
Ballistics	Science dealing with the motion of projectile like rockets bombs & shells
Balmaccan	A type of man's overcoat
Barbarism	Mixed Language
Barometer	An apparatus used for measuring the atmospheric pressure
Bellicose	Ready to fight
Benefactor	Kindly helper. One who makes a request or endowment
Benevolent	Kind hearted
Bevy	Group of girls or women larks. Flocks of quail
Bibliographer	One who writes big books
Bibliography	A list of books with details of authorship, editions, subject etc
Bibliophile	A person who loves books
Biblophile	One who loves the study of books
Bifurcate	Divided into two branches
Bigamy	The crime of having two life partners at a time
Bilingual	Spoken or written in two languages
Biography	Life of a person written by somebody
Biologist	One who studies the science of animals and plants
Biota	Animal and plant life of a religion or period
Black Box	An apparatus which records the fight data of an aeroplane and is also a voice recorder
Blackbinding	Kidnapping for selling into slavery
Blasphemer	One who speaks evil - Impcous one - irrevirent one
Blood Transfusion	The process the transfusing blood of one person into blood stream of another person
Boat Wrighter	Wagon maker
Bolo	Large single - adged military knife - Machete
Botanist	One who studies the science of plants
Boycott	To obstain from buying or using
Brettle	Easily broken
Buccal	Of the check of the sides of the mouth
Bureaucracy	A gout in which the whole power is vested in officials
Butcher	One whose business to a slaughter cattle for food
Bigamist	A person who marries someone else while already being married to someone

One Word Substitution – C

Cacophonous	Harsh or discordant sound
Cadaver	Dead body
Caduceus	Emblem of medical profession and US army medical corps
Calibre	Diameter of bore of gun - degree of merit
Calligraphy	Beautiful writing
Calorimeter	An instrument used for measuring quantities of heat
Canon	Church law body of principles

Carburator	An apparatus used in an internal combustion engine for charging air with petrol
Cardiac	Pertaining to the heart
Cardinal	Of prime importance
Cardiograph	A medical instrument for tracing heat movements
Caries	Dental decay
Carniology	Describe the habits, merits and demerits of a man by seeing his skull carniologist
Carnivore	Flesh eater – dogs, cats, lions
Carnivorous	An animal that eats human flesh
Carrion	Dead and putrifying flesh
Catastrophe	Denotes the last stage of a tradegy
Celibate	One who resolved not to marry
Centipede	An insect with many legs
Cervine	Of deers or the deer family - Deerlike
Chagrien	Vexation from humiliation or disappointment
Chandlier	Candle maker - Merchant - Dealer in supplies and provisions
Chemotherapy	Controls of infections by chemicals
Chiarascuro	Distribution of light and shade in a picture
Chiromanchy	Fortune telling through palm reading - palmistry
Choronology	Arrangements of events according to dates or times of occurance
Chronologer	One who writes the details of transactions which made in a country
Chronometer	An instrument kept on boardship for measuring accurate time
Cinematograph	It contains a series of lenses arranged to throw on screen an enlarged image of photography
Circumlocution	A round about way of speaking
Clarify	Make clear
Classic	That which is acclaimed as an excellent work
Clio	Greek muse of history
Coalesce	Grow into one - Blend - unite - fuse
Coercion	Intimidation by threat or duress - forceful - compulsion
Coeval	Of the same age or duration - Contemporary with
Cognomen	Surname or nickname
Collegues	Those who work in the same department
Colleiny	Complete with buildings and work - Caolmines
Comatose	In a coma - Lacking energy - Lethargic
Comely	Pleasing in appearance - fair - pretty
Commutator	Device for reversing direction of electrical current
Compensation	Money given for requisitioned property
Concatinate	Linked together
Concetric	Having the same centre
Conflagrative	Combustible - flammable - inflammable
Connoisseur	Expert in art - the fine arts
Contagious Disease	A disease which spreads by contact
Contemporary	A man living in the same age with another
Continent	Restrained in regard to desires or passion - especially to sexual desires

Convalescence	The gradual recovery from illness	Decelerate	Slow down
Converge	To meet in a point (Rays & illness)	Defendant	One who is sued by the plaintiff
Cooper	Maker of casks or barrels	Deism	Got birth and followed principles in a particular caste but telling, he is not god
Copy-right	Exclusive right to publish a book		
Coral reef	A chain of rocks laying at or near the sea	Deist	One who believes in the existence of god
Cosmopolitan	One who is free from national limitations	Delettante	An admirer by the people
		Deliquisic	Become liquid by absorbing moisture from the air - Melt away
Costegate	Correct by punishing		
Creditor	One to whom a debt is owing	Delittante	One who takes up an art - dabbler - a lover of fine arts
Credulity	Trust without proper evidence readiness to believe		
		Deluge	Anything that overwhelms like a flood - great flood - rain
Credulous	A person who readily believes others		
		Democracy	The gout formed by the people
Crescograph	Instrument used for measuring the growth of plants		
		Demography	Science of vital and social statistics
Cresendo	Gradual increase in force - volume - loudness	Demonology	Ralating to devils - ghost and other terror things
Crisis	Turning point of danger or disease	Depilate	Remove hair from
		Dermatologist	One who treats skin diseases
Cryogenics	Branch of physics dealing with very low temparature	Desiccate	Dry throughly - Remove moisture from
Cryptograph	Secret writing	Despondent	High - Spirited - Overflowing with enthusiasm - boiling up
Crystallography	Science of crystallization		
Cul-De-Sac	Dead end	Despotism	Is a form of government in which a single entity rules with absolute power.
Cygnet	Young swan		
Cynosoure	Centre of interest - something that strongly attracts attention by its brilliance		
		Detenu	One who detained in custody
		Dislectical (s)	Logical argumentation
Cytogenetics	Cell formation	Dialysis	The process for flood purification when the kidneys malfunction
Cytology	Dealing with cells		
One Word Substitution – D			
Debacle	Sudden collapse - general break-up - violent rush	Dilemma	A state of a person, who is asked to choose one of the two infavourable things
Debtor	One who owes money to another	Diminish	Make or become smaller
Decalogue	Ten commandments	Diminuendo	Gradual increase in force

Analogies and One Word

Dipsomania	Irristible craving for alcoholic drinks	Electrometer	Instrument used for measuring electricity
Dissuade	Persuade not to do something	Elegiac	Expressing sorrow or lamentation
Dividend	Sum payable as profit to an individual by a joint stock company	Elegy	A lament for the dead
		Elixir	Not clerical
Domicile	A place where one lives permanently	Ellipsis	The ommission from a sentence of a work or words that would comple the construction
Dorsal	Situated on bank		
Drinker's apparatus	Instrument used to help breathing in infantile paralysis	Etymology	Science relating to the formation and development of words
Dynamo	The origin of electricity in a dynamo is the transformation of mechanical energy into energy	Embezzle	Divert money fraudulently to one's own use
		Emeritus	Honourably discharged from service

One Word Substitution – E

Earth's Atmosphere	Covering of air which surrounds of earth	Emetic	Inducing vomiting - something that induces vomiting
Ebullient	Situated on the abdominal side		
		Emollient	Soothing to living tissue
Eccentric	That which is not placed centrally	Empericism	Belief based on experience or observation
Ecclisiologist	One who studies the science relating to the church	Encomium	Formal expression of high praise - eulogy
Eclectric	Persons with unusual or odd personality	Encroach	Make inroads on others property
Eclogue	A pastoral poem	Endemic	A disease which becomes prevalent in a particular area on account of its surroundings conditions
Ecology	Study of plants or of animal or of people or of institutions in relation to environment		
		Enduring	Long lasting
Edible	That which is fit to be eaten	Enjoin	Direct or order someone to do something
Effiminate	A person who is womanish in his habits		
Egoeism	Selfishness – opposed to altruism	Enthologist	One who studies the science of the variatees of human race
Egoism	Speaking too much of one self		
		Entomologist	One who studies about insects
Egoist	One who speaks using I and me always	Ephemeral	Transitory - short lived - lasting a very short time
Elastic	One which rescemes its normal shape and size after the stress is releases	Epicentre	(Of earthquake) is the point at which earthquake breakout

Epicure	A person who is very fond of sensous enjoyments	Exbiology	Science dealing with life or possibilities of life existing beyond the earth
Epidemic	A disease which attacks many people in a particular area in one time	Exegesis	Critical explanation or interpretation
Epilogue	A poem of speech at the end of the play	Exemplary	Fit to be
Epiphany	An appearance or manifestation	Exercism	Slogan to derive or get out of the dragon
Equanimity	Evenness of mind or temper	Exodus	Departure - Emigration (Usually of a large number of people)
Equigravisphere	A point in space where the gravity is constant		
Equine	Of horses - horselike - a horse	Exonerate	Free from blame - Exculpate
Equinox	When days and nights are equal (March 21 - September)	Explicit	Fully and clearly expressed
		Extempore	Speech delivered without any preparation
Esoteric	Known only a few - Reconcile	Extinguish	To put an end to
Estivate	Spend a hot or dry period in a prolonged state of torpor or dormancy		

One Word Substitution – F

Fanatic	One who passes interest in religion
Fatalism	Religion that which believes that god is everything
Fathom	Understand fully - unit of length equal to six feet
Fathometer	Instrument used for measuring the depth of the ocean
Fauna	Animals of a given region or period
Fealty	Sworn allegance to a lord
Fiduciary	Of the relationship between a trustee and his principal
Fertile	That which is productive
Fetish	Amulet object believed to have magic power
Filly	A young female horse
Fission	Cleaving or splitting into parts
Flock	Animals such as birds, sheep and goats keeping together in large number
Flora	Plants of a particular region or period
Flotsom	The thing which comes out from sea (Cannot stay in water)

Estuary	A broad channel formed by joining of the sea and river water
Ethologist	One who studies the science of character
Etiology	Study of causation. The study of the cause of disease
Etymologist	One who studies derivations of words - history of linguistic change
Eulogy	Speech or writing that praises - High praise - Encomium
Euphimism	Soften expression
Euphony	Melodious Music
Euthanasia	Mercy killing painless death to relieve suffering
Euthenics	Science of improving the environment
Exaggerate	Describe a thing beyond limits of truth
Exasphere	This is a outer most zone of the atmosphere and beings at about 40 miles above earth

Analogies and One Word

Fluctuating	Moving to & fro		Gynaecologist	One who treats femal diseases
Flux	Continuous change - instability - fusion			

One Word Substitution – H

Footpad	Robber, who goes on foot
Formidable	That which is heard tobe resisted
Fortissimo	Very loud
Fragile	That which can be easily broken
Funambulist	A rope dancer - who walks on thread
Fungi	A class of plants which have no chlorophyll
Fussion	Uniting by metting together

One Word Substitution – G

Galvanize	Startle into sudden activity - to coat with zinc
Galvanometer	A glass tube for measuring volume changes in chemical reactions between glasses
Gambrel	Type of roof
Gastronomy	Relating to taste (Food taste)
Genealogist	One who traces the history of the descent of families
Genealogy	Heredity, Hereditary
Genocide	international distriution of racial groups
Genuine	Authentic - free from pretense
Geologist	One who studies the internal structure of the earth (crust)
Germicide	Medicine that kills germs
Geysers	There are natural hot water springs
Glacier	A huge mass of snow moving slowly down the valley and stopes
Gnosticism	Heresay which is made up of a set of beliefs
Gourmet	Connoisseur of choice food
Graminuiorous	Animals that feed on grass
Gregarious	Animals living in flocks

Haemorrhage	Escape of blood to the ruptures of blood vessels inside the body
Hagiology	Relating to kings Hagiographic
Herbivore	Plant eater - hoofed mammals
Herbivorous	Animals eating herbs
Hedonist	One who devotes himself to pleasure
Hiatus	Gap - Missing part - Break in continuity - lacuna
Hibernate	To spend the winter in a dormant state
Hibernation	Condition of sleep during certain parts of the year
Hierarchy	Any system of persons or things passed on to other
Hieroglyphic	Pictographic script
Histrionics	Acting - Artificial behaviour or speech done for effect
Hodge-Podge	Heterogeneous mixture - Jumble
Holocaust	A sacrifice totally concerned by fire - Devastation
Holography	Making of true - three dimensional photographs by use of laser beams
Homely	Not beautiful - unattractive - plain
Homogenous	Things which are of the same kind and of the same dimensions
Homologous	Corresponding having same or similar relation
Homophone	Word pronounced the same as, but different in meaning spelled the same wayhood
Horologist	One who studies the art of clock making
Horticulture	An art of garden cultivation

Hostage	Persons given to another as pledge	Igloo	Eskimo home shaped hut or native house
Hullabaloo	Clamorous noise or disturbance - Uproar	Igneous	Of or about fire produced under intense heat
Hybrid	Anything derived from heterogeneous sources	Ill-omened	Ill fated-Unlucky
Hydraulics	Study of water or other liquid in Motion	Illegible	That which is incapable of being read
Hydrographer	One who knows the positions of lands and draws the maps	Illicit	Unlicensed-unlawful
		Imago	an insect in its sexually mature adult state
Hydrography	Description of oceans and lands and the oceans	Immiscible	Incapable of being mined
Hydrometer	Instrument used for measuring the specific gravity of liquids	Immutable	Unchangeable-unalterable-changeless
Hydrophobia	It is usually caused by the bite of mad dog	Implicit	Not fully and clearly expressed implied
Hydrophone	Instrument used for recording sound under water	Imply	Indicate without express statement
Hydroponics	Culture of plants without soil, with the help of chemical solutions containing nutrients	Impregnable	That which cannot be taken by force
		Improbable	That which is not likely to happen
Hydrostatics	Relating to water	Impromptu	Made or done without previous preparation - Extemporaneous
Hydrotropic	Turning towards or away from moisture		
Hygrometer	Instrument used for measuring humidity in air	Impenetrable	impossible to pass through or enter
Hymn	Song in praise of god		
Hyperbola	Curve with two distinct and similar branches	Inattentive	Not giving proper attention
		Inaudible	That which cannot be heard
Hypercriticism	Deep criticism		

One Word Substitution – I

Ichthyologist	An expert in fishes	Incarcerate	imprison or confine
Ichthyology	Study of fishes	Incarnadine	Blood red - crimson - flesh coloured - pale pink
Iconoclast	Destroyer of images attached on traditions		
Iconography	Teaching by pictures and models	Incinerate	Burn - Reduce to ashes
		Incognito	Travelling under a name other than one's own
Iconolater	Worshipper of idols or images		
Idol	Favorite - Any person or thing devotedly or excessively admired	Incombustible	Not inflammable

Analogies and One Word

Incompatible	Persons who cannot work or live together in harmony
Incomprehensible	That which cannot be understood
Iconoclast	A destroyer of images
Incorrigible	Incapable of being corrected
Incorruptible	very honest: incapable of being corrupted
Incredible	That which cannot be believed
Incriminate	Change with a crime or fault
Incumbent	Holding of an office - obligatory
Indescribable	That which is impossible to describe adequately
Inescapable	That which cannot escaped from
Inevitable	Sometimes which cannot fail to come to pass
Inexplicable	That which cannot be explained
Infallible	Incable of making mistakes
Infanticide	Murder or infants
Infections	That (disease) which is liable to spread
Inflammable	That which sets on fire easily
Inimitable	That which cannot be
Insolation	The sun's energy
Insoluble	That which cannot be dissolved in liquid
Insomnia	Loss of sleep
Inhalation	taking air into lungs - stimulus
Insurmountable	too great to be overcome
Interdiction	Prohibition prevention from participation in certain sacred acts
Interjection	A word exclamation
Internist	Medical student receiving training in a hospital
Intractable	That which cannot be controlled easily
Invertebrate	Without a backbone - without strength of characters
Invincible	That which cannot be defeated
Invulnerable	Incapable of being wounded
Ionosphere	The layer of the earth's atmosphere which contains a high concentration of ions and free electrons
Irrevocable	A decision on which one cannot go back
Isobel	Is a contour lines of equal rainfall
Isohyets	A line on a map connecting points having the same amount of rainfall in a given period
Isthmus	A narrow strip of land connecting two larger land masses
Itinerate	One who journeys from place to place

MUST REMEMBER

- An analogy is a parallel comparison between two different things, whereas a metaphor is more of a direct comparison between two things, often with one word being used to symbolically represent another.
- One word can often express an idea of phrase or clause and can help in writing or communicating precisely.

PRACTICE EXERCISE

I. Choose the option that best matches the analogy.

1. Drip : Gush
   (a) Cry : Laugh
   (b) Curl : Roll
   (c) Stream : Tributary
   (d) Dent : Destroy
2. Walk : Legs
   (a) Gleam : Eyes
   (b) Chew : Mouth
   (c) Dress : Hem
   (d) Cover : Book
3. Enfranchise : Slavery
   (a) Equation : Mathematics
   (b) Liberate : Confine
   (c) Bondage : Subjugation
   (d) Appeasement : Unreasonable
4. Union jack : Vexillology
   (a) Toad : Ornithology
   (b) Turtle : Microbiology
   (c) Gymnosperms : Botany
   (d) Friend : home Economics
5. Topaz : Yellow
   (a) Diamond : Carat
   (b) Jeweler : Clarity
   (c) Sapphire : Red
   (d) Amethyst : Purple
6. Lumen : Brightness
   (a) Candle : Light
   (b) Density : Darkness
   (c) Nickel : Metal
   (d) Inches : Length
7. Maceration : Liquid
   (a) Sublimation : Gas
   (b) Evaporation : Humidity
   (c) Trail : Path
   (d) Erosion : Weather
8. Clumsy : Botch
   (a) Wicked : Insinuate
   (b) Strict : Pamper
   (c) Willful : Heed
   (d) Lazy : Shirk
9. Fugitive : Flee
   (a) Parasite : Foster
   (b) Braggart : Boast
   (c) Sage : Stifle
   (d) Bystander : Procure
10. Chronological : Time
    (a) Virtual : Truth
    (b) Abnormal : Value
    (c) Marginal : Knowledge
    (d) Ordinal : Place
11. Soot : Grimy
    (a) Frost : Transparent
    (b) Sunshine : Fruitless
    (c) Rain : Sodden
    (d) Pall : Gaudy
12. Morbid : Unfavorable
    (a) Reputable : Favorable
    (b) Maternal : Unfavorable
    (c) Disputatious : Favorable
    (d) Vigilant : Unfavorable
13. Sullen : Brood
    (a) Lethargic : Cavort
    (b) Regal : Cringe
    (c) Docile : Obey
    (d) Poised : Blunder
14. Author : Literate
    (a) Cynic : Gullible
    (b) Hothead : Prudent
    (c) Saint : Notorious
    (d) Judge : Impartial
15. Massive : Bulk
    (a) Ultimate : Magnitude
    (b) Trivial : Importance
    (c) Anonymous : Luster
    (d) Gigantic : Size
16. Entice : Repel
    (a) Germinate : Sprout
    (b) Flourish : Fade
    (c) Officiate : Preside
    (d) Lubricate : Grease

17. Humdrum : Bore
    (a) Grim : Amuse
    (b) Nutritious : Sicken
    (c) Stodgy : Excite
    (d) Heartrending : Move
18. Hospitable : Courtesy
    (a) Morbid : Cheerfulness
    (b) Vindictive : Spite
    (c) Leisurely : Haste
    (d) Infamous : Honor
19. Reinforce : Stronger
    (a) Abound : Lesser
    (b) Dismantle : Longer
    (c) Wilt : Higher
    (d) Erode : Weaker
20. Braggart : Modesty
    (a) Fledgling : Experience
    (b) Embezzler : Greed
    (c) Wallflower : Timidity
    (d) Invalid : Malady

II. Find out the alternative which will replace the question mark.

1. Cup : Lip :: Bird : ?
   (a) Bush   (b) Grass
   (c) Forest   (d) Beak
2. Flow : River :: Stagnant : ?
   (a) Rain   (b) Stream
   (c) Pool   (d) Canal
3. Paw : Cat :: Hoof : ?
   (a) Lamb   (b) Elephant
   (c) Lion   (d) Horse
4. Ornithologist : Bird :: Archaeologist : ?
   (a) Islands
   (b) Mediators
   (c) Archealogy
   (d) Aquatic
5. Peacock : India :: Bear : ?
   (a) Australia   (b) America
   (c) Russia   (d) England
6. Reason : Sebtpo :: Think : ?
   (a) Sghmj   (b) Uijol
   (c) Uhnki   (d) Ujkpm
7. Carbon : Diamond :: Corundum : ?
   (a) Garnet   (b) Ruby
   (c) Pukhraj   (d) Pearl
8. Nation : Antino :: Hungry : ?
   (a) Hnugry   (b) Uhngyr
   (c) Yrnguh   (d) Unhgyr
9. Architect : Building :: Sculptor : ?
   (a) Museum   (b) Stone
   (c) Chisel   (d) Statue
10. Eye : Myopia :: Teeth : ?
    (a) Pyorrhoea   (b) Cataract
    (c) Trachoma   (d) Eczema
11. Conference : Chairman :: Newspaper : ?
    (a) Reporter   (b) Distributor
    (c) Printer   (d) Editor
12. Safe : Secure :: Protect : ?
    (a) Lock   (b) Sure
    (c) Guard   (d) Conserve
13. Master : Ocuvgt :: Labour : ?
    (a) Ncdqwt   (b) Nderwt
    (c) Nberwt   (d) Nedrwt
14. Microphone : Loud :: Microscope : ?
    (a) Elongate   (b) Investigate
    (c) Magnify   (d) Examine
15. Melt : Liquid :: Freeze : ?
    (a) Ice   (b) Condense
    (c) Solid   (d) Force
16. College : Student :: Hospital : ?
    (a) Nurse   (b) Doctor
    (c) Treatment   (d) Patient
17. Tree : Forest :: Grass : ?
    (a) Lawn   (b) Garden
    (c) Park   (d) Field
18. South : North-West :: West : ?
    (a) North   (b) South-West
    (c) North-East   (d) East
19. Cloth : Mill :: Newspaper : ?
    (a) Editor   (b) Reader
    (c) Paper   (d) Press
20. Country : President :: State : ?
    (a) Governer   (b) M.P
    (c) Legislator   (d) Minister

Analogies and One Word

21. Race : Fatigue :: Fast : ?
    (a) Food   (b) Laziness
    (c) Hunger   (d) Race
22. Peace : Chaos :: Creation : ?
    (a) Build   (b) Construction
    (c) Destruction   (d) Manufacture
23. Tiger : Forest :: Otter : ?
    (a) Cage   (b) Sky
    (c) Nest   (d) Water
24. Poles : Magnet :: ? : Battery
    (a) Cells   (b) Power
    (c) Terminals   (d) Energy
25. Cassock : Priest :: ? : Graduate
    (a) Cap   (b) Tie
    (c) Coat   (d) Gown

III. Choose the correct one word substitution for the given word/sentence.

1. Extreme old age when a man behaves like a fool
    (a) Imbecility   (b) Senility
    (c) Dotage   (d) Superannuation
2. That which cannot be corrected
    (a) Unintelligible (b) Indelible
    (c) Illegible   (d) Incorrigible
3. The study of ancient societies
    (a) Anthropology (b) Archaeology
    (c) History   (d) Ethnology
4. A person of good understanding knowledge and reasoning power
    (a) Expert   (b) Intellectual
    (c) Snob   (d) Literate
5. A person who insists on something
    (a) Disciplinarian (b) Stickler
    (c) Instantaneous (d) Boaster
6. State in which the few govern the many
    (a) Monarchy   (b) Oligarchy
    (c) Plutocracy   (d) Autocracy
7. A style in which a writer makes a display of his knowledge
    (a) Pedantic   (b) Verbose
    (c) Pompous   (d) Ornate
8. Words inscribed on tomb
    (a) Epitome   (b) Epistle
    (c) Epilogue   (d) Epitaph
9. One who eats everything
    (a) Omnivorous   (b) Omniscient
    (c) Irrestible   (d) Insolvent
10. The custom or practice of having more than one husband at same time
    (a) Polygyny   (b) Polyphony
    (c) Polyandry   (d) Polychromy
11. Tending to move away from the centre or axis
    (a) Centrifugal   (b) Centripetal
    (c) Axiomatic   (d) Awry
12. A person interested in collecting, studying and selling of old things
    (a) Antiquarian   (b) Junk-dealer
    (c) Crank   (d) Archealogist
13. That which cannot be seen
    (a) Insensible   (b) Intangible
    (c) Invisible   (d) Unseen
14. To slap with a flat object
    (a) Chop   (b) Hew
    (c) Gnaw   (d) Swat
15. Habitually silent or talking little
    (a) Servile   (b) Unequivocal
    (c) Taciturn   (d) Synoptic
16. One who cannot be corrected
    (a) Incurable   (b) Incorrigible
    (c) Hardened   (d) Invulnerable
17. Be the embodiment or perfect example of
    (a) Characterise (b) Idol
    (c) Personify   (d) Signify
18. A person not sure of the existence of god
    (a) Cynic   (b) Agnostic
    (c) Atheist   (d) Theist
19. A paper written by hand
    (a) Handicraft   (b) Manuscript
    (c) Handiwork   (d) Thesis
20. A place where bees are kept is called
    (a) An apiary   (b) A mole
    (c) A hive   (d) A sanctury
21. A religious discourse
    (a) Preach   (b) Stanza
    (c) Sanctorum   (d) Sermon

22. Parts of a country behind the coast or a river's banks
    (a) Isthmus   (b) Archipelago
    (c) Hinterland (d) Swamps
23. Study of the evolution of man as an animal
    (a) Archaeology (b) Anthropology
    (c) Chronology   (d) Ethnology
24. A person who speaks many languages
    (a) Linguist   (b) Monolingual
    (c) Polyglot   (d) Bilingual
25. One who does not believe in existence of god
    (a) Egoist   (b) Atheist
    (c) Stoic   (d) Naive
26. Giving undue favours to one's own kith and kin
    (a) Nepotism   (b) Favouritism
    (c) Wordliness (d) Corruption
27. Hater of learning and knowledge
    (a) Misologist (b) Bibliophile
    (c) Misogynist (d) Misanthropist
28. A person interested in reading books and nothing else
    (a) Book-keepr (b) Scholar
    (c) Book-worm   (d) Student
29. A place where monks live as a secluded community
    (a) Cathedral (b) Diocese
    (c) Convent   (d) Monastery
30. Incapable of being seen through
    (a) Ductile   (b) Opaque
    (c) Obsolete (d) Potable
31. One who does not care for literature or art
    (a) Primitive   (b) Illiterate
    (c) Philistine (d) Barbarian
32. A large sleeping-room with many beds
    (a) Bedroom (b) Dormitory
    (c) Hostel   (d) Basement
33. One who dabbles in fine arts for the love of it and not for monetary gains
    (a) Connoisseur   (b) Amateur
    (c) Professional (d) Dilettante
34. A school boy who cuts classes frequently is a
    (a) Defeatist (b) Sycophant
    (c) Truant   (d) Martinet
35. Ready to believe
    (a) Credulous   (b) Credible
    (c) Creditable (d) Incredible
36. Medical study of skin and its diseases
    (a) Dermatology (b) Endocrinology
    (c) Gynealogy   (d) Orthopaedics
37. A person who tries to deceive people by claiming to be able to do wonderful things
    (a) Trickster (b) Imposter
    (c) Magician   (d) Mountebank
38. A dramatic performance
    (a) Mask   (b) Mosque
    (c) Masque (d) Mascot
39. One who does not marry, especially as a religious obligation
    (a) Bachelor (b) Celibate
    (c) Vigin   (d) Recluse
40. Murder of a brother
    (a) Patricide (b) Regicide
    (c) Homicide   (d) Fratricide
41. Having superior or intellectual interests and tastes
    (a) Elite   (b) Highbrow
    (c) Sophisticated (d) Fastidious
42. To cause troops, et(c) to spread out in readiness for battle
    (a) Disperse   (b) Deploy
    (c) Collocate (d) Align
43. A voice loud enough to be heard
    (a) Audible   (b) Applaudable
    (c) Laudable (d) Oral
44. A light sailing boat built specially for racing
    (a) Canoe   (b) Yacht
    (c) Frigate (d) Dinghy
45. One who is in charge of museum
    (a) Curator   (b) Supervisor
    (c) Caretaker (d) Warden

HOTS

Choose the correct one word for given sentences.

1. A person living permanently in a certain place
   (a) Resident (b) Native
   (c) Domicile (d) Subject
2. Mania for stealing articles
   (a) Hypomania (b) Kleptomania
   (c) Logomania (d) Stelomania
3. One who loves mankind is called
   (a) Optimist (b) Philanthropist
   (c) Optometrist (d) Truant
4. A Government run by a dictator is termed as
   (a) Autocracy (b) Democracy
   (c) Oligracy (d) Theocracy
5. A remedy for all disease is
   (a) Medicine (b) Medical
   (c) Medica (d) Panacea

Phrasal Verbs, Idioms and Proverbs — 4

Learning Objectives : In this chapter, students will learn about:
- ✓ Concept of Phrasal Verbs
- ✓ Types of Phrasal Verbs
- ✓ Some common Idioms and their meanings

CHAPTER SUMMARY

Phrasal verbs are usually two-word phrases consisting of verb + adverb or verb + preposition. Study them as you come across them rather than trying to memorize many at once. If you think of each phrasal verb as a separate verb with a specific meaning, you will be able to remember it more easily. Like many other verbs, phrasal verbs often have more than one meaning. In short, a phrasal verb is a verb plus a preposition or adverb which creates a meaning different from the original verb.

Example: I 'ran into' my teacher at the movies last night. run + into = meet

Types of Phrasal Verb

1. The first type of phrasal verbs is called 'Intransitive verbs.' An intransitive verb cannot be followed by an object.
   Example: He suddenly 'showed up.' 'show up' cannot take an object
2. The second type of phrasal verbs is called 'Transitive verbs.' A transitive verb can be followed by an object.
   Example: I 'made up' the story. Here, 'story' is the object of 'make up'.
3. The third type of phrasal verbs is called 'Transitive verbs with fixed object in the middle of the verb.' The object is placed between the verb and the preposition.
   Example: I 'talked my mother into' letting me borrow the car.
   She 'looked the phone number up.'
4. The fourth type of phrasal verbs is called 'Transitive with fixed object after the verb.' The object is placed after the preposition.
   Example: I 'ran into an old friend' yesterday. They are 'looking into the problem.'
5. The fifth type of phrasal verbs is called 'Transitive with two objects, separable.
   Example: 'Put down to: Attribute to something.'
   Sarah's parents were really pleased and 'put her results down to' plenty of revising. The above example shows phrasal verbs that have two objects ('her results' and 'plenty of revising'). The example shows that the objects separate the verb ('and put her results down to') and the other comes after the verb itself ('plenty of revising').
   Interestingly, some transitive phrasal verbs can take an object in both places.
   Example: I 'looked the number up' in the phone book.
   I 'looked up the number' in the phone book.
   Note: Although many phrasal verbs can take an object in both places, you must put the object between the verb and the preposition if the object is a pronoun.
   Example: I 'looked the number up' in the phone book.
   I 'looked up the number' in the phone book.
   Correct: I 'looked it up' in the phone book.
   Incorrect: I looked up it in the phone book.

Phrasal Verbs with Their Meaning and Examples

Phrasal Verb	Meaning	Example
ask somebody out	invite on a date	Brian asked Judy out to dinner and a movie.
ask around	ask many people the same question	I asked around but nobody has seen my wallet.
add up to something	equal	Your purchases add up to $205.32.
back something up	reverse	You'll have to back up your car so that I can get out.
back somebody up	support	My wife backed me up over my decision to quit my job.
blow up	explode	The racing car blew up after it crashed into the fence.
blow something up	add air	We have to blow 50 balloons up for the party.
break down	stop functioning (vehicle, machine)	Our car broke down at the side of the highway in the snowstorm.
break down	get upset	The woman broke down when the police told her that her son had died.
break something down	divide into smaller parts	Our teacher broke the final project down into three separate parts.
break in	force entry to a building	Somebody broke in last night and stole our stereo.
break into something	enter forcibly	The firemen had to break into the room to rescue the children.
break something in	wear something a few times so that it doesn't look/feel new	I need to break these shoes in before we run next week.
break in	interrupt	The TV station broke in to report the news of the president's death.
break into	end a relationship	My boyfriend and I broke up before I moved to America.
break up	start laughing (informal)	The kids just broke up as soon as the clown started talking.
break out	escape	The prisoners broke out of jail when the guards weren't looking.
break out in something	develop a skin condition	I broke out in a rash after our camping trip.
bring somebody down	make unhappy	This sad music is bringing me down.

Phrasal Verb	Meaning	Example
bring somebody up	raise a child	My grandparents brought me up after my parents died.
bring something up	start talking about a subject	My mother walks out of the room when my father brings up sports.
bring something up	vomit	He drank so much that he brought his dinner up in the toilet.
call around	phone many different places/people	We called around but we weren't able to find the car part we needed.
call somebody back	return a phone call	I called the company back but the offices were closed for the weekend.
call something off	cancel	Jason called the wedding off because he wasn't in love with his fiancé.
call on somebody	ask for an answer or opinion	The professor called on me for question 1.
call on somebody	visit somebody	We called on you last night but you weren't home.
call somebody up	phone	Give me your phone number and I will call you up when we are in town.
calm down	relax after being angry	You are still mad. You need to calm down before you drive the car.
not care for somebody/something	not like (formal)	I don't care for his behaviour.
catch up	get to the same point as somebody else	You'll have to run faster than that if you want to catch up with Marty.
check in	arrive and register at a hotel or airport	We will get the hotel keys when we check in.
check out	leave a hotel	You have to check out of the hotel before 11:00 AM.
check somebody/something out	look at carefully, investigate	The company checks out all new employees.
check out somebody/something	look at (informal)	Check out the crazy hair on that guy!
cheer up	become happier	She cheered up when she heard the good news.
cheer somebody up	make happier	I brought you some flowers to cheer you up.
chip in	help	If everyone chips in we can get the kitchen painted by noon.

Phrasal Verbs, Idioms and Proverbs

Phrasal Verb	Meaning	Example
clean something up	tidy, clean	Please clean up your bedroom before you go outside.
come across something	find unexpectedly	I came across these old photos when I was tidying the closet.
come apart	separate	The top and bottom come apart if you pull hard enough.
come down with something	become sick	My nephew came down with chicken pox this weekend.
come forward	volunteer for a task or to give evidence	The woman came forward with her husband's finger prints.
come from somewhere	originate in	The art of origami comes from Asia.
count on somebody/something	rely on	I am counting on you to make dinner while I am out.
cross something out	draw a line through	Please cross out your old address and write your new one.
cut back on something	consume less	My doctor wants me to cut back on sweets and fatty foods.
cut something down	make something fall to the ground	We had to cut the old tree in our yard down after the storm.
cut in	interrupt	Your father cut in while I was dancing with your uncle.
cut in	pull in too closely in front of another vehicle	The bus driver got angry when that car cut in.
cut in	start operating (of an engine or electrical device)	The air conditioner cuts in when the temperature gets to 22°C.
cut something off	remove with something sharp	The doctors cut off the patient's leg because it was severely injured.
cut something off	stop providing	The phone company cut off our phone because we didn't pay the bill.
cut somebody off	take out of a will	My grandparents cut my father off when he remarried.
cut something out	remove part of something (usually with scissors and paper)	I cut this ad out of the newspaper.
do somebody/something over	beat up, ransack	He's lucky to be alive. His shop was done over by a street gang.

Phrasal Verb	Meaning	Example
do something over	do again	My teacher wants me to do my essay over because she doesn't like my topic.
do away with something	discard	It's time to do away with all of these old tax records.
do something up	fasten, close	Do your coat up before you go outside. It's snowing!
dress up	wear nice clothing	It's a fancy restaurant so we have to dress up.
drop back	move back in a position/group	Andrea dropped back to third place when she fell off her bike.
drop in/by/over	come without an appointment	I might drop in/by/over for tea sometime this week.
drop somebody/something off	take somebody/something somewhere and leave them/it there	I have to drop my sister off at work before I come over.
drop out	quit a class, school etc	I dropped out of Science because it was too difficult.
eat out	eat at a restaurant	I don't feel like cooking tonight. Let's eat out.
end up	eventually reach/do/decide	We ended up renting a movie instead of going to the theatre.
fall apart	break into pieces	My new dress fell apart in the washing machine.
fall down	fall to the ground	The picture that you hung up last night fell down this morning.
fall out	separate from an interior	The money must have fallen out of my pocket.
fall out	(of hair, teeth) become loose and unattached	His hair started to fall out when he was only 35.
figure something out	understand, find the answer	I need to figure out how to fit the piano and the bookshelf in this room.
fill something in	to write information in blanks, as on a form	Please fill in the form with your name, address, and phone number.
fill something out	to write information in blanks, as on a form	The form must be filled out in capital letters.
fill something up	fill to the top	I always fill the water jug up when it is empty.
find out	discover	We don't know where he lives. How can we find out?

Phrasal Verb	Meaning	Example
find something out	discover	We tried to keep the time of the party a secret, but Samantha found it out.
get something across/over	communicate, make understandable	I tried to get my point across/over to the judge but she wouldn't listen.
get along/on	like each other	I was surprised how well my new girlfriend and my sister got along/on.
get around	have mobility	My grandfather can get around fine in his new wheelchair.
get away	go on a vacation	We worked so hard this year that we had to get away for a week.
get away with something	do without being noticed or punished	Jason always gets away with cheating in his maths tests.
get back	return	We got back from our vacation last week.
get something back	receive something you had before	Liz finally got her Science notes back from my room-mate.
get back at sby	retaliate, take revenge	My sister got back at me for stealing her shoes. She stole my favourite hat.
get back into something	become interested in something again	I finally got back into my novel and finished it.
get on something	step onto a vehicle	We're going to freeze out here if you don't let us get on the bus.
get over something	recover from an illness, loss, difficulty	I just got over the flu and now my sister has it.
get over something	overcome a problem	The company will have to close if it can't get over the new regulations.
get round to something	finally find time to do (get around to something)	I don't know when I am going to get round to writing the thank you cards.
get together	meet (usually for social reasons)	Let's get together for a BBQ this weekend.
get up	get out of bed	I got up early today to study for my exam.
get up	stand	You should get up and give the elderly man your seat.
give somebody away	reveal hidden information about sby	His wife gave him away to the police.
give somebody away	take the bride to the altar	My father gave me away at my wedding.
give something away	ruin a secret	My little sister gave the surprise party away by accident.

Phrasal Verb	Meaning	Example
give something away	give something to somebody for free	The library was giving away old books on Friday.
give something back	return a borrowed item	I have to give these skates back to Franz before his hockey game.
give in	reluctantly stop fighting or arguing	My boyfriend didn't want to go to the ballet, but he finally gave in.
give something out	give to many people (usually at no cost)	They were giving out free perfume samples at the department store.
give something up	quit a habit	I am giving up smoking as of January 1st.
give up	stop trying	My maths homework was too difficult so I gave up.
go after somebody	follow somebody	My brother tried to go after the thief in his car.
go after something	try to achieve sthg	I went after my dream and now I am a published writer.
go against somebody	compete, oppose	We are going against the best soccer team in the city tonight.
go ahead	start, proceed	Please go ahead and eat before the food gets cold.
go back	return to a place	I have to go back home and get my lunch.
go out	leave home to go on a social event	We're going out for dinner tonight.
go out with somebody	date	Jesse has been going out with Luke since they met last winter.
go over something	review	Please go over your answers before you submit your test.
go over	visit somebody nearby	I haven't seen Tina for a long time. I think I'll go over for an hour or two.
go without something	suffer lack or deprivation	When I was young, we went without winter boots.
grow apart	stop being friends over time	My best friend and I grew apart after she changed schools.
grow back	regrow	My roses grew back this summer.
grow up	become an adult	When Jack grows up he wants to be a fireman.

Phrasal Verbs, Idioms and Proverbs

Phrasal Verb	Meaning	Example
grow out of something	get too big for	Elizabeth needs a new pair of shoes because she has grown out of her old ones.
grow into something	grow big enough to fit	This bike is too big for him now, but he should grow into it by next year.
hand something down	give something used to somebody else	I handed my old comic books down to my little cousin.
hand something in	submit	I have to hand in my essay by Friday.
hand something out	to distribute to a group of people	We will hand out the invitations at the door.
hand something over	give (usually unwillingly)	The police asked the man to hand over his wallet and his weapons.
hang in	stay positive (informal)	Hang in there. I'm sure you'll find a job very soon.
hang on	wait a short time (informal)	Hang on while I grab my coat and shoes!
hang out	spend time relaxing (informal)	Instead of going to the party we are just going to hang out at my place.
hang up	end a phone call	He didn't say goodbye before he hung up.
hold somebody/something back	prevent from doing/going	I had to hold my dog back because there was a cat in the park.
hold something back	hide an emotion	Jamie held back his tears at his grandfather's funeral.
hold on	wait a short time	Please hold on while I transfer you to the Sales Department.
hold onto somebody/something	hold firmly using your hands or arms	Hold onto your hat because it's very windy outside.
hold somebody/something up	rob	A man in a black mask held the bank up this morning.
keep on doing something	continue doing	Keep on stirring until the liquid comes to a boil.
keep something from somebody	not to tell	We kept our relationship from our parents for two years.
keep somebody/something out	stop from entering	Try to keep the wet dog out of the living room.
keep something up	continue at the same rate	If you keep those results up you will get into a great college.

Phrasal Verb	Meaning	Example
let somebody down	fail to support or help, disappoint	I need you to be on time. Don't let me down this time.
let somebody in	allow to enter	Can you let the cat in before you go to school?
log in (or on)	sign in (to a website, database etc)	I can't log in to Facebook because I've forgotten my password.
log out (or off)	sign out (of a website, database etc)	If you don't log off somebody could get into your account.
look after somebody/ something	take care of	I have to look after my sick grandmother.
look down on somebody	think less of, consider inferior	Ever since we stole that chocolate bar your dad has looked down on me.
look for somebody/ something	try to find	I'm looking for a red dress for the wedding.
look forward to something	be excited about the future	I'm looking forward to the Christmas break.
look into something	investigate	We are going to look into the price of snowboards today.
look out	be careful, vigilant, and take notice	Look out! That car's going to hit you!
look out for somebody/ something	be especially vigilant for	Don't forget to look out for snakes on the hiking trail.
look something over	check, examine	Can you look over my essay for spelling mistakes?
look something up	search and find information in a reference book or database	We can look her phone number up on the Internet.
look up to somebody	have a lot of respect for	My little sister has always looked up to me.
make something up	invent, lie about something	Josie made up a story about why we were late.
make up	forgive each other	We were angry last night, but we made up at breakfast.
make up with someone	reconcile with someone	I am happy that I and my sister made up after our arguement.
mix something up	confuse two or more things	I mixed up the twins' names again!
pass away	die	His uncle passed away last night after a long illness.

Phrasal Verb	Meaning	Example
pass out	faint	It was so hot in the church that an elderly lady passed out.
pass something out	give the same thing to many people	The professor passed the textbooks out before class.
pass something up	decline (usually something good)	I passed up the job because I am afraid of change.
pay somebody back	return owed money	Thanks for buying my ticket. I'll pay you back on Friday.
pay for something	be punished for doing something bad	That bully will pay for being mean to my little brother.
pick something out	choose	I picked out three sweaters for you to try on.
point somebody/something out	indicate with your finger	I'll point my boyfriend out when he runs by.
put something down	put what you are holding on a surface or floor	You can put the groceries down on the kitchen counter.
put somebody down	insult, make somebody feel stupid	The students put the substitute teacher down because his pants were too short.
put something off	postpone	We are putting off our trip until January because of the hurricane.
put something out	extinguish	The neighbours put the fire out before the firemen arrived.
put something together	assemble	I have to put the crib together before the baby arrives.
put up with somebody/something	tolerate	I don't think I can put up with three small children in the car.
put something on	put clothing/ accessories on your body	Don't forget to put on your new earrings for the party.
run into somebody/something	meet unexpectedly	I ran into an old school-friend at the mall.
run over somebody/something	drive a vehicle over a person or thing	I accidentally ran over your bicycle in the driveway.
run over/through something	rehearse, review	Let's run over/through these lines one more time before the show.
run away	leave unexpectedly, escape	The child ran away from home and has been missing for three days.
run out	have none left	We ran out of shampoo so I had to wash my hair with soap.

Phrasal Verb	Meaning	Example
send something back	return (usually by mail)	My letter got sent back to me because I used the wrong stamp.
set something up	arrange, organize	Our boss set a meeting up with the president of the company.
set somebody up	trick, trap	The police set up the car thief by using a hidden camera.
shop around	compare prices	I want to shop around a little before I decide on these boots.
show off	act extra special for people watching (usually boastfully)	He always shows off on his skateboard
sleep over	stay somewhere for the night (informal)	You should sleep over tonight if the weather is too bad to drive home.
sort something out	organize, resolve a problem	We need to sort the bills out before the first of the month.
stick to something	continue doing something, limit yourself to one particular thing	You will lose weight if you stick to the diet.
switch something off	stop the energy flow, turn off	The light's too bright. Could you switch it off.
switch something on	start the energy flow, turn on	We heard the news as soon as we switched on the car radio.
take after somebody	resemble a family member	I take after my mother. We are both impatient.
take something apart	purposely break into pieces	He took the car brakes apart and found the problem.
take something back	return an item	I have to take our new TV back because it doesn't work.
take off	start to fly	My plane takes off in five minutes.
take something off	remove something (usually clothing)	Take off your socks and shoes and come in the lake!
take something out	remove from a place or thing	Can you take the garbage out to the street for me?
take somebody out	pay for somebody to go somewhere with you	My grandparents took us out for dinner and a movie.
tear something up	rip into pieces	I tore up my ex-boyfriend's letters and gave them back to him.
think back	remember (often + to, sometimes + on)	When I think back on my youth, I wish I had studied harder.

Phrasal Verbs, Idioms and Proverbs

Phrasal Verb	Meaning	Example
think something over	consider	I'll have to think this job offer over before I make my final decision.
throw something away	dispose of	We threw our old furniture away when we won the lottery.
turn something down	decrease the volume or strength (heat, light etc)	Please turn the TV down while the guests are here.
turn something down	refuse	I turned the job down because I don't want to move.
turn something off	stop the energy flow, switch off	Your mother wants you to turn the TV off and come for dinner.
turn something on	start the energy, switch on	It's too dark in here. Let's turn some lights on.
turn something up	increase the volume or strength (heat, light etc)	Can you turn the music up? This is my favourite song.
turn up	appear suddenly	Our cat turned up after we put posters up all over the neighbourhood.
try something on	sample clothing	I'm going to try these jeans on, but I don't think they will fit.
try something out	test	I am going to try this new brand of detergent out.
use something up	finish the supply	The kids used all of the toothpaste up so we need to buy some more.
wake up	stop sleeping	We have to wake up early for work on Monday.
warm somebody/something up	increase the temperature	You can warm your feet up in front of the fireplace.
warm up	prepare body for exercise	I always warm up by doing sit-ups before I go for a run.
wear off	fade away	Most of my make-up wore off before I got to the party.
work out	exercise	I work out at the gym three times a week.
work out	be successful	Our plan worked out fine.
work something out	make a calculation	We have to work out the total cost before we buy the house.

Idioms and Proverbs

Idioms are words, phrases or expressions which are commonly used in everyday conversation by native speakers of English. They are often metaphorical and make the language more colourful. People use them to express something more vividly and often more briefly.

They serve as an image or mental picture.

Idioms beginning with A

- A big cheese: an important or a powerful person in a group or family.
- A bird's eye view: a view from a very high place which allows you to see a large area.
- A bone of contention: something that people argue for a long time.
- A cock and a bull story: a story or an explanation which is obviously not true.
- At the crack of the dawn: very early in morning.
- A cuckoo in the nest: someone in a group of people but not liked by them.
- A litmus test: a method which clearly proves something.
- As the crow flies: measuring distance between two places in a straight line.
- A dead letter: an argument or law not followed by anyone.
- At the drop of the hat: to do something easily and without any preparation.
- An early bird: someone who gets early in the morning.
- An educated guess: a guess which was likely to be correct.
- At the eleventh hour: too late.
- A queer fish: a strange person.
- A wakeup call: an event done to warn someone.
- A worm's eye view: having very little knowledge about something.
- A witch hunt: an attempt to find and punish those who have options that are believed to be dangerous.
- At the heels of: to follow someone.
- A dish fit for Gods: something of very high quality.
- A game of two equal halves: a sudden change in circumstances.
- Afraid of one's own shadow: to become easily frightened.
- Against the clock: to be in a hurry to do something before a particular time.
- Air one's dirty laundry: to make public something embarrassing that should be kept secret.
- All systems go: everything is ready.
- An arm and a leg: a large amount of money.
- Appear out of now here: to appear suddenly without warning.
- Apple of someone's eye: someone loved very much.
- Ask for the moon: to ask for too much.
- Asleep at the switch: not to be alert on opportunity.
- At sixes and sevens: to be lost and bewildered.
- At someone's beck and call: to be always ready to serve.
- At the bottom of the ladder: at the lowest level.
- A house of cards: a poor plan.
- At an arm's length: to keep at a distance.
- A boon in disguise: a benefit in loss.
- A bull in a China shop: an awkward person.
- A red letter day: an important day.
- A nine days wonder: pleasure for a short time.
- A bit under the weather: falling ill.

TRIVIA

The word nice was originally used for describing something foolish, stupid or senseless.

Idioms beginning with B

- Bad blood: feelings of hate between two families.
- Bend your ears: to talk to someone for a very long time about something boring.
- Bite your tongue: to stop yourself from saying something because it would be better not to.
- Black and blue: full of bruises.
- Blue blood: belonging to high social class.
- Be above board: to be honest and legal.

- Be bouncing off the walls: excited and full of nervous energy.
- Bow and scrap: try too hard to please someone in a position of authority.
- Brass monkey weather: extremely cold weather.
- Be tailor made: to be completely suitable for someone.
- Break the ice: to make more comfort or relaxed with a person whom you have not met earlier, to break the silence.
- Be as clear as mud: to be impossible to understand.
- Be on cloud nine: be very happy.
- Between the devil and deep blue sea: a type of situation where you must choose between two equally unpleasant situations.
- Be in the doldrums: not very successful or nothing new is taking place.
- Beat the drum: to speak eagerly about something you support.
- Be on the edge: to be nervous or worried about something.
- Be in seventh heaven: extremely happy.
- Be at each other's throat: two persons arguing angrily.
- Batten down the hatches: to prepare for trouble.
- Back the wrong horse: to support someone weak.
- Back to square one: to reach again to the starting point.
- Back to the salt mines: back to something that you don't want to do.
- Ball of fire: active and energetic.
- Beat one's head against the wall: to try to do something that is hopeless.
- Bark up the wrong tree: to make a wrong assumption.
- Batten down the hatches: prepare for difficult times.
- Beat one's brain out: to work hard.
- Begin to see the light: to begin to understand.
- Behind closed doors: done in secret.
- Bet on the wrong horse: to misread the future.
- Bent on doing: to be determined to do something.
- Bite off more than one can chew: to do more than one's ability.
- Bite the bullet: to face a difficult situation bravely.
- Bitter pill to swallow: an unpleasant fact that must be accepted.
- Black sheep of the family: worst member.
- Blessing in disguise: something that turns out to be good which earlier appeared to be wrong.
- Blind leading the blind: someone who does not understand something but tries to explain it to other.
- Blow one's own horn: to praise oneself.
- Blow someone's mind: excite someone.
- Bone of contention: subject matter of the fight.
- Bring home the bacon: to earn money to live.
- Blue in the face: exhausted and speechless.
- Break the back of: reduce the power of something.
- Burn a hole in one's pocket: to spend money quickly.
- Burn the midnight oil: to study till late of night.
- Bushman's holiday: a holiday where you spend doing same thing as you did at working days.
- Button's one lip: to keep quite.
- Break a leg: to wish good luck.

Idioms beginning with C
- Carrot and sticks: to use both awards as well as punishments to make someone do something.
- Cloak and dragger: when people behave in a very secret manner.
- Cards are stacked against: luck is against you.
- Crack a book: to open book to study.
- Cross a bridge before one comes to it: worry about the future in advance.
- Carry coals to new castle: to take something to a place or a person that has a lot of that thing already.
- Cast in the same mould: to be very similar.
- Change horses in midstream: to change plans.
- Cap it all: to finish.

- Cried with eyes out: cried a lot.
- Carry the can: If you carry the can, you take the blame for something, even though you didn't do it or are only partly at fault.
- Cast a long shadow: Something or someone that casts a long shadow has considerable influence on other people or events.
- Cat and dog life: If people lead a cat and dog life, they are always arguing.

Idioms beginning with D
- Drive a wedge between: to break relationship between the two.
- Dances to the tune: to always do what someone tells you to do.
- Dressed up to the nines: wearing fancy clothes.
- Dragging its feet: delaying in decision, not showing enthusiasm.
- Davey Jones' locker: Davey Jones' locker is the bottom of the sea or resting place of drowned sailors. ('Davy Jones' locker' is an alternative spelling.)
- Dancing on someone's grave: Celebrate someone's demise.
- Dog in the manger: If someone acts like a dog in the manger, they don't want other people to have or enjoy things that are useless to them.
- Don't cry over spilt milk: When something bad happens and nothing can be done to help it people say, 'Don't cry over spilt milk'.
- Don't wash your dirty laundry in public: People, especially couples, who argue in front of others or involve others in their personal problems and crises, are said to be washing their dirty laundry in public; making public things that are best left private.
- Donkey work: Donkey work is any hard, boring work or task.
- Don't throw bricks when you live in a glass house: Don't call others out on actions that you, yourself do. Don't be a hypocrite.

Idioms beginning with E
- Entering the 80th orbit: celebrating the 80th birthday.
- Eleventh hour decision: decision that is made at the last possible minute.
- End in smoke: to bear no result.
- Earth shattering: not at all surprising.
- Eat humble pie: to apologize humbly.
- Elephant in the room: An elephant in the room is a problem that everyone knows very well but no one talks about because it is taboo, embarrassing, etc.
- Egg on your face: If someone has egg on their face; they are made to look foolish or embarrassed.
- Eye for an eye: This is an expression for retributive justice, where the punishment equals the crime.
- Eyes are bigger than one's stomach: If someone's eyes are bigger than their stomach, they are greedy and take on more than they can consume or manage.

Idioms beginning with F
- From cradle to grave: during the whole span of your life.
- Face the music: to accept punishment for something you have done.
- Feel the pinch: to have problems with money.
- Fall on your own sword: to be cheated by someone you trust.
- Feather in one's cap: something that you achieve and proud of.
- Firing on all cylinders: work every possible way to succeed.
- French leave: absent without permission, to take French leave is to leave a gathering without saying goodbye or without permission.
- Fall on our feet: If you fall on your feet, you succeed in doing something where there was a risk of failure.
- Fall on your sword: If someone falls on their sword, they resign or accept the consequences of what they have done wrong.
- Fingers and thumbs: If you are all fingers and thumbs, you are being clumsy and not very skilled with your hands.
- Finger in the pie: If you have a finger in the pie, you have an interest in something.

- **Flash in the pan:** If something is a flash in the pan; it is very noticeable but doesn't last long, like most singers, who are very successful for a while, then forgotten.
- **Follow your nose:** When giving directions, telling someone to follow their nose means that they should go straight ahead.
- **Fool's paradise:** A fool's paradise is a false sense of happiness or success.
- **Foot in mouth:** This is used to describe someone who has just said something embarrassing, inappropriate, wrong or stupid.
- **For a song:** If you buy or sell something for a song, it is very cheap.
- **For donkey's years:** If people have done something, usually without much if any change, for an awfully long time, they can be said to have done it for donkey's years.

Idioms beginning with G
- **Get off the hook:** free from all obligations.
- **Give-up the ghost:** to die.
- **Got the slap on the wrist:** got light punishment.
- **Give someone a bird:** make fun.
- **Got the wind up:** to be scared.
- **Get a raw deal:** not treated equally.
- **Gift of the gab:** talent of speaking, if someone has the gift of the gab, they speak in a persuasive and interesting way.
- **Gives cold shoulder:** to ignore.
- **Get your wires crossed:** Misunderstand each other, especially when making arrangements. ('Get your lines crossed' is also used.)
- **Give me five:** If someone says this, they want to hit your open hand against theirs as a way of congratulation or greeting.
- **Give me a hand:** If someone gives you a hand, they help you.
- **Give someone a piece of your mind:** Criticize someone strongly and angrily.
- **Go bananas:** If you go bananas, you are wild with excitement, anxiety, or worry.
- **Go tell it to birds:** This is used when someone says something that is not credible or is a lie.
- **Go under the hammer:** If something goes under the hammer, it is sold in an auction.
- **Graveyard shift:** If you have to work very late at night, it is the graveyard shift.
- **Grease monkey:** A grease monkey is an idiomatic term for a mechanic.

Idioms beginning with H
- **Have ants in your pants:** not be able to keep still because you are very excited or worried about something.
- **Having a whole of a time:** to enjoy very much.
- **Hold one's horse:** be patient.
- **Have a big mouth:** one who gossips more or tells secret.
- **Himalayan blunder:** a serious mistake.
- **Have a one track mind:** think only of one thing.
- **Have clean hands:** be guiltless.
- **Have an egg on the face:** be embarrassed.
- **Have eyes bigger than stomach:** desiring more food than one can eat.
- **Heart missed a beat:** very excited.
- **Heart in the right place:** good natured.
- **Hit the nail on the head:** done the thing correctly.
- **Hand to mouth:** Someone who's living from hand to mouth, is very poor and needs the little money they have coming in to cover their expenses.
- **Have no truck with:** If you have no truck with something or someone, you refuse to get involved with it or them.
- **Hit the bull's-eye:** If someone hits the bull's-eye, they are exactly right about something or achieve the best result possible.
- **Hold water:** When you say that something does or does not 'hold water', it means that the point of view or argument put forward is or is not sound, strong or logical. For e.g. 'Saying we should increase our interest rates because everyone else is doing so will not hold water'.
- **Hornets' nest:** A hornets' nest is a violent situation or one with a lot of dispute. (If you create the problem, you 'stir up a hornets' nest'.)

Idioms beginning with I

- In dribs and drabs: in small amounts at a time
- In black and white: to give in writing
- In the blues: low spirited
- In cahoots with: in a partnership usually for a dishonest reason
- If the shoe fits, wear it: This is used to suggest that something that has been said might apply to a person.
- In droves: When things happen in droves, a lot happen at the same time or very quickly.
- In the doghouse: If someone is in the doghouse, they are in disgrace and very unpopular at the moment.

Idioms beginning with J

- Jack Frost: If everything has frozen in winter, then Jack Frost has visited.
- Jack the lad: A confident and not very serious young man who behaves as he wants to without thinking about other people is a Jack the lad.
- Jack-of-all-trades: A jack-of-all-trades is someone that can do many different jobs.
- Jam on your face: If you say that someone has jam on their face, they appear to be caught, embarrassed or found guilty.
- Jam tomorrow: This idiom is used when people promise good things for the future that will never come.
- Jane Doe: Name given to an unidentified female who may be party to legal proceedings, or to an unidentified person in hospital, or dead. John Doe is the male equivalent.
- Jekyll and Hyde: Someone who has a Jekyll and Hyde personality has a pleasant and a very unpleasant side to the character.
- Jersey justice: Jersey justice is very severe justice.
- Jet set: Very wealthy people who travel around the world to attend parties or functions are the jet set.
- Jet-black: To emphasise just how black something is, such as someone's hair, we can call it jet-black.
- Job's comforter: Someone who says they want to comfort, but actually discomforts people is a Job's comforter.
- Jobs for the boys: Where people give jobs, contracts, etc, to their friends and associates, these are jobs for the boys.
- Jockey for position: If a number of people want the same opportunity and are struggling to emerge as the most likely candidate, they are jockeying for position.
- Jog my memory: If you jog someone's memory, you say words that will help someone trying to remember a thought, event, word, phrase, experience, etc.
- John Doe: Name given to an unidentified male who may be party to legal proceedings, or to an unidentified person in hospital, or dead. Jane Doe is the female equivalent.
- Joe Public: Joe Public is the typical, average person.
- Johnny on the spot: A person who is always available; ready, willing, and able to do what needs to be done. ('Johnny-on-the-spot' is also used.)
- Johnny-come-lately: Someone who has recently joined something or arrived somewhere, especially when they want to make changes that are not welcome.
- Join the club: Said when someone has expressed a desire or opinion, meaning "That viewpoint is not unique to you". It can suggest that the speaker should stop complaining since many others are in the same position. Example: "If this train doesn't come, I'll be late for work!" "Join the club!"
- Joined at the hip: If people are joined at the hip, they are very closely connected and think the same way.
- Judge, jury and executioner: If someone is said to be the judge, jury, and executioner, it means they are in charge of every decision made, and they have the power to be rid of whomever they choose.

- Juggle frogs: If you are juggling frogs, you are trying to do something very difficult.
- Jump down someone's throat: If you jump down someone's throat, you criticise or chastise them severely.
- Jump on the bandwagon: If people jump on the bandwagon, they get involved in something that has recently become very popular.
- Jump ship: If you leave a company or institution for another because it is doing badly, you are jumping ship.
- Jump the broom: To jump the broom is to marry. (Jump over the broom, jump over the broomstick, jump the broomstick are also used.)
- Jump the gun: If you jump the gun, you start doing something before the appropriate time.
- Jump the track: Jumping the track is suddenly changing from one plan, activity, idea, etc, to another.
- Jump through hoops: If you are prepared to jump through hoops for someone, you are prepared to make great efforts and sacrifices for them.
- Jump to a conclusion: If someone jumps to a conclusion, they evaluate or judge something without a sufficient examination of the facts.
- Jumping Judas!: An expression of surprise or shock.
- Jungle out there: If someone says that it is a jungle out there, they mean that the situation is dangerous and there are no rules.
- Jury's out: If the jury's out on an issue, then there is no general agreement or consensus on it.
- Just around the corner: If something is just around the corner, then it is expected to happen very soon.
- Just coming up to: If the time is just coming up to nine o'clock, it means that it will be nine o'clock in a very few seconds. You'll hear them say it on the radio in the morning.
- Just deserts: If a bad or evil person gets their just deserts, they get the punishment or suffer the misfortune that it is felt they deserve.
- Just for the heck of it: When someone does something just for the heck of it, they do it without a good reason.
- Just for the record: If something is said to be just for the record, the person is saying it so that people know but does not necessarily agree with or support it.
- Just in the nick of time: If you do something in the nick of time, you just manage to do it just in time, with seconds to spare.
- Just off the boat: If someone is just off the boat, they are naive and inexperienced.
- Just what the doctor ordered: If something's just what the doctor ordered, it is precisely what is needed.
- Justice is blind : Justice is blind means that justice is impartial and objective.

Idioms beginning with K
- Kick up a row: to start a fight, to create disturbance.
- Keep ones eye on the ball: be ready for something.
- Kangaroo court: When people take the law into their own hands and form courts that are not legal, these are known as kangaroo court.
- Keep body and soul together: If you earn enough to cover your basic expenses, but nothing more than that, you earn enough to keep body and soul together.
- Keep your eye on the ball: If you keep your eye on the ball, you stay alert and pay close attention to what is happening.
- Know which way the wind blows: This means that you should know how things are developing and be prepared for the future.

Idioms beginning with L
- Loaves and fishes: done for material benefits.
- Like a shag on a rock: completely alone.
- Let someone slide: neglect something.
- Let the cat out of the bag: reveal a secret.
- Let nature take its course: to allow someone to live or die naturally.
- Like a sitting duck: totally unaware.
- Lion's share: a major share.

☞ Left to your own devices: If someone is left to their own devices, they are not controlled and can do whatever they want.

Idioms beginning with M

☞ Make castles in the air: plans or hopes that have very little chances of happening.

☞ Make a bee line for: to go directly towards something.

☞ Make ones bed and lie on it: to be responsible for what you have done and accept the results.

☞ Meet ones waterloo: meet ones final end.

☞ Monkey around: to waste time here and there.

☞ My hands are full: I am busy.

☞ Make a dry face: show disappointment.

☞ Make a monkey of someone: If you make a monkey of someone, you make them look foolish.

☞ Man of his word: A man of his word is a person who does what he says and keeps his Promises.

☞ Many moons ago: A very long time ago.

Idioms beginning with N

☞ Nobody's fool: one who can take care of himself.

☞ Not having a leg to stand for: not having proof.

☞ Never-never land: ideal best place.

☞ No love lost between: dislike.

☞ Needle in a haystack: If trying to find something is like looking for a needle in a haystack, it means that it is very difficult, if not impossible to find among everything around it.

☞ New brush sweeps clean: Someone with a new perspective can make great changes. However, the full version is 'a new brush sweeps clean, but an old brush knows the corners', which warns that experience is also a valuable thing.

☞ No smoke without fire: This idiom means that when people suspect something, there is normally a good reason for the suspicion, even if there is no concrete evidence. ('Where there's smoke, there's fire' is also used.)

Idioms beginning with O

☞ Once in a blue moon: very rarely

☞ On the bandwagon: doing something because others are also doing it

☞ Open Pandora's box: to discover more problems

☞ Over the moon: being too happy

☞ On its last legs: in a bad condition and will not last long

☞ Old flames die hard: It's very difficult to forget old things.

☞ On pins and needles: If you are on pins and needles, you are very worried about something.

☞ On the carpet: When you are called to the bosses office (since supposedly, they are the only ones who have carpet) and its definitely not for a good reason, i.e., you are in trouble, something has not gone according to plan and either maybe you are responsible and/or have some explaining to do.

☞ On the hook: If someone is on the hook, they are responsible for something.

☞ Only the wearer knows where the shoe pinches: This means that it's hard to know how much someone else is suffering.

Idioms beginning with P

☞ Pass muster: to be approved.

☞ Pick someone to pieces: to criticize sharply

☞ Paper over the cracks: to try to hide something.

☞ Put the cart before the horse: doing things in a wrong manner.

☞ Pull up the shocks: do things in the right manner and correctly.

☞ Parrot fashion: If you learn something parrots fashion; you learn it word for word

☞ Pay on the nail: If you pay on the nail, you pay promptly in cash.

☞ Pen is mightier than the sword: The idiom 'the pen is mightier than the sword' means that words and communication are morepowerful than wars and fighting.

☞ Pick someone's brains: If you pick someone's brains, you ask them for advice, suggestions and information about something they know about.

- Pieces of the same cake: Pieces of the same cake are things that have the same characteristics or qualities.
- Play fast and loose: If people play fast and loose, they behave in an irresponsible way and don't respect rules, etc.
- Poker face: Not showing any emotion.

Idioms beginning with Q
- Quarrel with bread and butter: Bread and butter, here, indicate the means of one's living. If a sub-ordinate in an organization is quarrelsome or if he is not patient enough to bear the reprimand he deserves, gets angry and retorts or provokes the higher-up, the top man dismisses him from the job. So, he loses the job that gave him bread and butter. Hence we say, he quarreled with bread and butter (manager or the top man) and lost his job
- Quiet as a cat: Make as little noise as possible and try to be unnoticeable.
- Quiet as a mouse: Make absolutely no noise.
- Queer fish: A strange person is a queer fish

Idioms beginning with R
- Round the twist: go crazy
- Read between the lines: read hidden meanings.
- Rack and ruin: If something or someone goes to rack and ruin, they are utterly destroyed or wrecked.
- Rain on your parade: If someone rains on your parade, they ruin your pleasure or your plans.
- Rake someone over the coals: If you rake someone over the coals, you criticize or scold them severely.
- Recipe for disaster: A recipe for disaster is a mixture of people and events that could only possibly result in trouble.
- Red carpet: If you give someone the red-carpet treatment, you give them a special welcome to show that you think they are important.
- Red herring: If something is a distraction from the real issues, it is a red herring.
- Red letter day: A red letter day is a one of good luck, when something special happens to you.
- Reduce to ashes: If something is reduced to ashes, it is destroyed or made useless.
- Round the houses: Do something in an inefficient way when there is a quicker, more convenient way.
- Rub shoulders: If you rub shoulders with people, you meet and spend time with them, especially when they are powerful or famous.
- Run into the sand: If something runs into the sand, it fails to achieve a result.

Idioms beginning with S
- Salt on the earth: fundamental good people
- Sands of time: tiny amounts of time
- Shake a leg: to go fast, hurry
- Spill the beans: to expose a secret
- Snake in the grass: a hidden but harmful person who seems harmless.
- Snake in the shoes: to be in a state of fear
- Stood to his guns: maintained to his opinion
- Showing the door: asking someone to leave
- Song and a dance: an excuse
- Salad days: Your salad days are an especially happy period of your life.
- Sail under false colours: Someone who sails under false colours is hypocritical or pretends to be something they aren't in order to deceive people.

Idioms beginning with T
- Threaded his way out: walked carefully through.
- Take the cloth: to become a priest.
- Talk turkey: to discuss a problem with a real intension to solve it.
- Tit for tat: an action done to revenge against a person who has done some wrong to you
- To crow over: to triumph over someone
- To blow a fuse: to turn someone angry
- Though thick and thin: under all conditions
- To bell the cat: to take great risks
- To look through coloured glasses: to look the things not as they are
- Taking to a brick wall: taking with a no response
- Turned a deaf ear: disregarded
- Take a back seat: choose to decrease involvement

- Tables are turned: When the tables are turned, the situation has changed giving the advantage to the party who had previously been at a disadvantage.
- Take someone under your wing: If you take someone under your wing, you look after them while they are learning something.
- Take your medicine: If you take your medicine, you accept the consequences of something you have done wrong.
- Talking to a brick wall: If you talk to someone and they do not listen to you, it is like talking to a brick wall.
- Taste of your own medicine: If you give someone a taste of their own medicine, you do something bad to someone that they have done to you to teach them a lesson.
- The apple does not fall far from the tree: Offspring grow up to be like their parents.
- Through thick and thin: If someone supports you through thick and thin, they support you during good times and bad.

Idioms beginning with U
- Upset the apple cart: to create difficulty
- Under a cloud: If someone is suspected of having done something wrong, they are under a cloud.
- Under fire: If someone is being attacked and criticized heavily, they are under fire.
- Under your nose: If something happens right in front of you, especially if it is surprising or audacious, it happens under your nose.
- Up for grabs: If something is up for grabs, it is available and whoever is first or is successful will get it.
- Up to the neck: If someone's in something up to the neck, they are very involved in it, especially when it's something wrong.
- Up a river without a paddle: If you up a river without a paddle, you are in an unfortunate situation, unprepared and with none of the resources to remedy the matter.
- Uncharted waters: If you're in uncharted waters, you are in a situation that is unfamiliar to you, that you have no experience of and don't know what might happen.
- Under lock and key: If something is under lock and key, it is stored very securely.

Idioms beginning with V
- Vale of tears: A catholic phrase meaning the world is a place of sorrow and suffering.
- Velvet glove: This idiom is used to describe a person who appears gentle, but is determined and inflexible underneath. ('Iron fist in a velvet glove' is the full form.)
- Vent your spleen: If someone vents their spleen, they release all their anger about something.
- Vicar of Bray: A person who changes their beliefs and principles to stay popular with people above them is a Vicar of Bray.
- Vicious circle: A vicious circle is a sequence of events that make each other worse- someone drinks because they are unhappy at work, then loses their job. 'Vicious cycle' is also used.
- Vinegar tits: A mean spirited women lacking in love or compassion.
- Virgin territory: If something is virgin territory, it hasn't been explored before.
- Voice in the wilderness: Someone who expresses an opinion that no one believes or listens to is a voice in the wilderness, especially if proved right later.
- Volte-face: If you do a volte-face on something, you make a sudden and complete change in your stance or position over an issue.
- Vultures are circling: If the vultures are circling, then something is in danger and its enemies are getting ready for the kill.

Idioms beginning with W
- Weight one's word: be careful to what one says
- Wait for a raindrop in the drought: When someone is waiting for a raindrop in the drought, they are waiting or hoping for something that is extremely unlikely to happen.
- Walking on broken glass: When a person is punished for something.
- Wet behind the ears: Someone who is wet behind the ears is either very young or inexperienced.

- Whale of a time: If you have a whale of a time, you really enjoy yourself.
- Work your fingers to the bone: If you work your fingers to the bone, you work extremely hard on something.
- Wrench in the works: If someone puts or throws a wrench, or monkey wrench, in the works, they ruin a plan.

Idioms beginning with X
- X factor: The dangers for people in the military that civilians do not face, for which they receive payment, are known as the X factor.
- X marks the spot: This is used to say where something is located or hidden.
- X-rated: If something is x-rated, it is not suitable for children.

Idioms beginning with Y
- Yah boo sucks: Yah boo sucks can be used to show that you have no sympathy with someone.
- Yank my chain: If some one says this to another person (i.e. stop yanking my chain) it means for the other person to leave the person who said it alone and to stop bothering them.
- Yell bloody murder: Protest angrily and loudly, or scream in fear.
- Yellow press: The yellow press is a term for the popular and sensationalist newspapers.
- Yellow streak: If someone has a yellow streak, they are cowardly about something.
- Yellow-bellied: A yellow-bellied person is a coward.
- Yen: If you have a yen to do something, you have a desire to do it.
- Yeoman's service: To do yeoman's service is to serve in an exemplary manner.
- Yes-man: Someone who always agrees with people in authority is a yes-man.
- Yesterday's man or Yesterday's woman: Someone, especially a politician or celebrity, whose career is over or on the decline is yesterday's man or woman.
- You are what you eat: This is used to emphasise the importance of a good diet as a key to good health.
- You can catch more flies with honey than with vinegar: This means that it is easier to persuade people if you use polite arguments and flattery than if you are confrontational.
- You can choose your friends, but you can't choose your family: Some things you can choose, but others you cannot, so you have to try to make the best of what you have where you have no choice.
- You can lead a horse to water, but you can't make it drink: This idiom means you can offer something to someone, like good advice, but you cannot make them take it.
- You can say that again: If you want to agree strongly with what someone has said, you can say 'You can say that again' as a way of doing so.
- You can't fight City Hall: This phrase is used when one is so cynical that one doesn't think one can change their representatives. The phrase must have started with frustration towards a local body of government.
- You can't have cake and the topping, too: This idiom means that you can't have everything the way you want it, especially if your desires are contradictory.
- You can't have your cake and eat it: This idiom means that you can't have things both ways. For example, you can't have very low taxes and a high standard of state care.
- You can't hide elephants in mouse holes: means that some issues/problems/challenges cannot be hidden/concealed but have to be faced and dealt with.
- You can't make a silk purse out of a sow's ear: If something isn't very good to start with, you can't do much to improve it.
- You can't make an omelette without breaking eggs: In order to achieve something or make progress, there are often losers in the process.
- You can't take it with you: To use up all you have before you die because it's no use to you afterwards.
- You can't teach an old dog new tricks: It is difficult to make someone change the way they do something when they have been doing it the same way for a long time.
- You can't un-ring a bell: Once something has been done, you have to live with the consequences as it can't be undone.

- You could have knocked me down with a feather: A person being very shocked or surprised.
- You do not get a dog and bark yourself: If there is someone in a lower position who can or should do a task, then you shouldn't do it.
- You get what you pay for: Something that is very low in price is not usually of very good quality.
- You reap what you sow: If you do bad things to people, bad things will happen to you, or good things if you do good things. It is normally used when someone has done something bad.
- You said it!: Agreeing completely with something just said.
- You scratch my back and I'll scratch yours: If you do something for me, they will return the favour.
- You what?: This is a very colloquial way of expressing surprise or disbelief at something you have heard. It can also be used to ask someone to say something again.
- You're toast: If someone tells you that you are toast, you are in a lot of trouble.
- You've got rocks in your head: Someone who has acted with a lack of intelligence.
- You've made your bed; you'll have to lie in it: To live with the consequences of their own actions.
- Young blood: Young people with new ideas and fresh approaches.
- Young Turk: Young person who is rebellious and difficult to control in a company, team or organisation.
- Your belly button is bigger than your stomach: Take on more responsibilities than you can handle.
- Your call: Up to your choice to make a decision on the matter.
- Your name is mud: If someone's name is mud, then they have a bad reputation.
- Your sins will find you out: This idiom means that things you do wrong will become known.

Idioms beginning with Z
- Zero hour: The time when something important is to begin is zero hour.
- Zero tolerance: If the police have a zero tolerance policy, they will not overlook any crime, no matter how small or trivial.
- Zigged before you zagged: Doing things in the wrong order.
- Zip it: This is used to tell someone to be quiet.
- Zip your lip: If someone tells you to zip your lip, they want to shut up or keep quiet about something. ('Zip it' is also used.)

MUST REMEMBER

→ Phrasal verbs are usually two-word phrases consisting of verb + adverb or verb + preposition.
→ Idioms are words, phrases or expressions which are commonly used in everyday conversation by native speakers of English. They are often metaphorical and make the language more colourful.

PRACTICE EXERCISE

I. Fill in the blanks with correct option.

1. Robert was expected to arrive at 8 o'clock, but he didn't turn _____ until midnight.
   (a) out (b) up
   (c) off (d) with

2. Peter needs either to get a raise or to get a better job, because he can't get _____ on his current salary.
   (a) by (b) out
   (c) in (d) off

3. Manuela and Glenda didn't like each other at first, but now they get _____.
   (a) over (b) across
   (c) away (d) along

4. The plane is scheduled to take _____ at 7 a.m.
   (a) away (b) to
   (c) off (d) with

5. We need milk, but we can do _____ beer.
   (a) without (b) along
   (c) away (d) off

6. The wedding was originally scheduled for June 12, but it has been put _____ until September 24.
   (a) out (b) away
   (c) off (d) up

7. Our alarm clock is set to go _____ at 6 a.m.
   (a) away (b) up
   (c) out (d) off

8. Gary asked Cynthia to marry him, but she turned him _____.
   (a) down (b) without
   (c) across (d) over

9. The emergency workers managed to put _____ the fire.
   (a) off (b) out
   (c) down (d) without

10. Everyone thought she was English, but she turned _____ to be Canadian.
    (a) up (b) off
    (c) by (d) out

11. The math teacher lets students chew gum in class, but the French teacher does not put _____ with it.
    (a) over (b) out
    (c) up (d) along

12. The university students want to do _____ with tuition, because they think education should be free.
    (a) away (b) out
    (c) up (d) off

13. Nelson is a creative liar who is always making _____ unusual excuses for not doing his work.
    (a) up (b) across
    (c) away (d) off

14. Paula always comes _____ as very sincere.
    (a) out (b) along
    (c) across (d) away

15. Tom and Carol often have heated arguments, but they always make _____ later.
    (a) down (b) away
    (c) up (d) along

16. We have to clean _____ the house before my parents arrive.
    (a) down (b) away
    (c) without (d) up

17. The police officer almost captured the criminals, but they managed to get _____.
    (a) without (b) over
    (c) along (d) away

18. I have come down with a cold, but I will get _____ it soon.
    (a) over (b) up
    (c) without (d) above

19. I'd like to stop smoking but I just can't _____ it up.
    (a) give (b) turn
    (c) put (d) hurry

20. I'm getting really unfit. I think I should _____ up a sport.
    (a) speak (b) take
    (c) put (d) hurry

21. I'm fed up hearing you talk all the time. Why don't you just _____ up and listen for once?
    (a) cheer (b) move
    (c) put (d) shut

22. He's a really irritating person. I don't see how you _____ up with him.
    (a) speak (b) move
    (c) put   (d) hurry
23. If you don't put any oil in the motor when the warning light comes on, it's likely to _____ up.
    (a) send   (b) seize
    (c) put   (d) set
24. There's not enough room for all my papers. I'm going to ask maintenance to _____ up some more shelves.
    (a) cheer (b) move
    (c) put   (d) hurry
25. If you ever come to my city you must _____ me up and we'll have dinner together.
    (a) speak (b) move
    (c) put   (d) look
26. Let's ask Andrew and see if he can _____ up with any good ideas.
    (a) come   (b) set
    (c) put   (d) turn
27. It was really embarassing. I'd had too much to drink and when we left the bar I was sure I was going to _____ up.
    (a) cheer (b) sign
    (c) throw (d) hurry
28. It's a difficult market to enter but we intend to _____ up a small subsidiary anyway.
    (a) cheer (b) turn
    (c) throw (d) set
29. When I saw that this course was available I rushed to _____ up for it.
    (a) cheer (b) sign
    (c) gee   (d) feel
30. That was a complete surprise - a total _____ up for the books.
    (a) speak (b) move
    (c) turn   (d) throw

II. Choose the correct option for the given proverb/idiom.

1. To make clean breast of
   (a) To gain prominence
   (b) To praise oneself
   (c) To confess without reserve
   (d) To destroy before it blooms
2. To keeps one's temper
   (a) To become hungry
   (b) To be in good mood
   (c) To preserve ones energy
   (d) To be aloof from
3. To catch a tartar
   (a) To trap wanted criminal with great difficulty
   (b) To catch a dangerous person
   (c) To meet with disaster
   (d) To deal with a person who is more than one's match
4. To drive home
   (a) To find one's roots
   (b) To return to place of rest
   (c) Back to original position
   (d) To emphasise
5. To have an axe to grind
   (a) A private end to serve
   (b) To fail to arouse interest
   (c) To have no result
   (d) To work for both sides
6. To cry wolf
   (a) To listen eagerly
   (b) To give false alarm
   (c) To turn pale
   (d) To keep off starvation
7. To end in smoke
   (a) To make completely understand
   (b) To ruin oneself
   (c) To excite great applause
   (d) To overcome someone
8. To be above board
   (a) To have a good height
   (b) To be honest in any business deal
   (c) They have no debts
   (d) To try to be beautiful
9. To put one's hand to plough
   (a) To take up agricultural farming
   (b) To take a difficult task
   (c) To get entangled into unnecessary things
   (d) Take interest in technical work
10. To pick holes
    (a) To find some reason to quarrel
    (b) To destroy something
    (c) To criticise someone
    (d) To cut some part of an item

11. To leave someone in the lurch
    (a) To come to compromise with someone
    (b) Constant source of annoyance to someone
    (c) To put someone at ease
    (d) To desert someone in his difficulties
12. To play second fiddle
    (a) To be happy, cheerful and healthy
    (b) To reduce importance of one's senior
    (c) To support the role and view of another person
    (d) To do back seat driving
13. To beg the question
    (a) To refer to
    (b) To take for granted
    (c) To raise objections
    (d) To be discussed
14. A black sheep
    (a) An unlucky person
    (b) A lucky person
    (c) An ugly person
    (d) None of these
15. A man of straw
    (a) A man of no substance
    (b) A very active person
    (c) A worthy fellow
    (d) An unreasonable person
16. To smell a rat
    (a) To see signs of plague epidemic
    (b) To get bad small of a bad dead rat
    (c) To suspect foul dealings
    (d) To be in a bad mood
17. To hit the nail right on the head
    (a) To do the right thing
    (b) To destroy one's reputation
    (c) To announce one's fixed views
    (d) To teach someone a lesson

III. **Choose the most appropriate option which explains the given idiom/phrase.**

1. Bid defiance
    (a) to obey
    (b) to ignore
    (c) to follow
    (d) none of these
2. Blow one's trumpet
    (a) To praise other
    (b) To praise leader
    (c) To praise ownself
    (d) To praise community
3. Bury the hatchet
    (a) to break peace
    (b) joint operation of killing
    (c) to make peace
    (d) none of these
4. Bring to book
    (a) To punish   (b) To serve
    (c) To praise   (d) To write a story
5. Blaze the trail
    (a) To stop a movement
    (b) To join a movement
    (c) To protect a movement
    (d) To start a movement
6. Broken Reed
    (a) Continue support
    (b) Support that failed
    (c) Support endlessly
    (d) None of these
7. By dint of
    (a) By force of
    (b) By permission of
    (c) By fear of
    (d) By blessing of
8. Charley horse
    (a) Very rapid   (b) Very weak
    (c) Stiffness   (d) Boldness
9. Cart before the horse
    (a) To be ready to go
    (b) To be very active
    (c) To do things in reverse order
    (d) To do things in right order
10. Chalk and Cheese
    (a) Different from each other
    (b) Having same properties
    (c) Having fun together
    (d) Making plans
11. Cry for the moon
    (a) To wish for something impossible
    (b) To wish for something accessible
    (c) To try to have something by bad means
    (d) None of above

12. Carry the day
    (a) To have great fun
    (b) To do something wrong
    (c) To win a victory
    (d) To lose something
13. Cloven hoof
    (a) the evil intention
    (b) the nice intention
    (c) to do something religious
    (d) to help someone silently
14. Cry over spilt milk
    (a) Approve   (b) Be happy
    (c) Praise   (d) Repent
15. If workers get a raw deal for long, they get frustrated.
    (a) receive the same wages
    (b) are unable to close their sales
    (c) are not treated as well as other people
    (d) get uncooked food
16. To fight tooth and nail means
    (a) To fight a losing battle
    (b) To oppose resolutely
    (c) To have a physical fight
    (d) To lodge a formal protest
17. To steer clear of means
    (a) drive carefully
    (b) avoid
    (c) explain clearly
    (d) escape
18. At last the rioters fell back.
    (a) fell on the ground
    (b) yielded
    (c) ran back
    (d) turned back

HOTS

Read the passages and choose the correct phrasal verbs that can replace the underlined portions/blanks.

1. Once the verdict of guilty was __1__, Tarun __2__ to prove that his brother __3__ for a crime that he did not commit.
   (a) Handed in   (b) Handed out
   (c) Handed down   (d) Handed
2. Once the verdict of guilty was __1__, Tarun __2__ to prove that his brother __3__ for a crime that he did not commit.
   (a) Waited about (b) Planned about
   (c) Set about   (d) Wished about
3. Once the verdict of guilty was __1__, Tarun __2__ to prove that his brother __3__ for a crime that he did not commit.
   (a) Frames
   (b) Are framed
   (c) Framed
   (d) Had been framed
4. You will never __4__ anything if you continue __5__ with that bunch of dropouts," said the Principal to Karun.
   (a) Meet up with (b) Achieve to
   (c) Amount to   (d) Refer to
5. You will never __4__ anything if you continue __5__ with that bunch of dropouts," said the Principal to Karun.
   (a) Hanging about (b) Hanging out
   (c) Hanging by   (d) Hanging for

Nouns and Pronouns 5

Learning Objectives : In this chapter, students will learn about:
- ✓ Kinds of Nouns
- ✓ Usage of Nouns
- ✓ Usage of Pronoun
- ✓ Functions of Nouns
- ✓ Pronoun and its Types

CHAPTER SUMMARY

Nouns are used to name persons, things, animals, places, ideas, or events. Nouns are the simplest among the parts of speech, which is why they are the first ones taught to students in primary school.
Example: '*Tom Hanks*' is very versatile.
(The italicized noun refers to a name of a person.)
Dogs can be extremely cute.
(In this example, the italicized word is considered a noun because it names an animal.)
It is my *birthday*.
(The word "birthday" is a noun which refers to an event.)

Types of Noun
The following some types of nouns.
Proper Noun: Proper nouns always start with a capital letter and refer to specific names of persons, places, or things.
Example: Volkswagen Beetle, Shakey's Pizza, Game of Thrones
Common Noun: Common nouns are just generic names of persons, things, or places.
Example: car, pizza parlor, TV series
Concrete Noun: This kind refers to nouns which you can perceive through your five senses.
Example: folder, sand, board
Abstract Noun: Abstract nouns are those which you can't perceive through your five senses.
Example: happiness, grudge, bravery

Count Noun: It refers to anything that is countable, and has a singular and plural form.
Example: kitten, video, ball
Mass Noun: Mass nouns are also called non-countable nouns, and they need to have "counters" to quantify them.
Example of Counters: kilo, cup, meter
Example of Mass Nouns: rice, flour, garter
Collective Noun: These nouns refer to a group of persons, animals, or things.
Example: Faculty (group of teachers), class (group of students), pride (group of lions)

TRIVIA

The word "selfie" was the Oxford Dictionary's Word of the Year in 2013 because the use of the term increased 17,000% from 2012 to 2013.

Pronouns
A pronoun replaces a noun in a sentence. Pronouns are used so that our language is not cumbersome with the same nouns being repeated over and over in a paragraph.
Some examples of pronouns include: I, me, mine, myself, she, her, hers, herself, we, us, ours and ourselves. You may have noticed that they tend to come in sets of four, all referring to the same person, group or thing:
He, him, his and himself, for example, all refer to a male person or something belonging to him. They, them, theirs and themselves all refer

to a group or something belonging to a group, and so on.

Types of Pronoun

There are five types of pronoun.
1. Personal Pronoun
2. Possessive Pronoun
3. Reflexive Pronoun
4. Relative Pronoun
5. Demonstrative Pronoun

Personal Pronoun

Personal pronoun describes the person speaking (I, me, we, us), the person spoken to (you), or the person or thing spoken about (he, she, it, they, him, her, them).

Example: 'He' helps poor.

The pronoun "he" in above sentence describes a person who helps poor.

Number	Person	Personal Pronoun	
		Subject	Object
Singular	1st Person	I	Me
	2nd Person	You	You
	3rd Person	He, She, It	Him, Her, It
Plural	1st Person	We	Us
	2nd Person	You	You
	3rd Person	They	Them

Example: 'She' is intelligent.
'They' are playing chess.
'He' sent 'me' a letter.
'It' is raining.
'We' love our country.
The teacher appreciated 'them.'
'I' met 'him' yesterday.
'He' gave 'her' a gift.
Did 'you' go home?

Possessive Pronoun

Possessive pronoun indicates close possession or ownership or relationship of a thing/person to another thing/person. yours, mine, his, hers, ours, theirs, hers are possessive pronouns.

Example: This book is 'mine.'

The pronoun 'mine' describes the relationship between the book and a person (me) who possesses this book or who is the owner of this book.

Number	Person	Possessive Pronoun
Singular	1st Person	Mine
	2nd Person	Yours
	3rd Person	Hers, his, its
Plural	1st Person	Ours
	2nd Person	Yours
	3rd Person	Theirs

Nouns and Pronouns

Example: That car is 'hers.'
Your book is old. 'Mine' is new.
The pen on the table is 'mine.'
The smallest cup is 'yours.'
The voice is 'hers.'
The car is 'ours' not 'theirs.'
I have lost my camera. May I use 'yours'?
They received your letter. Did you receive 'theirs'?

NOTE:
Possessive adjectives (my, her, your) may be confused with possessive pronouns. Possessive adjective modifies noun in terms of possession. Both possessive adjective and possessive pronoun show possession or ownership, but possessive adjective is used (with noun) to modify the noun while possessive pronoun is used instead (in place of) a noun.

Example: This is 'my' book. (Possessive adjective: 'my' modifies the noun 'book')
This book is 'mine'. (Possessive pronoun: 'mine' is used instead of noun "to whom the book belongs")

Reflexive Pronoun
Reflexive pronoun describes noun when a subject's action affects the subject itself. For examples, himself, yourself, herself, ourselves, themselves, itself are reflexive pronouns.

Reflexive pronouns always act as objects not subjects, and they require an interaction between the subject and an object.

Number	Person	Subject	Reflexive Pronoun
Singular	1st Person	I	Myself
	2nd Person	You	Yourself
	3rd Person	He, she, it	Himself, Herself, Itself
Plural	1st Person	We	Ourselves
	2nd Person	You	Yourselves
	3rd Person	They	Themselves

Example: I looked at 'myself' in the mirror.
You should think about 'yourself.'
They prepared 'themselves' for the competition.
She pleases 'herself' by thinking that she will win the prize.
He bought a car for 'himself.'
He locked 'himself' in the room.
He who loves only 'himself' is a selfish.

Intensive Pronoun
Reflexive pronoun can also be used to give more emphasis on subject or object. If a reflexive pronoun is used to give more emphasis on a subject or an object, it is called "Intensive Pronoun". Usage and function of intensive pronoun are different from those of reflexive pronoun.

For example, she 'herself' started to think about herself.

In the above sentence, the first "herself" is used as intensive pronoun while the second "herself" is used as reflexive pronoun.

See the following examples of intensive pronouns.

Example: I did it 'myself.' OR I 'myself' did it.
She 'herself' washed the clothes.
He 'himself' decided to go to New York.
She 'herself' told me.

Reciprocal Pronouns

Reciprocal pronouns are used when two subjects act in a same way towards each other, or, more subjects act in the same way to one another.

For example,'A loves B and B loves A.'Instead, we can say that 'A and B love each other.'

There are two reciprocal pronouns: Each other, One another

Example: John and Marry are talking to 'each other.'

The students gave cards to 'one another.'

The people helped 'one another' in the hospital.

Two boys were pushing 'each other.'

The car and the bus collided with 'each other.'

The students in the class greeted 'one another.'

Relative Pronouns

Relative Pronoun describes a noun, which is mentioned before and more information is to be given about it.

For example, 'It is the person, who helped her.'

In this sentence, the word 'who' is a relative pronoun, which refers to the noun (the person) which is already mentioned in the beginning of the sentence (It is the person) and more information (he helped her) is given after using a relative pronoun (who) for the noun (the person). Similarly, in the above sentence, the pronoun "who" joins two clauses which are "it is the person" and "who helped her".

The most commonly used five relative pronouns are 'who, whom, whose, which', that:

'Who' is for subject and "whom" is used for object. "who" and "whom" are used for people.

'Whose' is used to show possession and can be used for both people and things.

'Which' is used for things.

'That' is used for people and things.

Example: It is the girl 'who' got first position in class.

The man 'whom' I met yesterday is a nice person.

It is the planning 'that' makes succeed.

The boy 'who' is laughing is my friend.

It is the boy 'whose' father is doctor.

The car 'which' I like is red.

Demonstrative Pronoun

Demonstrative pronoun is a pronoun that points to a thing or things. For example, this, that, these, those, none, neither. These pronouns point to thing or things in short distance/time or long distance/time.

Short distance or time: This, these

Long distance or time: That, those

Demonstrative pronouns "this and that" are used for singular thing while 'these or those' are used for plural things.

Example: 'This' is black.

'That' is heavy.

Can you see 'these'?

Do you like 'this'?

John brought 'these.'

'Those' look attractive.

Have you tried 'this'?

Nouns and Pronouns

MUST REMEMBER

- Nouns are used to name persons, things, animals, places, ideas, or events.
- Proper nouns always start with a capital letter and refer to specific names of persons, places, or things.
- Abstract nouns are those which you can't perceive through your five senses.
- Mass nouns are also called non-countable nouns, and they need to have "counters" to quantify them.
- Pronouns are used so that our language is not cumbersome with the same nouns being repeated over and over in a paragraph.
- Possessive pronoun indicates close possession or ownership or relationship of a thing/person to another thing/person.
- Reflexive pronoun describes noun when a subject's action affects the subject itself.
- If a reflexive pronoun is used to give more emphasis on a subject or an object, it is called "Intensive Pronoun".
- Reciprocal pronouns are used when two subjects act in a same way towards each other, or, more subjects act in the same way to one another.
- Demonstrative pronoun is a pronoun that points to a thing or things.

PRACTICE EXERCISE

I. Fill in the blanks with the correct option.

1. There was a robbery at the ABC Bank. The thief ran off with a large _____ of cash.
   (a) pod (b) deck
   (c) bundle (d) none of these

2. For Christmas, I received in the mail a small _____ from my cousin. She sent me a woolen scarf.
   (a) deck (b) parcel
   (c) crowd (d) none of these

3. There was a _____ of cars on the road.
   (a) fleet (b) nest
   (c) swarm (d) none of these

4. The man never cleaned his office. He left a _____ of files and papers on his desk.
   (a) army (b) archipelago
   (c) stack (d) none of these

5. My friend's cat had a _____ of kittens on the weekend.
   (a) gaggle (b) litter
   (c) swarm (d) none of these

6. On Sunday, I went to Stanley Park and saw a _____ of dolphins in Lost Lagoon.
   (a) drove (b) school
   (c) brood (d) none of these

7. At the library, there is a _____ of useful educational resources, such as: books, audio tapes, dictionaries, computers, etc.
   (a) host (b) litter
   (c) nest (d) none of these

8. I was attacked by a _____ of bees.
   (a) swarm (b) deck
   (c) package (d) none of these

9. On the ferry ride from Victoria, I saw a _____ of whales in the ocean.
   (a) bundle (b) pack
   (c) pod (d) none of these

10. On a clear summer night you can see a _____ of stars.
    (a) galaxy (b) school
    (c) pod (d) none of these

11. A _____ of geese was heard a mile away.
    (a) litter (b) herd
    (c) gaggle (d) none of these

12. A _____ of children ran around in the classroom.
    (a) nest (b) bundle
    (c) group (d) none of these

13. The boy saw a _____ of sheep grazing in the fields.
    (a) bevy (b) flock
    (c) swarm (d) none of these

14. I love hiking in the spring because the mountains are covered with _____ of wild flowers.
    (a) bed (b) nest
    (c) deck (d) none of these

15. Last Sunday, I went with my friends to the park. We had to eat our lunch quickly because an _____ of ants attacked our food.
    (a) army (b) crowd
    (c) bevy (d) none of these

16. On a stormy night you could hear the howling of a _____ of wolves.
    (a) pack (b) bevy
    (c) swarm (d) none of these

17. A _____ of cows was transported to a farm in Texas for slaughter.
    (a) pod (b) herd
    (c) pack (d) none of these

18. I was so happy to see a _____ of quails on the country road.
    (a) crowd (b) archipelago
    (c) bevy (d) none of these

19. There was a _____ of visitors in the Vancouver Art Gallery on Sunday.
    (a) crowd (b) nest
    (c) school (d) none of these

20. My sister in Sweden took me on a boat cruise to see the famous _____. It is a group of small islands.
    (a) archipelago (b) horde
    (c) pack (d) none of these

Nouns and Pronouns

II. **Fill in the blanks with correct pronoun in the following sentences.**

1. Gary's mom asked _____ to clean the garage.
   (a) he (b) him
   (c) her (d) his
2. A student at an all boys high school should be on _____ best behavior.
   (a) their (b) his
   (c) him (d) her
3. Neither Mary nor _____ knew why the store was closed.
   (a) I (b) me
   (c) his (d) her
4. After school you and _____ must discuss a few things.
   (a) I (b) me
   (c) him (d) her
5. Everyone at the table has eaten _____ lunch earlier.
   (a) his or her (b) their
   (c) me (d) its

III. **Find out the pronoun(s) in each sentence and choose the correct option.**

1. When I looked over at the man, I noticed that he was reading a book.
   (a) I (b) I, he
   (c) him (d) none of these
2. I did not know the right answer.
   (a) him (b) I
   (c) answer (d) none of these
3. Why don't you go outside?
   (a) you (b) outside
   (c) go (d) none of these
4. Take Raman with you.
   (a) me (b) take
   (c) you (d) none of these
5. I like running fast.
   (a) I (b) run
   (c) run (d) none of these

IV. **Fill in the blank with the right pronoun.**

1. Did he see ___?
   (a) us (b) we
   (c) she (d) i
2. I took the bag from ___.
   (a) him (b) they
   (c) his (d) hers
3. My brother and ___ went to the park?
   (a) I (b) us
   (c) our (d) me
4. What did ___ do about the car?
   (a) them (b) they
   (c) us (d) he
5. What did ___ say about the work?
   (a) she (b) me
   (c) their (d) him
6. Where will ___ go from here?
   (a) you (b) us
   (c) our (d) their
7. Can ___ talk for a minute?
   (a) we (b) us
   (c) him (d) me
8. Is this house _____?
   (a) theirs (b) them
   (c) him (d) me
9. Why don't ___ have a seat?
   (a) you (b) us
   (c) her (d) them
10. Is that cup ___?
    (a) his (b) him
    (c) my (d) our

HOTS

I. Fill in the blanks with the correct noun.

1. On my African trip, I saw a _____ of lions.
   (a) bundle   (b) pride
   (c) pack   (d) none of these

2. I had so much fun in Hawaii swimming with a _____ of fish.
   (a) army   (b) school
   (c) bevy   (d) none of these

3. I like to play card games. So when I go camping, I usually take a _____ of cards with me.
   (a) school   (b) pack
   (c) herd   (d) none of these

4. I have lost a _____ of keys.
   (a) hive   (b) chain
   (c) bunch   (d) none of these

5. There seems to be a plan behind this chain of _____.
   (a) goodness   (b) series
   (c) events   (d) none of these

II. Choose the correct option to answer the following questions:

1. What is a noun?
   (a) A noun is a groups of people in the community.
   (b) A noun is a word or a group of words that represent a person, a place, a thing or activity, or a quality or idea.
   (c) A noun represent as the states of action.
   (d) A noun is an adverb.

2. 'That boy is my brother' represents the example for a _____.
   (a) Collective noun   (b) Abstract noun.
   (c) Proper noun.   (d) Countable noun

3. All these are types of nouns except _____.
   (a) Mass noun   (b) Concrete noun
   (c) Gender noun   (d) Common noun

4. Concrete noun can be described as _____.
   (a) A noun that has no plural form and cannot be used with numerical values.
   (b) A noun which names anything (or anyone) that you can perceive through your physical senses; touch, sight, taste, hearing or smell.
   (c) A noun referring to a person place, or thing in a general sense.
   (d) A noun referring to a particular unique person, place, animal, etc.

5. A noun that denotes an action idea quality or state is called _____.
   (a) Abstract noun
   (b) Proper noun
   (c) Common noun
   (d) Uncountable noun

6. Nouns can be classified into different main functions except _____.
   (a) Subject of a sentence
   (b) Direct object of a verb
   (c) Indirect object of a verb
   (d) Vocatives

7. A subject of a sentence is _____.
   (a) The element in the sentence with which the verb has grammatical agreement.
   (b) The action of the verb to the direct object.
   (c) Functions as the receiver of the action.
   (d) The beneficiary of the action.

8. Some nouns functions as the object of prepositions. An object of a preposition indicate location, direction and _____.
   (a) Possessive noun   (b) Time
   (c) Place   (d) Purpose

9. The sentence, the house is empty, represents _____.
   (a) The element in the sentence with which the verb has grammatical agreement.
   (b) Common noun as the subject agreement in a sentence.
   (c) The use of verb with a singular subject.
   (d) The main characteristic of proper noun in a sentence.

Nouns and Pronouns

10. Many English nouns would change form depending on their gender. An unmarried man is called a "bachelor" while an unmarried woman is called a _____.
    (a) Freethinker   (b) Spinster
    (c) Emperor   (d) Countess

III. **Choose the appropriate option to complete the sentences.**

1. We all told the boss that we wanted to have ____ salaries paid in advance but he just ignored ____.
   (a) ours / it   (b) his / we
   (c) their / our   (d) we / his
   (e) our / us

2. When the man asked me how I had got ____ address, I told him that I was given it by a relative of ____.
   (a) my / me   (b) his / his
   (c) mine / his   (d) his / him
   (e) him / him

3. Although ____ in the room seemed to follow ____ said by the speaker, he never intended to simplify his language.
   (a) no one / anything
   (b) anybody / anything
   (c) nobody / nothing
   (d) anyone / nothing
   (e) someone / something

4. I hope you will enjoy ____ at the re-union party this weekend because I won't be able to be there ____.
   (a) you / myself   (b) yourself / mine
   (c) yours / oneself (d) yourself / myself
   (e) you / me

5. We decided to do all the cooking ____ instead of hiring a catering company for the party.
   (a) of our own   (b) oneself
   (c) by ourselves   (d) ours
   (e) each other

6. Thousands of children nowadays prefer doing ____ homework with a background of pop-music to doing ____ in a quiet room.
   (a) theirs / them   (b) his / its
   (c) them / it's   (d) they / them
   (e) their / it

7. You and ____ brother need to take time to prepare ____ for the long journey which will start next month.
   (a) his / yourself
   (b) yours / ourselves
   (c) their / you
   (d) your / yourselves
   (e) her / by themselves

8. The students watched each gesture of ____ as if their teacher were a stranger.
   (a) them   (b) hers
   (c) him   (d) her
   (e) himself

9. Trademarks enable a company to distinguish ____ products from ____ of another company.
   (a) their / it   (b) it / that
   (c) our / this   (d) its / those
   (e) my / these

10. ____ cannot see through translucent materials, but light can pass through ____.
    (a) We / it   (b) Anything / their
    (c) One / them   (d) No one / its
    (e) Everyone / their

Verbs and Adverbs 6

Learning Objectives : In this chapter, students will learn about:
- ✓ Verbs and its different types
- ✓ Modal Auxiliaries
- ✓ Adverbs and its different kinds
- ✓ Uses of Adverbs

CHAPTER SUMMARY

Verbs express an action or state of being.
Example: Write, Read, Act.

Types of Verb
There are three types of verbs: action verbs, linking verbs, and helping verbs.

Action Verb
Action verbs express an action (give, eat, walk, etc.) or possession (have, own, etc.). Action verbs can be either transitive or intransitive.

Transitive Verb
A transitive verb always has a noun that receives the action of the verb, called the direct object.
Example: Reena raises her hand.
The verb is 'raises.' 'Her hand' is the object receiving the verb's action. Therefore, 'raises' is a transitive verb.

Transitive verbs sometimes have indirect objects, which name the object to whom or for whom the action was done.
Example: Abdus gave Sonal the pencil.
The verb is 'gave.' The direct object is 'the pencil.' (What did he give? The pencil.)
The indirect object is 'Sonal.' (To whom did he give it? To Sonal.)

Intransitive Verb
An intransitive verb never has a direct or indirect object. Although an intransitive verb may be followed by an adverb or adverbial phrase, there is no object to receive its action.
Example: Reeta rises slowly from her seat.

The verb is 'rises.' The phrase, slowly from her seat, modifies the verb, but no object receives the action.

Transitive or Intransitive
To determine whether a verb is transitive or intransitive, follow these two steps:
Step 1. Find the verb in the sentence.
Example:
1. Dustin will lay down his book. What is the action? will lay
2. His book will lie there all day. What is the action? will lie

Step 1. Ask yourself, "What is receiving the action of the verb?" If there is a noun to receive the action of the verb, then the verb is transitive. If there is no direct object to receive the action, and if the verb does not make sense with a direct object, then it is intransitive.
Example:
1. Dustin will lay down his book.
   Dustin will lay down what? his book.
   Since the verb can take a direct object, it is transitive.
2. His book will lie there all day.
   His book will lie what? nothing.
   It does not make sense to 'lie something.' Since the verb has no direct object, it is intransitive.

Linking Verb
A linking verb connects the subject of a sentence to a noun or adjective that renames or describes

Verbs and Adverbs 101

the subject. This noun or adjective is called the subject complement.

Example:
1. Jason became a business major.
   The verb, became, links the subject, Jason, to its complement, a business major.
2. Lisa is in love with Jason.
   The verb, is, links the subject, Lisa, to the subject complement, in love with Jason (describing Lisa).

The most common linking verb is the verb to be in all of its forms (am, are, is, was, were, etc.). This verb may also be used as a helping verb. 'To become' and 'to seem' are always linking verbs. Other verbs may be linking verbs in some cases and action verbs in others: to appear, to feel, to look, to remain, to stay, to taste, to continue, to grow, to prove, to sound, to smell, to turn.

Example: Libby appeared happy. (Appeared links Libby to the subject complement, happy.)
Action: Deon suddenly appeared. (Here, appeared is an intransitive action verb.)

Helping Verb

Helping verbs are used before action or linking verbs to convey additional information regarding aspects of possibility (can, could, etc.) or time (was, did, has, etc.). The main verb with its accompanying helping verb is called a verb phrase.

Example: Tarun is (helping verb) going (main verb) to Florida.

The trip might (helping verb) be (main verb) dangerous.

The following words, called modals, always function as helping verbs: can, may, must, shall, will, could, might, ought to, should, would

Example: Tanya could learn to fly helicopters. (Could helps the main verb, learn.)

Janine will drive to Delhi tomorrow. (Will helps the main verb, drive.)

Example: Jana 'is' moving to a new house. (Helping)

Jana 'is' ready to go. (Linking)

Dustin 'did' eat his vegetables! (Helping)

Dustin 'did' his homework last night. (Action)

TRIVIA

Microsoft founder Bill Gates bought 'Codex Leicester', one of Leonardo Di Vinci's scientific journals for a whopping $30.8 million in November 1994.

Adverbs

An adverb is used to change or qualify the meaning of an adjective, a verb, a clause, another adverb.

Example: Saurabh runs <u>fast</u>.

Sarita works <u>slowly</u>.

Kinds of Adverb

Adverb of Manner

Adverbs of Manner tell us the manner or way in which something happens. They answer the question "how?" Adverbs of Manner mainly modify verbs.

Example: He speaks 'slowly.' (How does he speak?)

They helped us 'cheerfully.' (How did they help us?)

James Bond drives his cars 'fast.' (How does James Bond drive his cars?)

We normally use Adverbs of Manner with dynamic (action) verbs, not with stative or state verbs.

Correct: He ran 'fast'. She came 'quickly'. They worked 'happily'.

Incorrect: She looked 'beautifully'. It seems 'strangely'. They are 'happily'.

Adverb of Place

Adverbs of Place tell us the place where something happens. They answer the question "where?" Adverbs of Place mainly modify verbs.

Example: Please sit 'here'. (Where should I sit?)

They looked 'everywhere'. (Where did they look?)

Two cars were parked 'outside'. (Where were two cars parked?)

Adverb of Time
Adverbs of Time tell us about the time that something happens. Adverbs of Time mainly modify verbs. They can answer the question "when?":

Example: He came 'yesterday'. (When did he come?)

I want it 'now'. (When do I want it?)

Adverb of Frequency
Adverbs of Frequency tell us how often something happens. They answer the question 'how often'. They modify verbs.

Example: They deliver the newspaper 'daily'. (How often do they deliver the newspaper?)

We 'sometimes' watch a movie. (How often do we watch a movie?)

Adverb of Degree
Adverbs of Degree tell us the degree or extent to which something happens. They answer the question "how much?" or "to what degree?". Adverbs of Degree can modify verbs, adjectives and other adverbs.

Example: She 'entirely' agrees with him. (How much does she agree with him?)

Mary is 'very' beautiful. (To what degree is Mary beautiful? How beautiful is Mary?)

He drove 'quite' dangerously. (To what degree did he drive dangerously? How dangerously did he drive?)

MUST REMEMBER

- Action verbs express an action or possession. Action verbs can be either transitive or intransitive.
- A transitive verb always has a noun that receives the action of the verb, called the direct object.
- An intransitive verb never has a direct or indirect object.
- A linking verb connects the subject of a sentence to a noun or adjective that renames or describes the subject.
- Helping verbs are used before action or linking verbs to convey additional information regarding aspects of possibility.
- An adverb is used to change or qualify the meaning of an adjective, a verb, a clause, another adverb.
- Adverbs of Manner tell us the manner or way in which something happens.
- Adverbs of Place tell us the place where something happens.
- Adverbs of Time tell us about the time that something happens.
- Adverbs of Frequency tell us how often something happens.
- Adverbs of Degree tell us the degree or extent to which something happens.

PRACTICE EXERCISE

I. Fill in the blanks with the correct option.

1. Have you ever ___ abroad?
   (a) go   (b) went
   (b) to   (d) been

2. She's ___ a shower at the moment.
   (a) taking   (b) taken
   (c) take   (d) takes

3. I always ___ before bed.
   (a) reading   (b) read
   (c) to read   (d) none of these

4. He will ___ you later.
   (a) to call   (b) calls
   (c) calling   (d) call

5. I don't know who ___ the chair.
   (a) break   (b) broke
   (c) breaking   (d) breaks

6. We've all been ___ about you.
   (a) to think   (b) thought
   (c) thinking   (d) thinks

7. Someone ___ moved my bag.
   (a) have   (b) having
   (c) has   (d) haves

8. We ___ playing cards all afternoon.
   (a) were   (b) was
   (c) be   (d) is

9. Those ___ the type I like.
   (a) isn't   (b) don't
   (c) won't   (d) aren't

10. James asked me ___ him.
    (a) to email   (b) emailing
    (c) emailed   (d) email

II. Fill in the blanks with the correct option.

1. He seems really competent but he's not. But he appears so assured that he'll ___ in a lot of people.
   (a) set   (b) take
   (c) put   (d) get

2. It's a really big assignment. I'm going to have to ___ in a lot of hard work.
   (a) set   (b) call
   (c) put   (d) get

3. You'll need to be able to demonstrate this without any errors so if I were you I'd ___ in some practice beforehand.

   (a) set   (b) call
   (c) come   (d) get

4. That's the usual company policy but it's not something that is ___ in stone.
   (a) set   (b) call
   (c) put   (d) get

5. There are 120 applicants for every vacancy so it's not very easy to ___ in.
   (a) call   (b) get
   (c) put   (d) give

6. I don't think I'll get the job but I decided to ___ in an application anyway.
   (a) set   (b) put
   (c) come   (d) call

7. Things were going very badly so we decided to ___ in an outside consultant.
   (a) give   (b) take
   (c) come   (d) call

8. The joint venture you are proposing is very interesting and we would really like to ___ in on it.
   (a) set   (b) come
   (c) put   (d) give

9. I tried to resist his arguments but in the end I had to ___ in on that point.
   (a) give   (b) take
   (c) be   (d) get

10. It's an excellent scheme and we would love to ___ in on it.
    (a) bring   (b) be
    (c) cave   (d) dig

11. He will not respond well to pressure. Give him an ultimatum and he's likely to ___ in and refuse to negotiate.
    (a) set   (b) be
    (c) put   (d) dig

12. They held out for some time but eventually had to ___ in and admit defeat.
    (a) set   (b) take
    (c) cave   (d) get

13. When he took over, he decided to ___ in some outside consultants to look over the business.
    (a) bring   (b) be
    (c) dig   (d) give

14. It's too much for our present team so I'm going to _____ some outside help.
    (a) give   (b) be
    (c) come   (d) get
15. The rest of the industry was prepared to agree to a minimum salary and we had to _____ in with what they wanted.
    (a) fall   (b) take
    (c) put   (d) get
16. It's time to get rid of the old team and _____ in some fresh ideas.
    (a) set   (b) be
    (c) come   (d) bring
17. I'm very unhappy with the service and I intend to _____ in a complaint.
    (a) cave   (b) take
    (c) dig   (d) put
18. I don't feel we can cope with this and I suggest we _____ in Judith to help us with this.
    (a) come   (b) give
    (c) bring (d) be
19. The company was in serious financial trouble so they decided to _____ in the receivers.
    (a) dig   (b) take
    (c) call   (d) be
20. It seems a shame to call off the project after all the hard work you have _____ in.
    (a) put   (b) give
    (c) cave   (d) dig

III. Fill in the blanks with the correct option.

1. _____ I met my childhood friend Meeta.
   (a) Yesterday   (b) Tomorrow
   (c) This Sunday (d) none of these
2. You need to run _____ to win this race.
   (a) slow   (b) steadily
   (c) fast   (d) none of these
3. I won't say it _____.
   (a) progressively   (b) repeatedly
   (c) necessarily   (d) none of these
4. Speak _____, I cannot hear you.
   (a) loudly   (b) slowly
   (c) hardly   (d) none of these
5. You should _____ smoke as it is dangerous for your health.
   (a) always   (b) usually
   (c) never   (d) none of these
6. We searched _____ but were unable to find her lost jewellery.
   (a) nowhere   (b) anywhere
   (c) everywhere
7. I hope to see you _____ !
   (a) soon   (b) never
   (c) random   (d) none of these
8. Deepak never dresses _____ for work.
   (a) formally   (b) coolly
   (c) dirtily   (d) none of these
9. The manager looked at me with an _____ expression when I reached late!
   (a) sad   (b) regret
   (c) angry (d) none of these

IV. Fill in the blanks with the most appropriate option.

1. When my teacher talks too _____, it's difficult to understand him.
   (a) quickly   (b) quietly
   (c) slowly   (d) none of these
2. I always study _____ for a big test.
   (a) goodly   (b) hardly
   (c) hard   (d) none of these
3. My dad used to shout _____ when he was angry.
   (a) loudly   (b) noise
   (c) loud   (d) none of these
4. Please try to behave _____ when you meet my family.
   (a) quickly   (b) softly
   (c) normally (d) none of these
5. She did _____ in her tennis match last week. She won.
   (a) bad   (b) goodly
   (c) well   (d) none of these
6. Please close the door _____ when you enter my room.
   (a) stupidly   (b) successfully
   (c) gently   (d) none of these
7. I'm sitting _____ so I don't want to move.
   (a) normally   (b) comfortably
   (c) quickly   (d) none of these
8. My husband sings _____ when he's in the shower. Even the neighbours can hear him.
   (a) bigly   (b) enthusiastically
   (c) quietly (d) none of these

9. She laughs ___ at my jokes.
   (a) happily (b) well
   (c) angrily (d) none of these
10. Sometimes I need my teacher to talk more ___ so I can hear her better.
    (a) loudly (b) successfully
    (c) slowly (d) none of these

V. Fill in the blanks by selecting the best adverb of frequency from the given options.

1. Carlos is an excellent student. He _____ goes to class.
   (a) always (b) usually
   (c) sometimes (d) seldom
   (e) never
2. I hate vegetables. I _____ eat carrots.
   (a) always (b) usually
   (c) sometimes (d) never
3. Robert goes to the gym only two or three times a year. He _____ goes to the gym.
   (a) always (b) never
   (c) usually (d) seldom
4. Harold never leaves the college on Friday. He _____ eats at the cafeteria on Fridays.
   (a) always (b) never
   (c) seldom (d) none
5. Ms. Biethan is always in a good mood. She is _____ sad.
   (a) always (b) usually
   (c) never (d) none of these
6. Teresa is not a pleasant person. She is _____ in a bad mood.
   (a) never (b) seldom
   (c) always (d) none of these
7. My sister usually drives to work with a friend. She _____ drives alone.
   (a) never (b) always
   (c) usually (d) seldom
8. I never lend money to Curtis. He _____ pays me back.
   (a) sometimes (b) always
   (c) never (d) usually
9. Susan goes to the beach whenever she can. She _____ misses a chance to go to the ocean.
   (a) never (b) always
   (c) usually (d) none of these
10. It almost always rains in Seattle. The sun _____ shines there.
    (a) always (b) usually
    (c) seldom (d) none of these

HOTS

I. Fill in the blanks with the correct verb.

1. I knew he would get promoted. It's good to see him _____ up the ladder.
   (a) speak (b) move
   (c) gee (d) throw
2. They badly need motivating. Perhaps you can _____ them up?
   (a) cheer (b) grow
   (c) gee (d) throw
3. They're so miserable. Perhaps you can _____ them up?
   (a) cheer (b) grow
   (c) put (d) give
4. What's taking them so long? Perhaps you can _____ them up?
   (a) speak (b) grow
   (c) give (d) hurry
5. We can't hear you at the back. Perhaps you could _____ up a bit?
   (a) speak (b) seize
   (c) put (d) throw

II. Fill in the blanks with a suitable Adverb of Frequency.

1. I _____ go to bed at 10 o'clock.
2. I have _____ been to the USA.
3. I have been to Australia just _____
4. I _____ take a bath before I go to bed.
5. My grandparents live in Kerala. I visit them _____

Adjectives   7

Learning Objectives: In this chapter, students will learn about:
- Adjectives of Quality
- Adjectives of Quantity
- Adjectives of Numbers
- Other key types of Adjectives

CHAPTER SUMMARY

Adjectives are used to describe (what kind of?) nouns and pronouns and to quantify (how much of?) and identify (which one?) them. In a nutshell, adjectives define nouns and give them characteristics to differentiate them from other nouns.

Example: He was wearing a blue shirt.
(Here 'blue' is an adjective as it is describing the noun 'shirt' by answering the question 'what kind of shirt?')
There are seven rooms in the house.
(Here 'Seven' is also an adjective as it's telling the quantity/the number of the noun 'rooms', answering the question 'how many rooms?')

Types of Adjective
There are five types of adjectives:

Adjective of Quality
These adjectives are used to describe the nature of a noun. They give an idea about the characteristics of the noun by answering the question 'what kind'. For example, Honest, Kind, Large, Bulky, Beautiful, Ugly.
Example: New Delhi is a 'large' city with many historical monuments.
Sheila is a 'beautiful' woman.

Adjective of Quantity
These adjectives help to show the amount or the approximate amount of the noun or pronoun. These adjectives do not provide exact numbers; rather they tell us the amount of the noun in relative or whole terms. For example, All, Half, Many, Few, Little, No, Enough, Great, etc.
Example: They have finished 'most' of the rice.
'Many' people came to visit the fair.

Adjective of Number
These adjectives are used to show the number of nouns and their place in an order. There are three different sections within adjectives of number.

Definite Numeral Adjective
Those which clearly denote an exact number of nouns or the order of the noun.
One, Two, Twenty, Thirty also known as Cardinals.
First, Second, Third, Seventh also known as Ordinals.

Indefinite Numeral Adjective
Those adjectives that do not give an exact numerical amount but just give a general idea of the amount. For example, Some, Many, Few, Any, Several, All.
Example: There were 'many' people present at the meeting.

Distributive Numeral Adjective
Those adjectives that are used to refer to individual nouns within the whole amount. For example, Either, Neither, Each, Another, Other.
Example: Taxes have to be paid by 'every' employed citizen.

Demonstrative Adjective

These adjectives are used to point out or indicate a particular noun or pronoun using the adjectives - This, That, These and Those.

Example: 'That' bag belongs to Neil.
Try using 'this' paintbrush in art class.
I really like 'those' shoes.
'These' flowers are lovely.

Interrogative Adjective

These adjectives are used to ask questions about nouns or in relation to nouns; they are. Where, What, Which and Whose.

Example: 'Where' did he say he was going?
'What' assignment did I miss out on?
'Which' is your favorite author?
'Whose' pen is this?

> **TRIVIA**
> "I am." is the shortest complete sentence in the English language.

Coordinate and Non-coordinate Adjectives

In some instances, we find that we need to use more than one adjective to describe a noun in a satisfactory manner. In these cases, commas are used to separate the adjectives but some series of adjectives do not require a comma. Therefore, we need to know the difference between Coordinate and Non-coordinate Adjectives.

Coordinate Adjectives are those words which can be re-arranged in the series easily and are still grammatically sound. This kind of series makes use of commas. This series can also insert 'and' between them and still be correct.

Example: She was a kind, generous, loving human being.
She was a generous, loving, kind human being.
She was a loving, kind and generous human being.

Here, we can see that all three sentences are grammatically correct. In this case, the adjectives only need to be separated by commas.

Non-coordinate Adjectives are those adjectives, which cannot be rearranged in the series. These do not use commas to separate the adjectives. Also, this kind of series do not make sense if we insert 'and' between them.

She has two energetic playful dogs. (Correct)
She has playful two energetic dogs. (Incorrect)
She has energetic and playful and two dogs. (Incorrect)

Here, we see that only the first sentence makes sense and is grammatically correct. The second and third ones are incorrect. Hence, the sentence uses non-coordinate adjectives and does not need commas.

There are certain rules regarding the placement of different kinds of adjectives in a sentence. The general order followed is as follows.

Determiner

Determiners include articles (the, a, an), demonstratives (this, that, these, those), possessives (my, mine, your, yours, -'s), quantifiers (all, many.), numerals (one, twenty, thirty-seven, etc.) and distributives (each, every, neither, either)

Example: The house

Observation/Quantity and Opinion

Then come the adjectives that give a quantity (also known as post-determiners) and subjective opinion to the noun, telling 'how much' and 'how was' the noun. For example, Few, Most, One, Three/ Beautiful, Ugly, Difficult.

Example: A beautiful house

Size of Noun

The position after Observations is for the adjectives that tell about the size of the noun, they can be used for an object as well as living thing. For example, Huge, Little, Bulky, Thin, Vast, Tiny, Lean, etc

Example: A beautiful little house.

Age of Noun

Then is the turn of the Adjectives that tell about the age of a noun either by itself or in relation to another noun. For example, Young, Old, Teenage, Mature, Recent, Bygone, etc.

Example: A beautiful little old house

Shape of Noun

Next are the adjectives that tell about the shape or appearance of the noun. For example: Circular, Crooked, Triangular, Oval, Wavy, Straight.

Example: A beautiful little old square house

Colour of Noun
After that are the adjectives that tell the shade and hue of a noun. For example, Pastel, Red, Blue, Metallic, Colourless, Translucent.

Example: The beautiful square blue coloured house

Origin of Noun
Next are the adjectives that show the different geographical locations associated with a noun. For example, Southern, Northern, Lunar, Mexican, French.

Example: The beautiful blue coloured Mexican house

Material of Noun
Next are the adjectives that talk about the raw material or texture of the objects or the behaviour of the living nouns. For example, Wooden, Plastic, Steely, Metallic, Cottony.

Example: The beautiful Mexican limestone house

Qualifier to Noun
Lastly, the qualifier or the grammatical modifier comes, which is an additional word or phrase provided to change the meaning of the noun in a sentence. For example, Pink + eye, Royal + treatment, Hot + fudge.

Example: The beautiful Mexican limestone doll house

- Adjectives are used to describe nouns and pronouns and to quantify and identify them.
- Coordinate Adjectives are those words which can be re-arranged in the series easily and are still grammatically sound.
- Non-coordinate Adjectives are those adjectives, which cannot be rearranged in the series.

PRACTICE EXERCISE

I. Fill in the blanks with the correct option.

1. Generally, girls are _____ than boys.
   (a) talkative   (b) more talkative
   (c) most talkative   (d) none of these

2. Cricket is an _____ game.
   (a) exciting   (b) excitinger
   (c) excitengest (d) none of these

3. Arpita is looking _____ in this dress.
   (a) gorgeous   (b) gorgeousest
   (c) gorgeouser (d) none of these

4. She has a very _____ voice.
   (a) sour   (b) bitter
   (c) sweet (d) none of these

5. Diamond is the _____ natural material.
   (a) hard   (b) harder
   (c) hardest (d) none of these

6. This exercise is quite _____
   (a) more simple (b) most simple
   (c) simple   (d) none of these

7. Rohan is a _____ boy.
   (a) trustworthy   (b) trustworthier
   (c) trustworthest (d) none of these

8. The entire staff of the hotel we stayed at was very _____.
   (a) friendly   (b) friendlier
   (c) friendliest (d) none of these

9. You are getting _____ all the time.
   (a) gooder (b) goodest
   (c) better (d) none of these

10. Your efforts to accomplish this project are _____.
    (a) outstandinger (b) outstandingest
    (c) outstanding   (d) none of these

II. Fill in the blanks with the correct option.

1. My elder brother is 25, he still feels _____ when he sees cockroach.
   (a) frightender (b) frightened
   (c) frightendest (d) none of these

2. Mr. Sharma felt very _____ when his son failed the final examination.
   (a) more disappointed
   (b) most disappointed
   (c) disappointed
   (d) none of these

3. I feel _____ on Sundays.
   (a) relaxed   (b) relaxing
   (c) relaxful (d) none of these

4. Rohan felt _____ when his manager shouted at him in front of his juniors.
   (a) proud   (b) honoured
   (c) ashamed (d) none of these

5. He is _____ so he avoids being photographed.
   (a) bashful (b) confident
   (c) bold   (d) none of these

6. It is always _____ to seek the advice of your elders in difficult times.
   (a) beneficial (b) useless
   (c) necessity   (d) none of these

7. We had a _____ time at the alumni meet.
   (a) least (b) great
   (c) cool   (d) none of these

8. John is very _____ about his wedding.
   (a) excited   (b) boring
   (c) interesting (d) None of these

9. He doesn't seem _____ in your offer.
   (a) interested (b) interesting
   (c) exciting   (d) none of these

10. The news of her death _____ us.
    (a) stunning (b) stunned
    (c) stunded   (d) none of these

HOTS

Read the passages that follow and choose the correct options that can replace the underlined portions.

Elephants are highly ____1____ with relatively large, ____2____ and ____3____ brains. They have reasoning capabilities, can learn skills and have emotions experiencing pain, suffering, sadness and grief and they are even ____4____ just like we are sometimes. They love to wallow in mud and swish their bodies with ____5____ sand. As their skin is ____6____ to the sun, the mud and sand form a sunscreen of sorts, protecting them from the sun's ____7____ rays. In the ____8____, clear stream, the elephants exhibit their ____9____ nature by spraying water over ____10____ visitors and by lying on their side in the stream.

1. (a) agile (b) lethargic (c) intelligent (d) gigantic
2. (a) complex (b) fast (c) simple (d) uncomplicated
3. (a) quick-witted (b) child-like (c) childish (d) slow - maturing
4. (a) depressing (b) mirthful (c) depressed (d) caring
5. (a) rocky (b) fluffy (c) grainy (d) silken
6. (a) soft (b) sensitive (c) thick (d) hard
7. (a) copious (b) lightning (c) celestial (d) harsh
8. (a) ample (b) cool (c) flowing (d) rising
9. (a) majestic (b) youthful (c) buoyant (d) playful
10. (a) irritating (b) unsuspecting (c) heedless (d) timid

Adjectives

Articles and Prepositions

Learning Objectives: In this chapter, students will learn about:
- ✓ Types of Articles
- ✓ Determiners and Quantifiers
- ✓ Uses of Preposition
- ✓ Uses of Articles
- ✓ Preposition and its types

CHAPTER SUMMARY

An article is used to modify a noun, which is a person, place, object, or idea. Technically, an article is an adjective, which is any word that modifies a noun. Usually adjectives modify nouns through description, but articles are used instead to point out or refer to nouns.

Types of Article
There are two types of articles that we use in writing and conversation to point out or refer to a noun or group of nouns: definite and indefinite articles.

Definite Articles
The article 'the', refers directly to a specific noun or groups of nouns.
Example: 'the' freckles on my face
'the' alligator in the pond
'the' breakfast burrito on my plate
Each noun or group of nouns being referred to - in these cases, freckles, alligator, and breakfast burrito is direct and specific.

Indefinite Articles
Indefinite articles are 'a' and 'an'. Each of these articles is used to refer to a noun, but the noun being referred to is not a specific person, place, object, or idea. It can be any noun from a group of nouns.
Example: 'a' Mercedes from the car lot
'an' event in history

In each case, the noun is not specific. The Mercedes could be any Mercedes car available for purchase, and the event could be any event in the history of the world.

Usage of Indefinite Article
Properly using a definite article is fairly straight-forward, but it can be tricky when you are trying to figure out which indefinite article to use. The article choice depends on the sound at the beginning of the noun that is being modified. There is a quick and easy way to remember this.

☞ If the noun that comes after the article begins with a vowel sound, the appropriate indefinite article to use is 'an.' A vowel sound is a sound that is created by any vowel in the English language: 'a,' 'e,' 'i,' 'o,' 'u,' and sometimes 'y' if it makes an 'e' or 'i' sound.

'an' advertisement on the radio (this noun begins with 'a,' which is a vowel)

Example: A boy, a cat, a dog, a fight, a gym, a horse, a joke, a kite, a lion, a mirror, a noise, a pin, a quilt, etc.

An apple, an elephant, an idiot, an orange, an umbrella, etc.

Note here that the usage is on the basis of sound and not on that of the letter the word starts with.

Example: 'An hour'
'An honest man'
'A one eyed dog'

☞ The words 'hour' and 'honest' both begin with a vowel sound, as the consonant 'h' is not pronounced. Similarly, the word 'one' begins with the consonant sound of 'w' and hence is written as 'a one eyed dog', not 'an one eyed dog'.

☞ Also, remember that we use 'a' and 'an' only before a singular noun. We can't use 'a' and 'an' before a plural noun.

Example: A book - correct

A books - incorrect

An egg - correct

An eggs – incorrect

☞ Tips to remember the differences in a nutshell
- a + singular noun beginning with a consonant: a bag, a pen, etc.
- an + singular noun beginning with a vowel: an egg, an orphan, etc.
- a + singular noun beginning with a consonant sound: a user (sounds like 'yoo-zer,' i.e., gives a 'y' sound, so 'a' is used), a university, a European, etc.
- an + nouns starting with silent 'h': an hour, an honest man, etc.

NOTE:
- These rules also apply in Acronyms.
  For example:
  He is 'a' DU (Delhi University) student.
  He is 'an' IIT (Indian Institute of Technology) graduate.
- The rule also applies when acronyms start with consonant letters but have vowel sounds.
  For example:
- She is 'an' MBA (Master of Business Administration).
- When/If the noun is modified by an adjective, the choice between 'a' and 'an' depends on the initial sound of the adjective that immediately follows the article.
  For example:
  'a' beautiful umbrella
  'an' unusual situation
  'a' European country (pronounced as 'yer-o-pi-an,' i.e., sounds like consonant 'y')
  A/An is used to indicate membership in a group.

For example:
- I am a journalist. (I am a member of a large group of professionals known as journalists.)
- She is an Indian. (She is a member of the people from India, known as Indians.)

Difference Between 'A' and 'The'

'The', as mentioned earlier, is used to give information about particular or known nouns. These are usually things that have been mentioned before or that the listener is familiar with. On the other hand, 'A' or 'an' are used to talk about things which are not particular. Usually, these are the things that haven't been mentioned before or that the listener is unfamiliar with.

Example: I went to see a tattoo artist.

The tattoo artist has given me an appointment next week.

It is clear that, in the first sentence, the speaker did not go to see a particular tattoo artist. He/she went to see any tattoo artist and was speaking to a friend about the same. The tattoo artist, in this case, has either not been mentioned before or is not that important, and therefore, their identity is unknown.

Whereas in the second sentence, the speaker refers to the tattoo artist that had already been mentioned before. The identity is already known; therefore, "the" has been used to refer to the tattoo artist.

Usage of Definite article 'the'
☞ Count and Uncountable Nouns

'The' can either be used with uncountable nouns or the article can be omitted entirely.
For example:

She liked to sail over the water. (Here, some specific body of water is being talked about.)

She liked to sail over water. (Here, no particular water is being talked about. It can refer to any water.)

'A'/'An' can be used only with single count nouns.

I need a bottle of juice.

I need an eraser.

Use of 'the' in case of geography

There are some specific rules for using 'the' with geographical nouns.

Articles and Prepositions

☞ Do not use 'the' before:
- Names of most countries/territories: India, Brazil, Canada; however, the Netherlands, the Dominican Republic, the Philippines, the United States
- Names of cities, towns, or states: Toronto, Delhi, Sao Paolo
- Names of streets: Callowhill Drive, Park Avenue
- Names of lakes and bays: Lake Michigan, Lake Ontario; except while referring to a group of lakes the Great Lakes
- Names of mountains: Mount Everest, Mount Fuji except with ranges of mountains like the Andes or the Rockies or unusual names like the Matterhorn
- Names of continents: Asia, Europe
- Names of islands (Easter Island, Maui, Key West) except with island chains like the Andaman Islands, the Canary Islands

☞ Use 'the' before:
- Names of rivers, oceans and seas: the Ganga, the Indian Ocean
- Points on the globe: the Equator, the South Pole
- Geographical areas: the South East, the Asia Pacific
- Deserts, forests, gulfs, and peninsulas: the Kalahari, the Sunderbans

TRIVIA

There is a word in English with seven-letters that contains ten words without rearranging any of the letters. The word is 'Therein'. Words within 'therein' are: The, There, He, In, Rein, Her, Here, Ere, Therein, Herein.

Omission of Articles

The usage of articles is one of the most confusing things to remember for many English learners. It is not always necessary to use articles everywhere. Our tip is to remember the cases where articles should not be used.

Do not use articles in the following cases:

☞ When you talk about things in general.
Example: I like birds.
(Here, the speaker wants to imply that he/she likes any bird in general, and not a specific type of a bird.)

☞ When talking about plural count nouns.
Example: Dogs make great pets.
(Here, you are not talking about one specific dog or one specific pet; you are talking about all dogs in general.)

☞ When talking about uncountable nouns.
Example: I love music.
(Here, the speaker is saying that he enjoys music, in general – not any specific kind of music or song.)

☞ When talking about specific days or holidays, geography, companies, languages.
Example: I have bought candles for Diwali.
(Here, the speaker is talking about the candles he has bought to use on the day of Diwali.)

☞ When talking about Geography.
Articles are not used before countries, states, cities, towns, continents, single lakes, single mountains.
Example: I live in Canada.
Mt. Rosa is part of the Alps mountain range.
(Here, Mt. Rosa is one mountain, whereas the Alps refer to a group of mountains.)

NOTE:

The United Arab Emirates, The Russian Federation, The People's Republic of China, The United Kingdom of Great Britain and Northern Ireland, The Dominion of Canada, etc., all contain articles because of the usage of common nouns such as kingdom, republic, states, united, dominion, emirates, etc.

The Netherlands, the Philippines, The Bahamas, The Maldives, etc. have 'the' before them due to the plural nature of the names of the countries.

The Ukraine, The Sudan, etc. are exceptions to all of these rules. It is perhaps, due to common use, or at least previous common use. There have been historical uses of articles before names of countries that don't fit into either category.

- When you talk about companies.
  Example: Steve Jobs founded Apple.
  I use Facebook every day.
  (Here, the speaker is referring to companies like Apple and Facebook.)
- When you talk about languages.
  Example: I speak Hindi.
  (Here, the speaker is talking about the language Hindi.)
- When you talk about places, locations, streets.
  Example: My house is located on Callowhill Drive.
  I left my pen at home.
  (Here, a street called Callowhill Drive and speaker's home are being talked about.)
- However, there are specific places that do need the use of an article.
  Example: the bank, the hospital, the post office, the airport, the train station, the bus stop, etc.
- When you talk about sports and physical activities.
  Example: I love to play cricket.
  She enjoys dancing.
  (Here, cricket and dancing are being talked about.)
- When there is a noun + number
  Example: She is staying at the Hilton hotel in room 127.
  The train to Montreal leaves from platform 9.
  (Here, the nouns are followed by numbers; hence, no article is used.)
- When talking about academic subjects.
  Example: I hate attending Mathematics classes.
  (Here, the Mathematics classes are being discussed.)

Usages of Articles

Article	Where to Use	Example
'A' / 'An'	When mentioning something for the first time.	I went for a movie.
	When talking about something which belongs to a set of the same thing.	This is a pen.
	When talking about someone who belongs to a certain group.	She is an engineer.
	When talking about a certain kind of a thing.	I've have made a great movie.
	When wanting to say that someone is a certain kind of person.	She is a shy girl.
'The'	When talking about a particular thing.	The movie that I went for was fantastic.
	When talking about something that you are sure of.	I cleared the interview.
	When there is only one such thing.	I don't like to go out in the sun.
No article is used	When talking about something in general.	Swimming is a great physical activity.
	When talking about cities, countries, streets, sports.	We visited France. We watched soccer together.

Determiners
Determiners are words which come at the beginning of a noun phrase. They tell us whether the noun phrase is specific or general.

Types of Determiner
Determiners are either specific or general.

Specific Determiner
- the definite article: the
- possessives: my, your, his, her, its; our, their, whose
- demonstratives: this, that, these, those
- interrogatives: which

We use a specific determiner when we believe the listener/reader knows exactly what we are referring to.

Example: Can you pass me 'the' salt please?
Look at 'those' lovely flowers.
Thank you very much for 'your' letter.
Whose coat is 'this'?

General Determiner
The general determiners are: a, an, any, another, other, what.

☞ When we are talking about things in general and the listener/reader does not know exactly what we are referring to, we can use an uncount noun or a plural noun with no determiner.

Example: Milk is very good for you. (= uncountable noun)

☞ Health and education are very important. (= 2 uncountable nouns)

Example: Girls normally do better in school than boys. (= plural nouns with no determiner)

☞ ... or you can use a singular noun with the indefinite article a or an.

Example: A woman was lifted to safety by a helicopter.
A man climbing nearby saw the accident.

☞ We use the general determiner 'any' with a singular noun or 'an' uncount noun when we are talking about all of those people or things.

Example: It's very easy. 'Any' child can do it. (= All children can do it)
With a full licence, you are allowed to drive 'any' car.
I like beef, lamb, pork – 'any' meat.

☞ We use the general determiner 'another' to talk about an additional person or thing.

Example: Would you like 'another' glass of wine?

☞ The plural form of another is other.

Example: I spoke to John, Helen and a few 'other' friends.

Quantifiers
We use quantifiers when we want to give someone information about the number of something: how much or how many.

A preposition is a word placed before a noun (or pronoun) to show in what relation the person or thing denoted by the noun stands to something else. The preposition is almost always before the noun or pronoun and hence it is called a preposition.

Prepositions
Prepositions are words which show the relationship between two words in a sentence. The relationship can include:
(i) direction
(ii) place (or a particular point or location)
(iii) time
(iv) manner
(v) cause
(vi) amount (or degree)

Forms of Preposition
There are five forms of prepositions:
- Simple Prepositions
- Compound Prepositions
- Double Prepositions
- Participle Prepositions
- Phrase Prepositions

Simple Prepositions
Simple prepositions are used in simple sentences.

Examples
Mohan lives <u>in</u> Delhi.
Radha is <u>at</u> her desk.

Compound Prepositions
Compound prepositions are formed by prefixing the preposition to a noun, an adjective or an adverb. Examples are: *about, across, among, around, between, beside, before...*

The girls are running <u>around</u> the table. [Here preposition around is formed by joining 'a + round'].

Please get <u>off</u> <u>of</u> the couch. [off and of form compound preposition]

Double Prepositions

A double preposition is two (prepositional) words used in a sentence to connect nouns, pronouns and phrases with other words in a sentence.

Examples are: *because of, outside of, out of, from behind* ...

Suddenly he walked <u>out of</u> the meeting.

He could not reach the theater <u>because of</u> the heavy rain.

Participle Prepositions

When participles are used as prepositions they form participle prepositions. A participle is a verb ending with 'ed' or 'ing'. Examples are: *Concerning, pending, considering assuming, barring, during, given, notwithstanding, provided, regarding*

<u>Considering</u> the circumstances; the school principal didn't announce punishment.

There was less probability of achievement, <u>notwithstanding</u> they decided to go ahead.

Phrase Prepositions

A prepositional phrase is a group of words containing a preposition, a noun or pronoun (object of the preposition), and any modifiers of the object. Examples are: *According to, in spite of, on account of, in front of, in order to, for the sake of, by means of, with reference to, in addition to, due to*

Meena is standing in the queue <u>on behalf of</u> her friends.

<u>As long as</u> you do not change the meaning, you can rephrase the sentence.

Types of Prepositions

There are mainly of five types of prepositions:
- Preposition of Place
- Preposition of Time
- Preposition of Direction
- Preposition of Movement
- Preposition of Position

☞ **Preposition of Place:** There are three prepositions of places.

- **At** is used for a point of place (for small towns, villages or less important or small places)

  Examples

  <u>At</u> home

  <u>At</u> the exit/entrance

  <u>At</u> work

  He lives <u>at</u> Meharauli in Delhi.

- **In** is used for spaces, for large places, countries, large towns, state of rest or position inside anything.

  Examples

  He lives <u>in</u> Delhi.

  He is <u>in</u> his room.

  He lives <u>at</u> Panji <u>in</u> Goa.

- **On** is used for surface tops

  Examples

  We sat <u>on</u> the ground.

  The book is lying <u>on</u> the table.

  Rama is <u>on</u> the way

  He is working <u>on</u> the computer

☞ **Preposition of Time:** There are two prepositions of Time.

- **At** is used to indicate precise time.

  Examples

  <u>At</u> ten o'clock

  He came <u>at</u> sunset

  <u>At</u> this moment...

  He will start <u>at</u> 5 pm.

- **In** is used to indicate a period of time.

  Examples

  Amitabh Bachchan was born <u>in</u> 1942.

  He was born <u>in</u> Ireland <u>in</u> the eighteenth century.

☞ **Preposition of Direction:** There are eight prepositions of direction.

- **To** is used to indicate a specific destination

  Examples

  I am going <u>to</u> my office.

- **Towards** is used to refer to direction of the destination.

  Examples

  I am going <u>towards</u> the station. [It

means I am not going to the station but in the same direction.]

- **From** is used for the point of departure.

  Examples

  He has come <u>from</u> the club.

- **Off** is used to indicate either *'being taken away from'* or *'down from'* i.e. when two things separate.

  Examples

  The cat fell <u>off</u> the tin roof.
  The aeroplane took <u>off</u> at 4 pm.

- **Against** is means *'pressing against'* i.e. used to indicate contact or pressure

  Examples

  The motorcycle leaned <u>against</u> the wall.

- **For** is used to indicate direction only when the verb indicates the beginning of a movement.

  Examples

  He is leaving <u>for</u> London today.

- **Out of** is used to indicate departure from a place/location

  Examples

  John went <u>out of</u> the classroom.

- **At** is used when we want to say *'face to face with'*

  Examples

  I was looking <u>at</u> the photograph.
  I was sitting <u>at</u> the table.

☞ **Preposition of Movement:** There are six prepositions of movement.

- **Into** refers to the movement towards the interior.

  Examples

  He jumped <u>into</u> the river.

- **Through/Across** is used to show the movement from one side to the other

  Examples

  He swam <u>across</u> the river.
  The hunters went <u>through</u> the forest.

- **Onto** is used to show the movement on an object.

  Examples

  The ball rolled <u>onto</u> the pavement.

- **Along** is used to show the movement that is 'adjacent in line' or say 'in the same line'

  Examples

  He walked <u>along</u> the bank of river.

- **In/On/By** is used to indicate a means of something.

  Examples

  He came <u>by</u> foot.

- **Up/Down** is used to show the movement across an upper or lower level

  Examples

  Jack and Jill climb <u>up</u> the hill.

☞ **Preposition of Position:** There are six prepositions of position.

- **Between** is used when we refer to persons.

  Examples

  What happened <u>between</u> these two I do not know.

- **Among** is used when we refer to more than two persons.

  Examples

  <u>Among</u> all the five brothers he is the best.

- **Over/Above:** Above means 'higher than' but over means 'vertically above'

  Examples

  They stay <u>above</u> the shop.
  The ceiling fan is <u>over</u> the table.

- **Below, Under:** Below means 'lower than' whereas under means 'vertically below'

  Examples

  I saw him standing <u>below</u> the building.
  The cat went <u>under</u> the floor.

  Exception: He is sitting <u>in</u> the shade of the tree. [Not under the shade.]

- **Beneath:** It means 'lower position/ layer/level', but generally it is used figuratively.

  Examples

  We sat <u>beneath</u> the apple tree.

- **Underneath:** It means 'directly below' something facing towards ground.

  Examples

  The tunnel goes right <u>underneath</u> the city.

MUST REMEMBER

- An article is used to modify a noun, which is a person, place, object, or idea.
- Indefinite articles are 'a' and 'an'. Each of these articles is used to refer to a noun, but the noun being referred to is not a specific person, place, object, or idea.
- Properly using a definite article is fairly straightforward, but it can be tricky when you are trying to figure out which indefinite article to use.
- If the noun that comes after the article begins with a vowel sound, the appropriate indefinite article to use is 'an.'
- Determiners are words which come at the beginning of a noun phrase. They tell us whether the noun phrase is specific or general.
- A preposition is a word placed before a noun (or pronoun) to show in what relation the person or thing denoted by the noun stands to something else.
- Compound prepositions are formed by prefixing the preposition to a noun, an adjective or an adverb.
- A double preposition is two (prepositional) words used in a sentence to connect nouns, pronouns and phrases with other words in a sentence.
- A prepositional phrase is a group of words containing a preposition, a noun or pronoun and any modifiers of the object.

PRACTICE EXERCISE

I. Fill in the blanks with the most suitable article.

1. I want to buy _____ laptop computer next week.
   (a) a
   (b) an
   (c) the
   (d) none of these

2. Can you please go to _____ grocery store on Fifth Street and buy 2 cartons of milk?
   (a) a
   (b) an
   (c) the
   (d) none of these

3. Please meet me at the train station in _____ hour from now.
   (a) a
   (b) an
   (c) the
   (d) none of these

4. I like to watch tennis on television. It is _____ very good game.
   (a) a
   (b) an
   (c) the
   (d) none of these

5. My brother won an award for being _____ best speller in our school.
   (a) a
   (b) an
   (c) the
   (d) none of these

6. I couldn't believe my eyes when I saw _____ elephant crossing the road in front of my school yesterday.
   (a) a
   (b) an
   (c) the
   (d) none of these

7. Hello, my name is Bob! I have nothing to do tonight, so if you're not busy, would you like to watch _____ movie or something with me?
   (a) a
   (b) an
   (c) the
   (d) none of these

8. How much will it cost to go on _____ holiday to Bali?
   (a) a
   (b) an
   (c) the
   (d) none of these

9. Can you please help me pick out _____ birthday present for my father?
   (a) a
   (b) an
   (c) the
   (d) none of these

10. _____ President of the United States will be visiting Australia next week.
    (a) a
    (b) an
    (c) the
    (d) none of these

II. Fill in the blanks with a, an, the. Write (d) where no article is required.

1. I need _____ egg for this recipe, but we're out.
   (a) an
   (b) a
   (c) the
   (d) none of these

2. I need _____ milk for this recipe, but we're out.
   (a) a
   (b) an
   (c) the
   (d) none of these

3. I need _____ potato for this recipe, but we're out.
   (a) an
   (b) a
   (c) the
   (d) no article

4. Is that _____ '8' or _____ 'B'? I can't read it.
   (a) a/an
   (b) an/a
   (c) an/the
   (d) no article

5. Is that _____ 'U' or _____ 'O'? I can't read it.
   (a) an/a
   (b) a/the
   (c) a/an
   (d) no article

6. He is from _____ European country, but I don't know which one.
   (a) a
   (b) an
   (c) the
   (d) no article

7. I enjoyed _____ DVD you gave me for my birthday.
   (a) the
   (b) an
   (c) a
   (d) no article

8. If I were rich, I would buy _____ apartment in Manhattan and _____ house in Hawaii.
   (a) an
   (b) a
   (c) the
   (d) no article

9. Do you know _____ name of her perfume?
   (a) a
   (b) an
   (c) the
   (d) no article

10. This school has _____ great teachers.
    (a) a (b) an (c) the (d) no article

III. **Fill in the blanks with a suitable article. If no article is required, choose (d) no article.**

1. I will give you _____ pen and _____ notebook.
   (a) a, an (b) a, a (c) a, the (d) no article
2. _____ house has windows.
   (a) An (b) A (c) The (d) No article
3. _____ house built of _____ stone is colder than one built of _____ brick.
   (a) A, no article, no article
   (b) An, a, no article
   (c) A, the, the
   (d) No article
4. You write on _____ blackboard with _____ chalk.
   (a) a, an (b) a, the (c) a, no article (d) no article
5. I want to listen to _____ music.
   (a) a (b) an (c) the (d) no article
6. _____ sugar is sweet.
   (a) an (b) a (c) the (d) no article
7. There are usually _____ flowers in _____ garden.
   (a) any (b) some, the (c) all (d) no article
8. I want _____ milk and _____ piece of bread.
   (a) a, an (b) no article, a (c) a, the (d) no article
9. Do you take _____ sugar in _____ tea?
   (a) a, an
   (b) a, the
   (c) an, the
   (d) no article, no article
10. There is _____ mud on my shoes.
    (a) some (b) any (c) all (d) no article
11. Letters should be written in _____ ink.
    (a) a, (b) an (c) the (d) no article
12. _____ friend of mine bought _____ books today.
    (a) a, an (b) a, the (c) a, some (d) no article
13. The coal mine gives us _____ coal.
    (a) a (b) an (c) the (d) no article
14. _____ book on _____ mathematics is too difficult for him.
    (a) the, no article (b) a, an (c) a, the (d) no article
15. I put _____ butter into my soup.
    (a) any
    (b) all
    (c) some
    (d) no article
16. _____ ring made of _____ gold costs more than one made of _____ silver.
    (a) a, no article, no article
    (b) a, an, the
    (c) an, the, few
    (d) No article
17. _____ good worker is never late for _____ work.
    (a) A, An
    (b) A, The
    (c) A, no article
    (d) no article
18. _____ Books are printed on _____ paper.
    (a) a, an
    (b) a, the
    (c) an, an
    (d) no article, no article
19. To eat _____ fruit is good for _____ health.
    (a) a, the
    (b) a, an
    (c) a, a
    (d) no article, no article
20. I take _____ cup of tea with _____ sugar.

Articles and Prepositions

(a) a, no article (b) a, an
(c) a, the (d) no article

IV. Choose the correct preposition to fill in the blanks.

1. You must be back _____ four o'clock.
   (a) in (b) by
   (c) for (d) to
2. Workout is necessary _____ health.
   (a) by (b) to
   (c) for (d) in
3. The Woman is looking _____ her diamond ring.
   (a) to (b) at
   (c) inside (d) in
4. The Woman is holding a cup of tea _____ her hands.
   (a) into (b) in
   (c) on (d) by
5. What are you doing _____ coming Sunday?
   (a) on (b) in
   (c) to (d) from
6. The Moon is a barren, rocky world _____ air and water.
   (a) from (b) without
   (c) to (d) in
7. The dog ran _____ the cat.
   (a) without (b) into
   (c) from (d) behind
8. Sweater will protect you _____ cold.
   (a) from (b) with
   (c) to (d) for
9. Students are responsible _____ any kind irresponsible behaviour.
   (a) to (b) with
   (c) for (d) from
10. Ramesh is sitting _____ of the laptop.
    (a) into (b) in front of
    (c) to (d) with
11. I will meet you _____ 7:00 PM.
    (a) in (b) on
    (c) at (d) none of these
12. Let's meet _____ Wednesday.
    (a) on (b) at
    (c) in (d) none of these
13. I am going to Japan _____ seven days.
    (a) in (b) at
    (c) on (d) none of these
14. I met John _____ my friend's party.
    (a) in (b) at
    (c) on (d) none of these
15. She was sitting _____ her car.
    (a) at (b) on
    (c) in (d) none of these
16. Being a nurse is hard work, especially if you're _____ call all the time.
    (a) in (b) with
    (c) on (d) none of these
17. She's the kind of girl who knows everything _____ everyone.
    (a) about (b) on
    (c) in (d) none of these
18. She is, _____ a doubt, the best student in the class.
    (a) without (b) outside
    (c) about (d) none of these
19. _____ our visit to Japan, we saw a lot of interesting places.
    (a) While (b) During
    (c) Through (d) None of these
20. _____ the year, I've spoken to her five times.
    (a) In (b) During
    (c) Throughout (d) None of these
21. Will you be _____ home today?
    (a) at (b) in
    (c) on (d) none of these
22. He is never late. He always comes _____ time.
    (a) at (b) on
    (c) in (d) none of these
23. How many students are _____ your class?
    (a) in (b) at
    (c) on (d) none of these
24. The teacher wrote something _____ the board.
    (a) at (b) in
    (c) on (d) none of these
25. Many people work _____ this building.
    (a) at (b) in
    (c) on (d) none of these

26. It's _____ time you told him the truth!
    (a) on   (b) about
    (c) in   (d) none of these
27. The soccer player was ejected because he had done something that was _____ the rules.
    (a) without   (b) outside
    (c) against   (d) none of these
28. Another way of saying 'old-fashioned' is '_____ the times'.
    (a) beside   (b) behind
    (c) outside   (d) none of these
29. You shouldn't pick _____ him just because he's different.
    (a) on   (b) to
    (c) with   (d) none of these
30. The animal hospital is somewhere _____ that big blue building.
    (a) around   (b) about
    (c) on   (d) none of these
31. I'll arrive sometime _____ 8 and 9 am.
    (a) in   (b) next to
    (c) between   (d) on
32. The shops here are open _____ 9 am until 5 pm.
    (a) from   (b) at
    (c) on   (d) for
33. They should be ready to go _____ 20 minutes.
    (a) on   (b) in
    (c) by   (d) to
34. She wants to stay _____ home tonight.
    (a) to   (b) of
    (c) at   (d) in
35. Did you watch the football _____ TV last night.
    (a) by   (b) on
    (c) in   (d) to
36. Do you always come to work _____ bike.
    (a) in   (b) on
    (c) by   (d) of
37. I read the news _____ the newspaper.
    (a) on   (b) by
    (c) in   (d) to
38. I'll be in the office _____ 5 pm.
    (a) on   (b) for
    (c) until   (d) since
39. You must have this report finished ___ Monday.
    (a) while   (b) by
    (c) at   (d) since
40. I haven't had a call from him _____ last Wednesday.
    (a) since   (b) on
    (c) in   (d) for
41. I really care _____ what happens to him.
    (a) about   (b) of
    (c) at   (d) to
42. I heard that he died _____ a heart attack.
    (a) to   (b) about
    (c) of   (d) for
43. Please apologise to them _____ me.
    (a) for   (b) of
    (c) to   (d) by
44. I saw a car collide _____ a motorbike.
    (a) against   (b) on
    (c) with   (d) to
45. "I don't agree ___ banning smoking in bars.
    (a) in   (b) about
    (c) with   (d) for
46. I ran _____ Tom while I was in the library. I haven't seen him for ages.
    (a) in   (b) at
    (c) into   (d) on
47. I'm very satisfied _____ my exam results.
    (a) for   (b) in
    (c) with   (d) on
48. I've noticed a big improvement _____ my English.
    (a) in   (b) at
    (c) for   (d) about
49. There's a real lack _____ cheap restaurants around here.
    (a) from   (b) by
    (c) about   (d) of
50. She has a lot of admiration _____ all that you have done.
    (a) on   (b) for
    (c) from   (d) of

Articles and Prepositions

HOTS

Choose the appropriate quantifier to complete the following sentences.

1. We have interviewed twenty candidates for the vacant position, but _____ of them was actually a good fit.
   - (a) most
   - (b) neither
   - (c) much
   - (d) none
   - (e) no

2. Oakland is about to go bilingual, with two official languages, but _____ of them is English.
   - (a) both
   - (b) none
   - (c) neither
   - (d) either
   - (e) no

3. On some computers there are keys which can have as many as five different functions _____.
   - (a) either
   - (b) each
   - (c) none
   - (d) every
   - (e) both

4. _____ argument could move _____ man from this decision.
   - (a) No / either
   - (b) Every / both
   - (c) No / neither
   - (d) Each / all
   - (e) Each / both

5. _____ Peter _____ Michael come here quite often but _____ of them gives us help.
   - (a) Both / and / either
   - (b) Neither / nor / both
   - (c) Both / and / neither
   - (d) Either / or / all
   - (e) Both / or / any

6. He gave _____ of us advice about our present goals.
   - (a) every
   - (b) each
   - (c) the whole
   - (d) much
   - (e) no

7. The Blues won the football match, but _____ players played well; In fact they _____ played quite badly.
   - (a) each / each
   - (b) neither of / both
   - (c) all / all
   - (d) neither of the / all
   - (e) none of the / all

8. There were _____ people on the beach, so we weren't completely alone.
   - (a) a few
   - (b) fewer
   - (c) fewest
   - (d) very little
   - (e) only a little

9. The two brothers got up at 8:30 that day. _____ of them were tired, because _____ of them had slept well.
   - (a) Both / neither
   - (b) Neither / neither
   - (c) Either / none
   - (d) None / either
   - (e) All / both

10. Everyone should have a check up with the dentist _____ six months.
    - (a) another
    - (b) each
    - (c) every
    - (d) all
    - (e) the whole

Conjunctions and Punctuations

Learning Objectives : In this chapter, students will learn about:
- ✓ Basic concept of Conjunction
- ✓ Types of Conjunction
- ✓ Common Punctuation marks

CHAPTER SUMMARY

A conjunction connects words, phrases, clauses or sentences. For example: and, but, or, nor, for, yet, so, although, because, since, unless, when, while, where.

Types of Conjunction
There are three types of conjunctions:
- Coordinating Conjunction
- Subordinate Conjunction
- Correlative Conjunction

Coordinating Conjunction
Coordinating conjunctions (called coordinators) join words, phrases (which are similar in importance and grammatical structure) or independent clauses. Coordinating conjunctions are short words i.e. and, but, or, nor, for, so, yet. They join two equal parts of a sentence i.e. Word + word, Phrase + phrase, Clause + clause, Independent clause + independent clause.

Example: She likes pizza and cake. (pizza and cake)
I bought a table and a chair. (table and chair)
He may come by bus or car. (bus or car)
She likes tea and coffee. (tea and coffee)
He may be in the room or on the roof. (Phrase + phrase)
What you eat and what you drink affect your health. (Clauses + clause)
In the following examples, conjunction joins two independent clauses. Independent clause is a clause which can stand alone as a sentence and have complete thought on its own.

Example: I called him but he didn't pick up the phone.
I advised him to quit smoking, but he didn't act upon my advice.
He fell ill, so he thought he should go to a doctor.
He shouted for help, but no body helped him.
He wants to become a doctor, so he is studying Biology.
The cat jumped over the mouse but the mouse ran away.
Coordinating conjunctions always come between the words or clauses that they join. A comma is used with conjunction if the clauses are long or not well-balanced. If both clauses have same subjects, the subject of 2nd clause may not be written again.

Example: She worked hard and succeeded.
The player stopped and kicked the ball.
He fell ill but didn't go to doctor.
Marry opened the book and started to study.

TRIVIA
Marcel Proust's 'Remembers of Things Past' is the longest book in the world at 9,609,000 characters. The book is highly inspired by Proust's personal experiences.

Subordinating Conjunction
Subordinating conjunctions (called subordinators) join subordinate clause (dependent

clause) to main clause. For example, although, because, if, before, how, once, since, till, until, when, where, whether, while, after, no matter how, provided that, as soon as, even if.

Main Clause + Subordinate Clause

Subordinate Clause + Main Clause

☞ Subordinate clause is combination of words (subject and verb) which cannot stand alone as a complete sentence. Subordinate clause is also called dependent clause because it is dependent on main clause. Subordinate clause usually starts with relative pronoun (which, who, that, whom, etc). Subordinate clause gives more information in relation to main clause to complete the thought.

☞ Subordinating conjunction always comes before the subordinate clause, no matter the subordinate clause is before main clause or after the main clause.

Example: He does not go to school because he is ill.

I will call you after I reach home.

I bought some cookies while I was coming back from my office.

They played football although it was raining.

Although it was raining, they played 'football'.

As far as I know, this exam is very difficult.

I have gone to every concert since I have lived in New York.

You can get high grades in exam, provided that you work hard for it.

Correlative Conjunction

These are paired conjunctions which join words, phrases or clauses which have reciprocal or complementary relationship. The most commonly used correlative conjunctions are as follows:

Either … or

Neither … nor

Whether … or

Both … and

Not only … But also

Example: Neither John nor Marry passed the exam.

Give me either a cup or a glass.

Both red and yellow are attractive colours.

I like neither tea nor coffee.

He will be either in the room or in the hall.

John can speak not only English but also French.

☞ Correlative Conjunctions are generally not used to link sentences themselves, instead they link two or more words of equal importance within the sentence itself. Some of the more commonly used correlative conjunctions are - Both the shoes and the dress were completely overpriced.

This is an example of using the correlative conjunctions 'both/and' in a sentence. As you can see in this sentence, the 'shoes' and the 'dress' were equally important elements that needed to be given the same importance.

☞ The 'either/or' conjunctions are used to suggest a choice between two options. For example, They should either change their strategy or just forfeit the game.

☞ Here the choice being suggested is between - 'change their strategy' or 'forfeit the game'.

☞ The correlative conjunctions 'just as/so' are used to link two phrases that have a similar theme or are referring to a similar thing together. This conjunction is used to show the correspondence between two phrases or words. For example, Just as she loves hiking so she enjoys travelling as well.

☞ 'Neither/nor' are conjunctions that are used to deny or negate words and phrases. In the case of 'neither', it gives two options that are both negated. 'Nor' is the negative form of 'or'. For example, He neither helps around the house nor does he look for a job.

☞ The correlative conjunctions 'not only/ but' are used to show an additional and important element in the sentence that is used to indicate excess when combined with the first element. For example, Not only does he play the lead guitar but he is also the band's songwriter. For instance, in this sentence the fact that he is a guitarist and a song writer are equally important but when shown together, they indicate an excess of talent in the person.

☞ 'Whether/or' is used as a conjunction to show two different options in the sentence. The conjunction can be used both in a manner of negation and confirmation. For example, It doesn't matter whether the roses are fresh or if they are drooping, just buy them.

Punctuations

Punctuation is the system of signs or symbols to show how a sentence is constructed and how it should be read.

Sentences are building blocks to construct written expression. Punctuation shows how the sentence should be read and makes the meaning clear. Every sentence should include at least a capital letter at the start, and a full stop, exclamation mark or question mark at the end. This basic system indicates that the sentence is complete.

Punctuation Signs

(i) comma (,)
(ii) full stop (.)
(iii) exclamation mark (!)
(iv) question mark (?)
(v) semi-colon (;)
(vi) colon (:)
(vii) apostrophe (')
(viii) quotation marks (" ")
(ix) hyphen (-)
(x) brackets ( ) or [ ]
(xi) slash (/)

Comma (,)

☞ The comma is useful in a sentence when the writer wishes to:
  (i) pause before proceeding
  (ii) add a phrase that does not contain any new subject
  (iii) separate items on a list
  (iv) use more than one adjective (a describing word, like beautiful)

Example: In the following sentence, the phrase or clause between the commas gives us more information behind the actions of the boy, the subject of the sentence:

The boy, who knew that his mother was about to arrive, ran quickly towards the opening door.

Note that if the phrase or clause were to be removed, the sentence would still make sense although there would be a loss of information. Alternatively, two sentences could be used: The boy ran quickly towards the opening door. He knew that his mother was about to arrive.

☞ Commas are also used to separate items in a list.

Example: The shopping trolley was loaded high with bottles of beer, fruit, vegetables, toilet rolls, cereals and cartons of milk.

Note that in a list, the final two items are linked by the word 'and' rather than by a comma.

☞ Commas are used to separate adjectives.

Example: The boy was happy, eager and full of anticipation at the start of his summer holiday.

☞ As commas represent a pause, it is good practice to read your writing out loud and listen to where you make natural pauses as you read it. More often than not, you will indicate where a comma should be placed by a natural pause. Although, the 'rules' of where a comma needs to be placed should also be followed.

Example: However, it has been suggested that some bees prefer tree pollen.

Full Stop (.)

☞ A full stop should always be used to end a sentence. The full stop indicates that a point has been made and that you are about to move on to further explanations or a related point.

Less frequently, a series of three full stops (an ellipsis) can be used to indicate where a section of a quotation has been omitted when it is not relevant to the text.

Example: "The boy was happy… at the start of his summer holiday."

☞ A single full stop may also be used to indicate the abbreviation of commonly used words as in the following examples:

Example: Telephone Number = Tel. No.
September = Sept.
Pages = pp.

Exclamation Mark (!)
☞ An exclamation mark indicates strong feeling within a sentence, such as fear, anger or love. It is also used to accentuate feeling within the written spoken word.

Example: "Help! I
　　　　　love you!"

☞ In this way, it can also be used to indicate a sharp instruction.

Example: "Stop! Police!"
or to indicate humour
"Ha! Ha! Ha!"

☞ The exclamation mark at the end of a sentence means that you do not need a full stop.

Exclamation marks are a poor way of emphasising what you think are important points in your written assignments; the importance of the point will emphasise itself without a sequence of !!! in the text. An exclamation mark should only be used when absolutely essential, or when taken from a direct quote. The exclamation mark should be used sparingly in formal and semi-formal writing.

Question Mark (?)
The question mark simply indicates that a sentence is asking a question. It always comes at the end of a sentence:

Example: Are we at the end?

Note that the question mark also serves as a full stop.

Semi-colon (;)
The semi-colon is perhaps the most difficult sign of punctuation to use accurately. If in doubt, avoid using it and convert the added material into a new sentence.

As a general rule, the semi-colon is used in the following ways:

☞ When joining two connected sentences.

Example: We set out at dawn; the weather looked promising.

☞ Assertive behaviour concerns being able to express feelings, wants and desires appropriately; passive behaviour means complying with the wishes of others.

☞ The semi-colon can also be used to assemble detailed lists.

Example: The conference was attended by delegates from Paris, France; Paris, Texas; London, UK; Stockholm, Sweden; Colombo, Sri Lanka; and Mumbai, India.

Colon (:)
The colon within a sentence makes a very pointed pause between two phrases. There are two main uses of the colon:

☞ It is most commonly used when listing.

Example: She placed the following items into the trolley: beer, fruit, vegetables, toilet rolls, cereals and cartons of milk.

☞ It can also be used within a heading or descriptive title.

Example: Human Resource Management: Guidelines for Telephone Advisors

Apostrophe (')
The apostrophe, sometimes called an inverted comma has two main uses.

☞ The apostrophe indicates possession or ownership.

Example: The girl's hat was green, (girl is in the singular).

This shows the reader that the hat belongs to the girl.

The girls' hats were green, (girls in this instance are plural, i.e. more than one girl, more than one hat). This indicates that the hats belong to the girls.

☞ Another use of the apostrophe is to indicate where a letter is omitted:

Example: We're going to do this course. (We are going to do this course.)

Isn't this a fine example of punctuation? (Is not this a fine example of punctuation?)

The time is now 7 o' clock. (The time is now 7 of the clock)

☞ Note that a common mistake is to confuse its with it's.

It indicates to the reader that a letter has been omitted.

Example: 'It's a lovely day' is an abbreviated way of saying: It is a lovely day.

Note that in most formal writings, the practice of using abbreviated words is inappropriate.

Quotation or Speech Marks ("....")

Quotation or speech marks are used to:
- To mark out speech
- When quoting someone else's speech

    Example: My grandpa said, "Share your chocolates with your friends."

    "George, don't do that!"

    "Will you get your books out please?" said Mrs Jones, the teacher, "and quieten down!"

- It is worth noting that to report an event back does not require speech or quotation marks.

    Example: Mrs Jones told the pupils to take out their books and to quieten down.

Hyphen (-)

- The hyphen is used to link words together.

    Example: sub-part

    eighteenth-century people

    week-end

    second-class post

    gender-neutral

    non-verbal

    The hyphen is also used when a word is split between two lines. The hyphen should be placed between syllables at the end of the upper line and indicates to the reader that the word will be completed on the next line.

    Computer applications such as Word Processors can be set to automatically hyphenate words for you, although it is more common to use extra spacing to avoid hyphenation.

Brackets ( )

Brackets always come in pairs ( ) and are used to make an aside, or a point which is not part of the main flow of a sentence. If you remove the words between the brackets, the sentence should still make sense.

Example: "The strategy (or strategies) chosen to meet the objectives may need to change as the intervention continues."

Square Brackets [...]

A different set of square brackets [ ] can be used:
- to abbreviate lengthy quotations
- to correct the tense of a quotation to suit the tense of your own sentence
- to add your own words to sections of an abbreviated quotation

    Example: To abbreviate lengthy quotations in an essay or report

    "We can define class as a large-scale grouping of people who share common economic resources, that strongly influence the types of lifestyle they are able to lead. Ownership of wealth, together with occupation, are the chief basis of class differences. The major classes that exist in Western societies are an upper class [...]; a middle class [...] and a working class [...]."

- To adjust a quotation to suit your own sentence

    Example: if you were writing about class structure, you might use the following:

    The "[o]wnership of wealth, together with occupation, are the chief basis of class differences".

    Note, that when using square brackets, only the occasional letter as in the above example or the occasional word (for example, when changing the tense of the sentence) would be placed in square brackets in this way.

MUST REMEMBER

- A conjunction connects words, phrases, clauses or sentences.
- Coordinating conjunctions join words, phrases or independent clauses.
- Coordinating conjunctions always come between the words or clauses that they join.
- Subordinating conjunctions join subordinate clause to main clause.
- Subordinate clause is combination of words which cannot stand alone as a complete sentence. Subordinate clause is also called dependent clause because it is dependent on main clause.
- Correlative Conjunctions are generally not used to link sentences themselves, instead they link two or more words of equal importance within the sentence itself.
- Punctuation is the system of signs or symbols to show how a sentence is constructed and how it should be read.
- The full stop indicates that a point has been made and that you are about to move on to further explanations or a related point.
- An exclamation mark indicates strong feeling within a sentence, such as fear, anger or love.
- The hyphen should be placed between syllables at the end of the upper line and indicates to the reader that the word will be completed on the next line.

PRACTICE EXERCISE

I. Fill in the blanks with the correct option.

1. _____ being very rich, he never shows off.
   (a) Other than   (b) Instead
   (c) Despite   (d) Otherwise

2. I am not feeling well, _____ I will come to the party.
   (a) because   (b) since
   (c) however   (d) unless

3. _____ I had my lunch, I didn't miss the Pizza.
   (a) Although   (b) Finally
   (c) Moreover   (d) Already

4. She never helps anyone _____ having a lot of money.
   (a) otherwise   (b) inspite of
   (c) however   (d) instead

5. You shouldn't go out _____ it's raining heavily.
   (a) for   (b) because
   (c) already   (d) but

6. My mother _____ I went to the market for shopping.
   (a) or   (b) either
   (c) neither   (d) and

7. Thomas was not telling the truth. _____ he was shouting at me.
   (a) Provided   (b) Although
   (c) Moreover   (d) In order to

8. Please come on time, _____ we may miss the flight.
   (a) otherwise   (b) so
   (c) therefore   (d) but

9. We should avoid oily food _____ be healthy.
   (a) finally   (b) consequently
   (c) in order to   (d) for

10. I will give you my car _____ you come back before 5'o clock.
    (a) as   (b) although
    (c) because   (d) provided

11. _____ my mother was sleeping, I prepared tea on my own.
    (a) As   (b) Besides
    (c) Unless   (d) Despite

12. He apologised _____ his bad behavior.
    (a) for   (b) since
    (c) because   (d) as

13. He was satisfied _____ not overjoyed.
    (a) yet   (b) as
    (c) but   (d) still

14. _____ his sister, he is very naughty.
    (a) Likely   (b) Unlike
    (c) Similar   (d) Differently

15. After months of studying hard, Meeta _____ cleared IAS examination.
    (a) initially   (b) consequently
    (c) therefore   (d) finally

16. _____ it is very cold there, we have postponed our visit.
    (a) Since   (b) Due to
    (c) Yet   (d) Because of

17. Radha knows French; _____, we have selected her to head our operations in France.
    (a) therefore   (b) moreover
    (c) otherwise   (d) provided

18. Mohan worked very sincerely and was _____ promoted.
    (a) yet   (b) although
    (c) besides   (d) consequently

19. _____ my family, I will also invite my close friends on my anniversary.
    (a) Aside   (b) Besides
    (c) Despite   (d) In spite of

20. We have a test on Monday ___ I'll have to study this weekend.
    (a) and   (b) but
    (c) so   (d) because

21. I like coffee ___ I don't like tea.
    (a) and   (b) but
    (c) so   (d) because

22. I cannot swim ___ I can ski.
    (a) and   (b) but
    (c) so   (d) because

23. I want a new TV ___ the one I have now is broken.
    (a) and   (b) but
    (c) so   (d) because

Conjunctions and Punctuations

24. I had to work on Saturday ___ I couldn't go to John's party.
    (a) and (b) but
    (c) so (d) because
25. My name is Jim ___ I'm your new teacher.
    (a) and (b) but
    (c) so (d) because
26. I was cold ___ I turned on the heater.
    (a) and (b) but
    (c) so (d) because
27. We'll have to go shopping ___ we have nothing for dinner.
    (a) and (b) but
    (c) so (d) because
28. The history test was difficult ___ the English one was easy.
    (a) and (b) but
    (c) so (d) because
29. We didn't go to the beach yesterday ___ it was raining.
    (a) and (b) but
    (c) so (d) because
30. Wait here ___ I get back.
    (a) as soon as (b) until
    (c) Either (a) or (b) (d) none of these
31. I'll visit you ___ I have time.
    (a) when (b) whenever
    (c) Either (a) or (b) (d) none of these
32. We'll be ready ___ the time you get back.
    (a) by (b) before
    (c) Either (a) or (b) (d) none of these
33. We'll leave ___ we're ready.
    (a) as soon as (b) when
    (c) Either (a) or (b) (d) none of these
34. I'll be glad ___ it's finished.
    (a) when (b) before
    (c) Either (a) or (b) (d) none of these
35. We must finish it ___ we leave.
    (a) before (b) until
    (c) Either (a) or (b) (d) none of these
36. I hurt myself ___ I was playing tennis.
    (a) whenever (b) while
    (c) Either (a) or (b) (d) none of these
37. I'll give her the message ___ she arrives.
    (a) a moment (b) the moment
    (c) Either (a) or (b) (d) none of these
38. I'll be ready when she ___.
    (a) arrives (b) will arrive
    (c) Either (a) or (b) (d) none of these
39. I'll only pay you ___ you finish the work.
    (a) if (b) unless
    (c) Either (a) or (b) (d) none of these
40. We turned back ___ it was raining.
    (a) because (b) because of
    (c) Either (a) or (b) (d) none of these

II. Select the correctly punctuated sentence.

1. (a) Spain is a beautiful country; the beache's are warm, sandy and spotlessly clean.
   (b) Spain is a beautiful country: the beaches are warm, sandy and spotlessly clean.
   (c) Spain is a beautiful country, the beaches are warm, sandy and spotlessly clean.
   (d) Spain is a beautiful country; the beaches are warm, sandy and spotlessly clean.
2. (a) The children's books were all left in the following places: Mrs. Smith's room, Mr. Powell's office and the caretaker's cupboard.
   (b) The children's books were all left in the following places; Mrs. Smith's room, Mr. Powell's office and the caretaker's cupboard.
   (c) The childrens books were all left in the following places: Mrs. Smiths room, Mr. Powells office and the caretakers cupboard.
   (d) The children's books were all left in the following places, Mrs. Smith's room, Mr. Powell's office and the caretaker's cupboard.
3. (a) She always enjoyed sweets, chocolate, marshmallows and toffee apples.
   (b) She always enjoyed: sweets, chocolate, marshmallows and toffee apples.
   (c) She always enjoyed sweets chocolate marshmallows and toffee apples.
   (d) She always enjoyed sweet's, chocolate, marshmallow's and toffee apple's.
4. (a) Sarah's uncle's car was found without its wheels in that old derelict warehouse.
   (b) Sarah's uncle's car was found without its wheels in that old, derelict warehouse.

(c) Sarahs uncles car was found without its wheels in that old, derelict warehouse.
   (d) Sarah's uncle's car was found without it's wheels in that old, derelict warehouse.

5. (a) I can't see Tim's car, there must have been an accident.
   (b) I cant see Tim's car; there must have been an accident.
   (c) I can't see Tim's car there must have been an accident.
   (d) I can't see Tim's car; there must have been an accident.

6. (a) Paul's neighbours were terrible; so his brother's friends went round to have a word.
   (b) Paul's neighbours were terrible: so his brother's friends went round to have a word.
   (c) Paul's neighbours were terrible, so his brother's friends went round to have a word.
   (d) Paul's neighbours were terrible so his brother's friends went round to have a word.

7. (a) Tims gran, a formidable woman, always bought him chocolate, cakes, sweets and a nice fresh apple.
   (b) Tim's gran a formidable woman always bought him chocolate, cakes, sweets and a nice fresh apple.
   (c) Tim's gran, a formidable woman, always bought him chocolate cakes sweets and a nice fresh apple.
   (d) Tim's gran, a formidable woman, always bought him chocolate, cakes, sweets and a nice fresh apple.

8. (a) After stealing Tims car, the thief lost his way and ended up the chief constable's garage.
   (b) After stealing Tim's car the thief lost his way and ended up the chief constable's garage.
   (c) After stealing Tim's car, the thief lost his way and ended up the chief constable's garage.
   (d) After stealing Tim's car, the thief lost his' way and ended up the chief constable's garage.

9. (a) We decided to visit: Spain, Greece, Portugal and Italy's mountains.
   (b) We decided to visit Spain, Greece, Portugal and Italys mountains.
   (c) We decided to visit Spain, Greece, Portugal and Italy's mountains.
   (d) We decided to visit Spain Greece Portugal and Italy's mountains.

10. (a) That tall man, Paul's grandad, is this month's winner.
    (b) That tall man Paul's grandad is this month's winner.
    (c) That tall man, Paul's grandad, is this months winner.
    (d) That tall man, Pauls grandad, is this month's winner.

11. (a) Many students prefer online classes to on-campus classes; however, on-campus classes do have the advantages of providing human contact and immediate feedback.
    (b) The study of writing can be quite rewarding; especially to those who actually write.
    (c) If good students study two hours for every hour they spend in class; they can expect to do well.
    (d) The professor was only a few minutes late; but the students had already left the classroom.

12. (a) After studying the problem for several years, the college worked on a plan to address it.
    (b) After studying the problem, for several years the college worked on a plan to address it.
    (c) The college, after studying the problem for several years, worked on a plan to address it.
    (d) All three sentences are correctly punctuated with commas.

13. (a) Professor Loren Pillar, Chair of the Animal Husbandry Department at Enormous State University recently resigned from his position as Director of Research for Global Dominance, a multi-national conglomerate that has come under criticism from animal-rights activists for animal experimentation.

Conjunctions and Punctuations

(b) Professor Loren Pillar, Chair of the Animal Husbandry Department at Enormous State University recently resigned from his position as Director of Research for Global Dominance, a multi-national conglomerate that has come under criticism from animal-rights activists for animal experimentation.

(c) Professor Loren Pillar, Chair of the Animal Husbandry Department at Enormous State University, recently resigned from his position as Director of Research for Global Dominance, a multi-national conglomerate, that has come under criticism from animal-rights activists for animal experimentation.

(d) Professor Loren Pillar, Chair of the Animal Husbandry Department at Enormous State University, recently resigned from his position as Director of Research for Global Dominance, a multi-national conglomerate that has come under criticism from animal-rights activists for animal experimentation.

14. (a) The student wrote that "Each of the experiments was successful."
    (b) The student wrote that, "Each of the experiments was successful."
    (c) The student wrote that each of the experiments was successful.
    (d) The student wrote "Each of the experiments was successful."

15. (a) Only three social science disciplines are represented at our college are psychology, sociology, and anthropology.
    (b) Only three social science disciplines are represented at our college: psychology, sociology, and anthropology.
    (c) Only three social science disciplines are psychology, sociology, and anthropology are represented at our college: .
    (d) All of the above sentences are punctuated correctly.

III. Choose the correct option for the following questions.

1. Which of the following comma rules is incorrect?
   (a) Place commas after introductory elements in sentences.
   (b) Place commas after items in a series.
   (c) Place a comma before coordinating conjunctions that join independent clauses.
   (d) Set off restrictive, essential elements with commas.

2. Which of the following possessives is correctly punctuated?
   (a) The library lost all its books.
   (b) That's anyones' guess.
   (c) That car is not your's.
   (d) That car is not their's

3. Which types of punctuation are generally used to separate independent clauses in declarative sentences in academic writing?
   (a) commas and quotation marks
   (b) periods and semi-colons
   (c) commas and periods
   (d) colons and quotation marks

4. How many commas should the following sentence contain?
   "He stops fights ejects drunks soothes hysteria cures headaches and tends bar."
   John Steinbeck, Cannery Row
   (a) one   (b) two
   (c) three   (d) four

5. Which of the following sentences contains a comma error?
   (a) While Washington managed to lose most of the battles he engaged in, he also managed to win the war.
   (b) The loss of New York City and Philadelphia in 1777 should have ended the rebellion, but four years later, George Washington stood upon a battlefield in Virginia watching Britain's most powerful army in the colonies parade past him in surrender.
   (c) We have put Washington's image on monuments and mountains, on currency and coins, and on stamps and postmarks; we have filled our country, our pockets, and our envelopes with memorials large and small to this essential man.
   (d) Washington's greatest quality might have been his belief in his own abilities, in the lesser men who served with him, that attribute all too often led to personal failure and military disaster.

HOTS

I. Choose the correct option based on the instructions provided.

1. Choose the correct closing:
   (a) Sincerely yours:
   (b) Sincerely Yours,
   (c) Sincerely yours,
   (d) Sincerely Yours:

2. Choose the correct sentence:
   (a) Employees of the Company were laid off with little hope of returning to work.
   (b) Employees of the company were laid off with little hope of returning to work.
   (c) Employees of the company were Laid Off with little hope of returning to work.

3. Choose the correct sentence:
   (a) "You must understand," he pleaded, "That I need more time to pay you."
   (b) "You must understand," he pleaded, "that I need more time to pay you."
   (c) "You must understand," he pleaded. "That I need more time to pay you."

4. Choose the correct sentence:
   (a) Mark Paxton, the Vice President of the Company, embezzled over one million dollars.
   (b) Mark Paxton, the Vice President of the company, embezzled over one million dollars.
   (c) Mark paxton, the vice president of the company, embezzled over one million dollars.
   (d) Mark Paxton, the vice president of the company, embezzled over one million dollars.

5. Choose the correct sentence:
   (a) The West, especially California, is famous for its cutting-edge technology.
   (b) The west, especially California, is famous for its cutting-edge technology.

6. Choose the correct sentence:
   (a) The president of the United States wields much power.
   (b) The President Of The United States wields much power.
   (c) The President of the United States wields much power.

7. Choose the correct sentence:
   (a) She said: "bees are not the only insects that sting."
   (b) She said: "Bees are not the only insects that sting."
   (c) She said, "Bees are not the only insects that sting."
   (d) She said, "bees are not the only insects that sting."

8. Choose the correct opening:
   (a) My dear Mr. simpson:
   (b) My Dear Mr. Simpson:
   (c) My Dear Mr. Simpson:
   (d) My dear Mr. Simpson:

9. Choose the correct sentence:
   (a) I enjoy Summer more than any other Season.
   (b) I enjoy summer more than any other season.
   (c) I enjoy Summer more than any other season.

10. Choose the correct sentence:
    (a) I live in the Northeastern part of the State where the climate is colder.
    (b) I live in the northeastern part of the state where the climate is colder.
    (c) I live in the Northeastern part of the state where the climate is colder.

II. Choose the option that shows correct punctuation and capitalization for the italic words.

1. The boys were taken to Dean Jefferson's office to explain *their, fight*?
   (a) their, fight.   (b) their fight?
   (c) Their Fight.   (d) their fight.

2. "Will you please drop this letter in the mailbox for me on your way to *school dad* asked Christian.
   (a) school?" Dad   (b) school?" dad
   (c) school" Dad   (d) school? Dad

Conjunctions and Punctuations

3. *Dawson's* plan is to hire more employees to get the job done.
   (a) Dawsons' (b) Dawso'ns
   (c) Dawsons (d) None of these
4. "Don't even think about parking *Here*," the sign commanded.
   (a) Here (b) here,
   (c) here" (d) here,"
5. *Toms'* wife works in the same office as my brother.
   (a) Toms (b) To'ms
   (c) Tom's (d) None of these
6. My favorite Teenage Mutant Ninja Turtle *is Michelangelo.*
   (a) is michelangelo?
   (b) is, Michelangelo.
   (c) Is Michelangelo?
   (d) None of these
7. "*Don't give* up now," the coach told us.
   (a) don't give (b) "don't give
   (c) Don't give (d) None of these
8. "I fell asleep last night while I was studying for the math *test*," *said* Jacob to his classmate sitting next to him.
   (a) test", said (b) test" said
   (c) test," said, (d) None of these
9. "Do you think it's *okay*" asked Emily, "if I wear this outfit to school tomorrow?"
   (a) okay (b) okay,"
   (c) okay." (d) okay,
10. *Ann'as* mother's shopping list is too long.
    (a) Anna's (b) Annas
    (c) Annas' (d) None of these

Question Tags

10

Learning Objectives : In this chapter, students will learn about:
- Rules of making Question Tags

CHAPTER SUMMARY

Question tags are short questions at the end of statements. They are mainly used in speech when we want to confirm that something is true or not, or to encourage a reply from the person we are speaking to.

We use tags in spoken English but not in formal written English. They are not really questions but are a way of asking the other person to make a comment and so keep the conversation open.

Making a tag is very mechanical. To make a tag, use the first auxiliary. If there is no auxiliary, use do, does or did. With a positive sentence, make a negative tag and with a negative sentence, make a positive tag.

Example: It's beautiful, isn't it?
He has been, hasn't he?
You can, can't you?
You know him, don't you?
He will come, won't he?
It isn't very good, is it?
It hasn't rained, has it?
Seema doesn't know Sohan, does she?
They didn't leave, did they?
He won't do it, will he?

TRIVIA

All of the roles in Shakespeare's plays were originally acted by men and boys. In England at that time, it wasn't proper for females to appear on stage.

Notice these:
There isn't an ATM here, is there?
Let's have a cup of coffee, shall we?
To reply, use the same auxiliary:
It's beautiful, isn't it? ~ Yes, it is. I think it's fabulous.
It isn't very good, is it? ~ No, it isn't. In fact, it's terrible.

Rules of Making Question Tags

Rule 1. A positive statement is followed by a negative question tag.

Example: Jack is from Spain, 'isn't he'?
Mary can speak English, 'can't she'?

Rule 2. A negative statement is followed by a positive question tag.

Example: They aren't funny, 'are they'?
He shouldn't say things like that, 'should he'?

Rule 3. When the verb in the main sentence is in the present simple, we form the question tag with do/does.

Example: You play the guitar, 'don't you'?
Alison likes tennis, 'doesn't she'?

Rule 4. If the verb is in the past simple we use did.

Example: They went to the cinema, 'didn't they'?

She studied in New Zealand, 'didn't she'?

Rule 5. When the statement contains a word with a negative meaning, the question tag needs to be positive.

Example: He hardly ever speaks, 'does he'?

They rarely eat in restaurants, 'do they'?

Although, the rules are very simple and mechanical, in order to use them easily in conversation, they have to be automatic. So you need to hear and practice them very often. Take a look at the exceptions below.

■ Some verbs/expressions have different question tags.

Example: I am - I am attractive, aren't I?

Positive imperative – Stop daydreaming, will/won't you?

Negative imperative – Don't stop singing, will you?

Let's – Let's go to the beach, shall we?

Have got (possession) – He has got a car, hasn't he?

There is/are – There aren't any spiders in the bedroom, are there?

This/that is – This is Paul's pen, isn't it?

Intonation

■ When we are sure of the answer and we are simply encouraging a response, the intonation in the question tag goes down:

Example: This is your car, isn't it?

(Your voice goes down when you say isn't it.)

■ When we are not sure and want to check information, the intonation in the question tag goes up:

Example: He is from France, isn't he?

(Your voice goes up when you say isn't he.)

➡ Question tags are short questions at the end of statements.
➡ We use tags in spoken English but not in formal written English.

PRACTICE EXERCISE

I. Fill in the blanks with the correct question tag.

1. She's from a small town in China, _____ ?
   - (a) isn't she
   - (b) is she
   - (c) if she is not
   - (d) none of these
2. They aren't on their way already, _____ ?
   - (a) aren't they
   - (b) are they
   - (c) if they are not
   - (d) none of these
3. We're late again, _____ ?
   - (a) isn't we
   - (b) are we
   - (c) aren't we
   - (d) none of these
4. I'm not the person with the tickets, _____ ?
   - (a) I am
   - (b) am I
   - (c) if I am not
   - (d) none of these
5. Julie isn't an accountant, _____ ?
   - (a) isn't she
   - (b) she is not
   - (c) is she
   - (d) none of these
6. The weather is really bad today, _____ ?
   - (a) it is not
   - (b) isn't it
   - (c) if it is not
   - (d) none of these
7. He's very handsome, _____ ?
   - (a) aren't they
   - (b) isn't he
   - (c) if he is not
   - (d) none of these
8. They aren't in Mumbai at the moment, _____ ?
   - (a) aren't they
   - (b) if they are not
   - (c) are they
   - (d) none of these
9. You aren't from Brazil, _____ ?
   - (a) are you
   - (b) are not you
   - (c) if you are not
   - (d) none of these
10. John's a very good student, _____ ?
    - (a) is he
    - (b) isn't he
    - (c) if he is not
    - (d) none of these
11. I like chocolate very much, _____ ?
    - (a) don't I
    - (b) I don't
    - (c) if I am not
    - (d) none of these
12. She doesn't work in a hotel, _____ ?
    - (a) does she
    - (b) she does
    - (c) if she is not
    - (d) none of these
13. They need some new clothes, _____ ?
    - (a) aren't they
    - (b) are they
    - (c) don't they
    - (d) none of these
14. We live in a tiny flat, _____ ?
    - (a) are not we
    - (b) don't we
    - (c) if we are not
    - (d) none of these
15. She studies very hard every night, _____ ?
    - (a) doesn't she
    - (b) does she
    - (c) if she does not
    - (d) none of these
16. David and Julie don't take Chinese classes, _____ ?
    - (a) do they
    - (b) do they not
    - (c) if they do not
    - (d) None of these
17. I often come home late, _____ ?
    - (a) do I
    - (b) don't I
    - (c) if they do not
    - (d) none of these
18. You don't like spicy food, _____ ?
    - (a) don't they
    - (b) do they
    - (c) if they do not
    - (d) none of these
19. She doesn't cook very often, _____ ?
    - (a) isn't she
    - (b) is she
    - (c) does she
    - (d) none of these
20. We don't watch much TV, _____ ?
    - (a) isn't she
    - (b) are they
    - (c) do we
    - (d) none of these

II. Choose the correct option to make question tag.

1. He won't be late, _____ he?
   - (a) will
   - (b) don't
   - (c) isn't
   - (d) won't
2. You've had a great time in Mallorca, _____ you?
   - (a) have
   - (b) haven't
   - (c) had
   - (d) hadn't
3. She won't believe this story, _____ she?
   - (a) won't
   - (b) will
   - (c) won't
   - (d) is
4. You'll join us tonight, _____?
   - (a) aren't you
   - (b) don't you
   - (c) shall you
   - (d) won't you
5. I'll be 13 tomorrow, _____ I?
   - (a) won't
   - (b) am
   - (c) shall
   - (d) aren't

Question Tags

6. You do have sugar in your coffee, _____ you?
   (a) don't (b) haven't
   (c) aren't (d) isn't
7. What a pleasant holiday this one has been, _____ it?
   (a) doesn't (b) isn't
   (c) wasn't (d) hasn't
8. They've got too much luggage, _____?
   (a) don't they (b) isn't it
   (c) got they not (d) haven't they
9. We can go out now; the danger is over, _____?
   (a) hasn't it (b) isn't it
   (c) is it (d) isn't he
10. You have no money to lend me, _____ you?
    (a) do (b) don't
    (c) haven't (d) can't
11. He played well yesterday, _____?
    (a) doesn't he (b) didn't he
    (c) had he (d) isn't it
12. You hardly ever panic, _____ you?
    (a) have (b) aren't
    (c) do (a) don't
13. It rained all day yesterday, _____?
    (a) isn't it (b) didn't they
    (c) it didn't (d) didn't it
14. You'd never say such a thing behind my back, _____ you?
    (a) had (b) did
    (c) would (d) should
15. Life _____ different in a hundred years' time, won't it?
    (a) will not be (b) will be
    (c) will not (d) would be
16. You haven't been to Italy, _____?
    (a) you haven't (b) haven't you
    (c) have you (d) you have
17. They won't do that, _____?
    (a) did they (b) will they
    (c) will they not (d) won't they
18. You've never had a girlfriend before, _____ you?
    (a) have (b) had
    (c) hadn't (d) haven't
19. We've met before, _____?
    (a) are we (b) didn't we
    (c) aren't we (d) haven't we
20. He'd done that before, _____ he?
    (a) didn't (b) wouldn't
    (c) had (d) hadn't

III. Fill in the blanks with the correct question tag.

1. You wanted that, _____?
   (a) would you (b) didn't you
   (c) wouldn't you (d) do you
2. He saw that _____?
   (a) is he (b) won't he
   (c) didn't he (d) doesn't he
3. You know that's right _____?
   (a) would you (b) wouldn't you
   (c) don't you (d) didn't you
4. He will be coming _____?
   (a) is he (b) did he
   (c) doesn't he (d) won't he
5. After all this time you'd think he'd have forgotten _____?
   (a) didn't you (b) wouldn't you
   (c) don't you (d) do you
6. The amount he is suffering from hay fever he needs to see a doctor _____?
   (a) doesn't he (b) did he
   (c) won't he (d) is he
7. You may think you know the answer but you don't _____?
   (a) don't you (b) would you
   (c) wouldn't you (d) do you
8. After working so hard he didn't deserve to fail the exam _____?
   (a) doesn't he (b) did he
   (c) won't he (d) is he
9. You wouldn't report me, _____?
   (a) don't you (b) would you
   (c) wouldn't you (d) do you
10. He isn't going to like this, _____?
    (a) didn't he (b) did he
    (c) won't he (d) is he

11. The train arrived late, _____ ?
    (a) doesn't it   (b) couldn't it
    (c) didn't it
12. They look good, _____ ?
    (a) don't they   (b) didn't they
    (c) look they   (d) none of these
13. They are good, _____ ?
    (a) aren't they   (b) are they
    (c) can they   (d) none of these
14. Nine years ago they became friends, ____ ?
    (a) don't they   (b) didn't they
    (c) aren't they   (d) none of these
15. She won't be able to see him tonight, _____ ?
    (a) will she   (b) can she
    (c) does she   (d) none of these
16. They may not listen to you, _____ ?
    (a) do they   (b) will they
    (c) don't they   (d) none of these
17. Tim should work harder, _____ ?
    (a) shouldn't he   (b) didn't he
    (c) should he   (d) none of these
18. We were often bored, _____ ?
    (a) didn't we   (b) were we
    (c) weren't we   (d) none of these
19. He's good, _____ ?
    (a) doesn't he   (b) is he
    (c) isn't he   (d) none of these
20. He went to school this morning, _____ ?
    (a) can't he   (b) didn't he
    (c) doesn't he   (d) none of these
21. Tony can't swim, _____ ?
    (a) does he   (b) can't he
    (c) can he   (d) none of these
22. These trousers don't fit, _____ ?
    (a) does it   (b) fitn't they
    (c) do they   (d) none of these
23. It tastes funny, _____ ?
    (a) is it   (b) does it
    (c) doesn't it   (d) none of these
24. You have seen him, _____ ?
    (a) don't you   (b) haven't you
    (c) can't you   (d) none of these
25. We must hurry, _____ ?
    (a) mustn't we   (b) didn't we
    (c) don't we   (d) none of these

HOTS

Fill in the blanks with the correct question tag.

1. We shall see, _____ ?
   (a) don't we   (b) shan't we
   (c) shall we   (d) none of these
2. He reads a lot of magazines, _____ ?
   (a) hasn't he   (b) didn't he
   (c) doesn't he   (d) none of these
3. He didn't help him, _____ ?
   (a) does he   (b) didn't he
   (c) did he   (d) none of these
4. He has to work late tonight, _____ ?
   (a) doesn't he   (b) hasn't he
   (c) does he   (d) none of these
5. She cries a lot, _____ ?
   (a) didn't she   (b) doesn't she
   (c) isn't she   (d) none of these

Tenses

Learning Objectives: In this chapter, students will learn about:
- ✓ Basic concepts of Tenses
- ✓ Different types of Tenses
- ✓ Concept of Conditional Sentences

CHAPTER SUMMARY

An aspect of verb which tells the time of an action is called tense. Aspect describes the degree of progress or completion of an action.

Kinds of Tense
There are mainly three kinds of tenses.
(i) Present tense
(ii) Past tense
(iii) Future tense

Each of present, past and future tense is further divided into four kinds:
(i) Simple (Indifinite)
(ii) Continuous (progressive)
(iii) Perfect
(iv) Perfect Continuous (Perfect progressive)

Present Simple Tense
It is used to express an action in present time, habitual or usual actions or daily event or universal fact. For example, a student says, "I go to school". It is a daily activity of a student to go to school, so such actions are expressed by present simple tense. Another example is, "I work in a factory". It tells about a usual action of a person that he works in a factory on regular basis.

Rule: 1st form of verb or base verb is used as main verb in a sentence.

Positive Sentence
- Subject + Main verb + Object
- Subject + 1st form of verb (or base verb) + Object

Note:
If the subject in a sentence is 'he, she, it, singular or proper noun' then 's' or 'es' is added to the first form of verb or base form in the sentence.

Example: I write a letter.
He gets up early in the morning.
Sun rises in east.

Negative Sentence
- Subject + auxiliary verb + not + Main verb + object
- Subject + Do not/Does not + 1st form of verb (base form) + object

Example: I do not write a letter.
He does not get up early in the morning.
Sun does not rise in east.

Note:
In negative sentence, auxiliary verb 'do or does' along with 'not' is used. If the subject in a sentence is 'he, she, it, singular or proper noun', then 'Does not' is used after the subject in a sentence. If subject is 'I, we, they, you or plural' then 'Do not' is used after subject in sentence. 's' or 'es' is not added to main verb in negative sentence

Interrogative Sentence
- Auxiliary verb + Subject + Main verb + Object

- Do/Does + Subject + 1st form of verb (or base verb) + Object

  Example: Do I write a letter?
  Does he get up early in the morning?
  Does sun rise in east?

> **Note:**
> If the subject in a sentence is 'he, she, it, singular or proper noun,' the sentence is started with Auxiliary verb 'Does'. If the subject in a sentence is 'I, we, they, you or plural,' the sentence is started with auxiliary verb 'Do'. 's' or 'es' is not added to main verb in Interrogative sentence.

Example: I sing a song.
He drinks water.
I do not sing a song.
He does not drink water.
Do I sing a song?
Does he drink water?

Present Continuous Tense

It is used to express a continued or ongoing action at present time. It expresses an action which is in progress at the time of speaking. For example, a person says, "I am writing a letter". It means that he is in the process of writing a letter right now. Such actions, which are happening at time of speaking, are expressed by present continuous tense. Present Continuous tense is also called Present Progressive tense.

> **Rule:** Auxiliary verb 'am' or 'is' or 'are' is used in sentence. 1st form of verb or base verb + ing (present participle) is used as main verb in sentence.

Positive Sentence

- Subject + auxiliary verb + main verb-ing (Present participle) + object
- Subject + am/is/are + (1st form of verb or base verb + ing) + object
- If the subject is 'I' then auxiliary verb 'am' is used after subject in sentence.
- If the subject is 'He, She, It, singular or proper name' then auxiliary verb 'is' is used after subject in sentence.
- If subject is 'You, They or plural' then auxiliary verb 'are' is used after subject in sentence.
- The participle 'ing' is added to the 1st form of verb i.e. going (go) writing (write)

  Example: I am playing cricket.
  He is driving a car.
  They are reading their lessons.

Negative Sentence

- Subject + auxiliary verb + not + main verb-ing (Present participle) + object
- Subject + am/is/are + not + (1st form of verb + ing) + object

> Rules for using auxiliary verbs (am or is or are) after subject in negative sentences are same as mentioned above.

Example: I am not playing cricket.
He is not driving a car
They are not reading their lessons.

Interrogative Sentence

- Auxiliary verb + Subject + main verb-ing (Present participle) + object
- Am/is/are + Subject + (1st form of verb or base verb + ing) + object

  For making interrogative sentences, the sentence is started with auxiliary verb rather than putting auxiliary verb inside the sentence. If the subject is 'I' the sentence starts with auxiliary verb 'am'. If the subject is 'He, She, It, singular or proper name' the sentence starts with auxiliary verb 'is'. If subject is 'You, They or plural' the sentence starts with auxiliary verb 'are'.

  Example: Am I playing cricket?
  Is he driving a car?
  Are they reading their lessons?

Present Perfect Tense

It is used to express an action, which happened or completed in past but usually at a short time before now (near past) - not a very long time before now. Specific time, such as, two years ago, last week or that day is usually not used in the sentences using this tense. It means that this tense expresses the action, whose time when it happened, is not exactly specified but it

Tenses

sounds to refer to some action that happened or completed in near past.

Rule: Auxiliary verb 'has or have' is used in sentence. 3rd form of verb (past participle) is used as main verb in sentence.

Positive Sentence
- Subject + Auxiliary verb + main verb (past participle) + Subject
- Subject + has/have + 3rd form of verb or past participle + subject

    If the subject is 'He, She, It, singular or proper name' then auxiliary verb 'has' is used after subject in sentence.

    If subject is 'You, They or plural' then auxiliary verb 'have' is used after subject in sentence.

    Example: I have eaten the meal.
    She has learnt a lesson.

Negative Sentence
- Subject + Auxiliary verb + not + main verb (past participle) + Subject
- Subject + has/have + not + 3rd form of verb or past participle + subject

    Rules for using auxiliary verb 'has or have' in negative sentence are same as mentioned above.

    Example: I have not eaten meal.
    She has not learnt a lesson.

Interrogative Sentence
- Auxiliary verb + Subject + main verb (past participle) + Subject
- Has/have + Subject + 3rd form of verb or past participle + subject

    Interrogative sentence starts with auxiliary verb. If the subject is 'He, She, It, singular or proper name' then the sentence starts with auxiliary verb 'has'.

    If subject is 'You, They or plural' then the sentence starts with auxiliary verb 'have'.

    Example: Have I eaten meal?
    Has she learnt a lesson?

Present Perfect Continuous Tense
It is used to express a continued or ongoing action that started in past and is continued until now. There will be a time reference, such as 'since 1980, for three hours etc' from which the action has been started. A sense of time reference is found in these sentences which gives an idea that action has been continued from some time in past till now. Such time reference or sense of time reference is the identity of Present perfect continuous tense because it tells that an action has started from a particular time in past. For example, 'He has been studying in this school since 2005', so that means that he has started his education in this school in 2005 and he is studying in this school till now.

Note:
If there is no time reference or sense of time reference, then it is not Present perfect continuous tense because there is no hint about the time of action when it started in past and it seems just an ongoing action at present time which resembles 'present Continuous tense.' So the reference of time differentiates between Present perfect continuous tense and Present continuous tense.

Rule: An auxiliary verb 'has been or have been' is used in sentence. 1st form of verb (base verb) +ing (present participle) is used as main verb in sentence. 'Since' or 'for' is used before the 'time reference' in sentence. If the time reference is exactly known such as 1995, 4 O'clock then 'since' is used before the time in sentence. If the time reference is not exactly known such as three hours, six years, four days, then 'for' is used before the time in sentence. Time reference such as '3 hours' or '5 days' is not exactly known because we don't know about which three hours a day is told in sentence or about which 5 days in a month is told in sentence. While the year 1995 is exactly known time.

Positive Sentence
- Subject + Auxiliary verb + main verb (Present participle) + Object + Time reference
- Subject + has been/have been + (1st form of verb or base verb + ing) + object + time reference

If the subject is 'He, She, It, singular or proper name' then auxiliary verb 'has been' is used after subject in sentence.

If subject is 'You, They or plural' then auxiliary verb 'have been' is used after subject in sentence.

Example: He has been watering the plants for two hours.

I have been studying since 3 O'clock

Negative Sentence
- Subject + Not between the Auxiliary verb + main verb (present participle) + Object + Time reference
- Subject + has not been/have not been + (1st form of verb or base verb + ing) + object + time reference

To make negative sentence, the word 'not' is written between the auxiliary verbs, so it becomes 'has not been or have not been'. The rule for using auxiliary verb 'has been or have been' in negative sentences is as same as mentioned above.

Example: He has not been watering the plants for two hours.

I have not been studying since 3 O'clock.

Interrogative Sentence
- Auxiliary verb + Subject + Auxiliary verb + main verb (present participle) + object + time reference
- Has/have + Subject + been + (1st form of verb or base verb + ing) + object + time reference

Interrogative sentence starts with auxiliary verb. If the subject is 'He, She, It, singular or proper name' then the sentence starts with auxiliary verb 'has' and auxiliary verb 'been' is used after subject

If subject is 'You, They or plural' then the sentence starts with auxiliary verb 'have' and 'been' is used after subject

Example: Has he been watering the plants for two hours?

Have I been studying since 3 O'clock?

Past Simple Tense

It is used to express an action that happened or completed in past, usually a very little time before speaking, or action which is just completed. Time of action is not specified in terms of long time ago or short ago but it make a sense that the action has done a little time ago. For example, a person says, 'I watched a movie', it means the speaker of this sentence watched a movie a little time ago or little time ago in the same day.

Rule: 2nd form of verb (past simple) is used as main verb in the positive sentences and base form is used in negative and interrogative sentences.

Positive Sentence
- Subject + main verb (past simple) + object
- Subject + 2nd form of verb (past simple) + object

Example: I killed a snake.

He ate a mango.

Negative Sentences
- Subject + (auxiliary verb + not) main verb (base form) + object
- Subject + did not + 1st form of verb or base form + object

In negative sentence, 'did not' is written and the 1st form of verb (base verb) is used instead of using 2nd form (or past simple verb).

Example: I did not kill a snake.

He did not eat the mango.

Interrogative Sentence
- Auxiliary verb + subject + main verb (base verb) + object
- Did + subject + 1st form of verb (or base verb) + object

Interrogative sentence starts with "did" and the 1st form of verb (base verb) is used instead of using 2nd form (or past simple verb).

Example: Did I kill a snake?

Did he eat the mango?

Past Continuous Tense

It is used to express a continued or ongoing action in past, an ongoing action which occurred in past and completed at some point in past. It expresses an ongoing nature of an action in past. For example, "he was laughing."

Tenses

This sentence shows ongoing action (laughing) of a person which occurred in the past. Past continuous tense is also called past progressive.

Rule: Auxiliary verb 'was or were' is used in sentence. 1st form of verb or base verb + ing (present participle) is used as main verb in sentence.

Positive Sentence
- Subject + auxiliary verb + Main Verb (present participle) + object
- Subject + was/were + (1st form of verb or base verb + ing) +object

  If the subject is 'he, she, It, I, singular or proper noun' then auxiliary verb 'was' is used. If subject is 'you, we, they or plural' then auxiliary verb "were" is used.

  Example: She was crying yesterday.
  They were climbing on a hill.

Negative Sentence
- Subject + auxiliary verb + NOT + Main verb (present participle) + object
- Subject + was/were + NOT + (1st form of verb or base verb +ing) +object

  Rules for using auxiliary verb after subject are same as mentioned above.

  Example: She was not crying yesterday.
  They were not climbing on a hill.

Interrogative Sentence
- Auxiliary verb + Subject + Main verb (present participle) + object
- Was/were + Subject + (1st form of verb or base verb +ing) + object

  The interrogative sentence starts with the auxiliary verb. If the subject is 'he, she, It, I, singular or proper noun' then the sentence starts with auxiliary verb 'was'. If subject is 'you, we, they or plural' then the sentence starts with auxiliary verb 'were'.

  Example: Was she crying yesterday?
  Were they climbing on a hill?

Past Perfect Tense

It is used to express an action which has occurred in past (usually, a long time ago) and action which has occurred in past before another action in past.

Example: I had lived in America. (The sense of time in this sentence refers to a completed action in past and especially a long time ago)

The students had gone before the teacher came. (The first part of sentence 'The student has gone' is sentence of past perfect tense, it says about an action which occurred before another action in the past, which is 'the teacher came'. The second part 'the teacher came' is a sentence using past simple tense. So such a sentence which expresses an action in past before another action in past comprises two parts where the first part of sentence is past perfect tense)

Rule: Auxiliary verb 'had' is used in sentence. 3rd form of verb (past participle) is used as main verb in sentence.

Positive Sentence
- Subject + auxiliary verb + main verb (past participle) + object
- Subject + had + 3rd form of verb or past participle + object

  Example: He had taken the exam last year.
  A thief had stolen my watch.

Negative Sentence
- Subject + auxiliary verb + NOT + main verb (past participle) + object
- Subject + had + not + 3rd form of verb or past participle + object

  'Not' is written after auxiliary verb in negative sentence.

  Example: He had not taken the exam last year.
  A thief had not stolen my watch.

Interrogative Sentence
- Auxiliary verb + subject + main verb (past participle) + object
- Had + subject + 3rd form of verb or past participle + object

  Interrogative sentence starts with auxiliary verb "had"

  Example: Had he taken the exam last year.
  Had a thief stolen my watch?

Past Perfect Continuous Tense

It is used to express a continued or ongoing action that started in past and continued until sometime in past (Remember, an ongoing action in past which continued till some time in past). There will be a time reference, such as 'since 1980, for three hours etc' from which the action had started. A sense of time reference is found in these sentences which shows that an action had started in the past and continued till some time in past. Such time reference or sense of reference is the identity of Present perfect continuous tense because it tells that action has started from a particular time in past or for some time period. For example, 'He had been studying in this school since 2005', so that means that he had started his education in this school in 2005 and he studied in this school till sometime in past.

Note:
If there is no time reference or sense of time reference, then it is not Past perfect continuous tense because there is no hint about the time of action when it started in past or continued for some time period, so it seems just an ongoing action in past which resembles 'past continuous tense'. So, the reference of time differentiates between Past perfect continuous tense and Past continuous tense.

Rule: An auxiliary verb 'had been' is used in sentence. 1st form of verb (base verb) + ing (present participle) is used as main verb in sentence. 'Since' or 'for' is used before the 'time reference' in sentence. If the time reference is exactly known such as 1995, 4 O'clock then 'since' is used before the time in sentence. If the time reference is not exactly known, such as, three hours, six years, four days, then 'for' is used before the time in sentence. Time reference such as 3 hours or 5 days is not exactly known because we don't know about which three hours a day is told in sentence or about which 5 days in a month is told in sentence. While the year 1995 is exactly known time.

Positive Sentence
- Subject + Auxiliary verb + main verb (Present participle) + Object + Time reference
- Subject + had been + (1st form of verb or base verb + ing) + object + time reference

Example: I had been waiting for him for one hour.

She had been playing chess since 7 O'clock.

Negative Sentence
- Subject + Not between the Auxiliary verbs + main verb (present participle) + Object + Time reference
- Subject + had not been + (1st form of verb or base verb + ing) + object + time reference

To make negative sentence, the word 'not' is added inside auxiliary verb, so it becomes 'had not been'.

Example: I had not been waiting for him for one hour.

She had not been playing chess since 7 O'clock.

Interrogative Sentence
- Auxiliary verb + Subject + Auxiliary verb + main verb (present participle) + object + time reference
- Had + Subject + been + (1st form of verb or base verb+ing) + object + time reference

Interrogative sentence starts with auxiliary verb 'had' and auxiliary verb 'been' is used after subject in sentence.

Example: Had I been waiting for him for one hour?

Had she been playing chess 7 O'clock?

Future Simple Tense

It is used to express an action which has not occurred yet and will occur after saying or in future. For example, 'I will go to zoo tomorrow.' In this sentence, the person intends for tomorrow's visit to zoo. In short, these sentences express actions which will be done in future.

Rule: Auxiliary verb 'will' is used in sentence. 1st form of verb or base form is used as main verb in sentence.

Positive Sentence
- Subject + auxiliary verb + main verb (present participle) + object
- Subject + will + (1st form of verb or base form + ing) + object

  Example: I will buy a computer tomorrow.
  They will come here.

Negative Sentence
- Subject + auxiliary verb + not + main verb (present participle) + object
- Subject + will + not + (1st form of verb or base form + ing) + object

  To make negative sentence, 'not' is written after auxiliary verb in sentence.

  Example: I will not buy a computer tomorrow.
  They will not come here.

Interrogative Sentence
- Auxiliary verb + subject + main verb (present participle) + object
- Will + subject + (1st form of verb or base form + ing) + object

  Interrogative sentence starts with auxiliary verb 'will'

  Example: Will I buy a computer tomorrow?
  Will they come here?

Future Continuous Tense
It is used to express a continued or an ongoing action in future. For example, 'I will be waiting for you tomorrow'; it conveys ongoing nature of an action (waiting) which will occur in future.

Rule: Auxiliary verb 'will be' is used in sentence. 1st form of verb + ing (present participle) is used as main verb in sentence.

Positive Sentence
- Subject + auxiliary verb + main verb (present participle) + object
- Subject + will be + 1st form of verb or base form + ing (present participle) + object

  Example: I will be waiting for you.
  You will be feeling well tomorrow.

Negative Sentence
- Subject + not between auxiliary verbs + main verb (present participle) + object
- Subject + will not be + 1st form of verb or base form+ing (present participle) + object

  To make negative sentence, 'not' is written between auxiliary verbs 'will and be' in sentence.

  Example: I will not be waiting for you.
  You will not be feeling well tomorrow.

Interrogative Sentence
- Auxiliary verb + subject + auxiliary verb + main verb (present participle) + object
- Will + subject + be+ 1st form of verb or base form+ing (present participle) + object

  Interrogative sentence starts with auxiliary verb "will" and auxiliary verb "be" comes after subject in interrogative sentence

  Example: Will I be waiting for you?
  Will you be feeling well tomorrow?

Future Perfect Tense

It is used to express an action which will occur in future and is thought to be completed in future. It expresses a sense of completion of an action which will occur in future.

Example: 'John will have gone tomorrow'. It shows a sense of completion of an action (go) which will occur in future (tomorrow).

Rule: Auxiliary verb 'will have' is used in sentence. 3rd form of verb or past participle form of verb is used as main verb in sentence.

Positive Sentence
- Subject + auxiliary verb + main verb (past participle) + object
- Subject + will have + 3rd form of verb or past participle + object

  Example: She will have finished the work by Wednesday.
  I will have left for home by the time he gets up.
  You will have started a job.

Negative Sentence
- Subject + Not between auxiliary verbs + main verb (past participle) + object
- Subject + will not have + 3rd form of verb or past participle + object

    Example: She will have finished the work by Wednesday.

    I will have left for home by the time he gets up.

    You will not have started a job.

Interrogative Sentence
- Auxiliary verb + Subject + auxiliary verb + main verb (past participle) + object
- Will + Subject + have + 3rd form of verb or past participle + object

    Example: Will she have finished the work by Wednesday?

    Will I have left for home by the time he gets up?

    Will you have started a job?

TRIVIA
The only 15 letter word that can be spelt without repeating a letter is uncopyrightable.

Future Perfect Continuous Tense

It is used to express a continued or ongoing action that will start in future and is thought to be continued till sometime in future. (Remember, an ongoing action in future which will continue till some time in future). There will be a time reference, such as 'since 2015, for three hours' from which the action will start in future and will continue. A sense of time reference is found which gives an idea that action will start at some time in future and will continue for some time. Such time reference or sense of time reference is the identity of Future perfect continuous tense because it tells that action will start at a particular time in future. For example, 'He will have been studying in this school since 2015', so that means that he will start studying in this school in 2015 and will study in this school till sometime in future.

Note:
If there is no time reference or sense of time reference, then it is not future perfect continuous tense because there is no hint about the time of action when it will start in future and it seems just an ongoing action in future which resembles 'future continuous tense.' So the reference of time differentiates between Future perfect continuous tense between future continuous tense.

Rules: An auxiliary verb 'will have been' is used in sentence. 1st form of verb (base verb) +ing (present participle) is used as main verb in sentence. 'Since' or 'for' is used before the 'time reference' in sentence. If the time reference is exactly known such as 2015, 4 O'clock then 'since' is used before the time in sentence. If the time reference is not exactly known such as three hours, six years, four days, then 'for' is used before the time in sentence. Time reference such as 3 hours or 5 days is not exactly known because we don't know about which three hours a day is told in the sentence or about which 5 days in a month is told in the sentence while the 2015 is exactly known time.

Positive Sentence
- Subject + Auxiliary verb + main verb (Present participle) + Object + Time reference
- Subject + will have been + (1st form of verb or base verb + ing) + object + time reference

    Example: I will have been waiting for him for one hour.

    She will have been playing football since 2015.

Negative Sentence
- Subject + Not inside Auxiliary verbs + main verb (present participle) + Object + Time reference
- Subject + will not have been + (1st form of verb or base verb + ing) + object + Time reference

To make negative sentence, the word 'not' is added inside auxiliary verb, so it becomes 'will not have been'.

Example: I will not have been waiting for him for one hour.

She will not have been playing football since 2015.

Interrogative Sentence

- Auxiliary verb + Subject + auxiliary verb + main verb (present participle) + object + time reference

- Will + Subject + have been + (1st form of verb or base verb + ing) + object + time reference

Interrogative sentence starts with auxiliary verb "will" and auxiliary verb "have been" is used after subject in sentence.

Example: Will I have been waiting for him for one hour?

Will she have been playing football since 2015?

- An aspect of verb which tells the time of an action is called tense.
- Present Continuous tense is also called Present progressive tense.
- For making interrogative sentences, the sentence is started with auxiliary verb rather than putting auxiliary verb inside the sentence.
- To make negative sentence, the word 'not' is written between the auxiliary verbs, so it becomes 'has not been or have not been'.

PRACTICE EXERCISE

I. Choose the correct option to complete the following sentences.

1. I _____ for them for an hour now. I can't wait any longer.
   (a) wait
   (b) am waiting
   (c) have been waiting
   (d) none of these

2. I hope _____ some interesting read in the new bookshop.
   (a) to find   (b) find
   (c) found   (d) none of these

3. Jane _____ TV for hours; that's why her eyes are red.
   (a) is watching   (b) watch
   (c) has been watching   (d) none of these

4. Unless John _____ harder, he won't get this job.
   (a) tried   (b) will try
   (c) tries   (d) none of these

5. Stop _____ that terrible noise.
   (a) making   (b) make
   (c) made   (d) none of these

6. He will see you as soon as Mr. Brown _____.
   (a) leaves   (b) will leave
   (c) left   (d) none of these

7. I realized that my parents _____ me and my brother.
   (a) have adopted   (b) had adopted

8. No one _____ text to me like that.
   (a) has ever spoken
   (b) ever spoke

9. We normally live with our parents but for these two months we _____ in our aunt's flat.
   (a) live   (b) are living

10. We _____ to the theatre tonight.
    (a) go   (b) are going

11. _____ this evening?
    (a) What do you do
    (b) What are you doing

12. Don't shout unless you _____ to be arrested.
    (a) want   (b) will want

13. I _____ asleep when somebody broke the glass in our front door.
    (a) fell   (b) was falling
    (c) had fallen   (d) none of these

14. Jim ought _____ languages if he wants to get a job with an international company.
    (a) to learn   (b) learn

15. Look! It's Tom! I _____ him for ages.
    (a) haven't seen   (b) saw

II. Choose the correct option to fill in the blanks with the correct form of the verbs given in brackets.

1. Next week we _____ into our new house. (move)
   (a) will move   (b) had move
   (c) do move   (d) moved

2. He was sure that he _____ that man before. (see)
   (a) will see   (b) had seen
   (c) has seen   (d) seen

3. What _____ have for breakfast? (you, have)
   (a) will you   (b) do you
   (c) did you   (d) are you

4. She _____ a bath when the telephone _____ (have, ring).
   (a) will have, rang
   (b) is having, rang
   (c) was having, rang
   (d) were having, rang

5. She _____ the piano for eight years. (play)
   (a) will play   (b) play
   (c) have played (d) played

6. He _____ never on time. (be)
   (a) is   (b) are
   (c) did   (d) am

7. You look terrible. _____ (you, drink)?
   (a) do you drink   (b) did you drink
   (c) have you drunk   (d) will you drink

8. He realized that he _____ his keys. (lose)
   (a) has lost   (b) have lost
   (c) had lost   (d) lost

Tenses

9. I _____ very angry with you if you do not stop smoking. (be)
   (a) will be   (b) had been
   (c) do be   (d) should be

10. They _____ for her for some time when she finally _____ (wait, arrive).
    (a) had, arrived
    (b) had arrived, lost
    (c) have been waiting, arrived
    (d) had been waiting, arrived

III. Choose the most suitable option to fill in the blanks.

1. Two children and one adult _____ in a fire last night.
   (a) died   (b) have died
   (c) are dying   (d) will die

2. Sam _____ the marathon for the first time in 2009.
   (a) has run   (b) runs
   (c) ran   (d) is running

3. I _____ English tea. Is it good?
   (a) drink   (b) 've never drunk
   (c) have drunk   (d) am drinking

4. We _____ Mrs. Stewart when we were in California.
   (a) will meet   (b) are meeting
   (c) met   (d) have met

5. He's not happy because his brother _____ his computer.
   (a) doesn't use (b) using
   (c) has used   (d) will use

6. If it's sunny tomorrow, maybe we _____ go to the beach.
   (a) went   (b) will go
   (c) don't go   (d) go

7. I _____ my exercise because I didn't understand the questions.
   (a) didn't do   (b) will do
   (c) did   (d) won't do

8. She _____ the piano very well.
   (a) play   (b) playing
   (c) will play   (d) plays

9. My brother _____ football in the same club as me.
   (a) play   (b) plays
   (c) is playing   (d) played

10. I _____ in a first-class hotel: it's too expensive for me.
    (a) 'm going to sleep (b) 've never slept
    (c) sleep   (d) am sleeping

11. He often _____ to the cinema because he loves movies.
    (a) going   (b) go
    (c) is going   (d) goes

12. She's shocked because she _____ a terrible accident.
    (a) has seen   (b) is going to see
    (c) sees   (d) saw

13. They _____ their new car two weeks ago.
    (a) bought   (b) will buy
    (c) buy   (d) have bought

14. Please be quiet! The baby _____ .
    (a) sleeps   (b) has slept
    (c) is sleeping (d) sleep

15. I _____ to the cinema tonight: I've got a lot of work to finish.
    (a) went   (b) 'm going
    (c) will go   (d) 'm not going

16. I'm very happy: my favourite singer _____ to my town next October for a big concert.
    (a) doesn't come
    (b) isn't going to come
    (c) has come
    (d) is going to come

17. Speak loudly I can't hear you because your dog _____ too much noise.
    (a) made   (b) has made
    (c) makes   (d) is making

18. My mother _____ 42 years old next Saturday.
    (a) will be   (b) is
    (c) was   (d) will have

19. My sister _____ hamburgers: she thinks they're bad for her.
    (a) is eating   (b) doesn't eat
    (c) eats   (d) will eat

20. For dinner last night, we _____ fish and chips.
    (a) are having (b) had
    (c) have had   (d) will have

HOTS

Fill in the blanks with the correct tense form of the verbs given in brackets.

1. I (have) _____ the same car for more than ten years. I'm thinking about buying a new one.
2. I (love) _____ chocolate since I was a child. You might even call me a "chocoholic."
3. Lately, I (think) _____ about changing my career because I (become) _____ dissatisfied with the conditions at my company.
4. John (work) _____ for the government since he graduated from Harvard University. Until recently, he (enjoy) _____ his work, but now he is talking about retiring.
5. How long (be) _____ in Canada?

Tenses

Voices and Narration 12

Learning Objectives : In this chapter, students will learn about:
- ✓ Voice and its two different types – Active and Passive
- ✓ Reporter Speech – Direct and Indirect
- ✓ Vocabulary

CHAPTER SUMMARY

Voice is the form of verb which expresses whether the person or thing denoted by the subject does something or something is done to it.

Types of Voice
There are two types of voice - (i) Active voice, (ii) Passive voice
For example, Saurabh speaks English fluently. English is spoken fluently by Saurabh.

Active Voice
(i) In 'active voice,' subject acts upon object, while in 'passive voice' object is acted upon by subject. It can also be said, in 'active voice' subject does a work on object, while in 'passive voice' object is worked on by subject.
(ii) The normal structure of an active voice sentence is subject + verb + object but in passive the normal structure of sentence is reversed according to certain rules and becomes like object + verb + subject.
(iii) The real meaning of a sentence does not change if the sentence is expressed either by active voice or by passive voice. The active voice is mostly used in writing because it gives a direct and more concise meaning.

Passive Voice
Passive voice is used sometimes due to the following reasons:

- When intentionally hiding the subject of a sentence.

  Example: A student who failed in exam might say, some chapters were not studied. Women were not treated as equal.

- When passive voice better explains thought of a sentence.

  Example: 'Cloth is sold in yards,' is more meaningful than to say, 'Shop keepers sell cloth in yards.'

- When passive voice better emphasizes the main thought of the sentence.

  Example: A man who is being teased by another person might say in anger, 'You will be beaten by me.'

- When subject is not exactly known.

  Example: 'His watch was stolen.' It is not known who stole his watch; the subject (thief) is not exactly known, so it is better to use passive voice for such a sentence.

TRIVIA

A 672-sided shape is called a "hexahectaheptacontakaidigon"

Fundamental Rules
Fundamental Rules for changing from active voice to passive voice (:)

Rule 1: The places of subject and object are interchanged i.e. the object shifts to the place of subject and subject shifts to the place of object in passive voice.
Example: I write a letter. (Active voice)
A letter is written by me. (Passive voice)
Subject (I) of sentence shifted to the place of object (letter) and object (letter) shifted to the place of subject (I) in passive voice.

Rule 2: Sometimes subject of sentence is not used in passive voice. Subject of sentence can be omitted in passive voice, if without subject it can give enough meaning in passive voice.
Example: Cloth is sold in yards. (Passive voice)

Rule 3: 3rd form of verb (past participle) is always used as main verb in sentences of passive voice for all tenses. Base form of verb or present participle will never be used in passive voice.

Rule 4: The word 'by' is used before subject in sentences in passive voice.
Example: He sings a song. (Active voice)
A song is sung by him. (Passive voice)

Rule 5: The word 'by' is not always used before subject in passive voice. Sometimes words 'with, to,' etc may also be used before subject in passive voice.
Example: The water fills the tub. (Active voice)
The tub is filled with water. (Passive voice)
He knows me. (Active voice)
I am known to him. (Passive voice)

Rule 6: Auxiliary verbs are used in passive voice according to the tense of sentence.

> **Note:**
> First 5 rules are usually same for all tenses in passive voice. Rule No. 6 is about the use of auxiliary verb in passive voice which differs for each tense. The auxiliary verbs of passive voice are used according to the tense of sentence in its active voice form.

Passive Voice for All Tenses

Present Simple Tense (Passive Voice)
Auxiliary verb in passive voice: am/is/are
Example: He sings a song. (Active voice)
A song is sung by him. (Passive voice)
He does not sing a song. (Active voice)
A song is not sung by him. (Passive voice)
Does he sing a song? (Active voice)
Is a song sung by him? (Passive voice)

Present Continuous Tense (Passive Voice)
Auxiliary verb in passive voice: am being/is being/are being
Example: I am writing a letter. (Active voice)
A letter is being written by me. (Passive voice)
I am not writing a letter. (Active voice)
A letter is not being written by me. (Passive voice)
Am I writing a letter? (Active voice)
Is a letter being written by me? (Passive voice)

Present Perfect Tense (Passive Voice)
Auxiliary verb in passive voice: has been/have been
Example: She has finished her work. (Active voice)
Her work has been finished by her. (Passive voice)
She has not finished her work. (Active voice)
Her work has not been finished by her. (Passive voice)
Has she finished her work? (Active voice)
Has her work been finished by her? (Passive voice)

Past Simple Tense (Passive Voice)
Auxiliary verb in passive voice: was/were
Example: I killed a snake. (Active voice)
A snake was killed by me. (Passive voice)
I did not kill a snake. (Active voice)
A snake was not killed by me. (Passive voice)
Did I kill a snake? (Active voice)
Was a snake killed by me? (Passive voice)

Past Continuous Tense (Passive Voice)
Auxiliary verb in passive voice: was being/were being
Example: He was driving a car. (Active voice)
A car was being driven by him. (Passive voice)
He was not driving a car. (Active voice)
A car was not being driven by him. (Passive voice)

Was he driving a car? (Active voice)
Was a car being driven by him? (Passive voice)

Past Perfect Tense (Passive Voice)
Auxiliary verb in passive voice: had been
Example: They had completed the assignment. (Active voice)
The assignment had been completed by them. (Passive voice)
They had not completed the assignment. (Active voice)
The assignment had not been completed by them. (Passive voice)
Had they completed the assignment? (Active voice)
Had the assignment been completed by them? (Passive voice)

Future Simple Tense (Passive Voice)
Auxiliary verb in passive voice: will be
Example: She will buy a car. (Active voice)
A car will be bought by her. (Passive voice)
She will not buy a car. (Active voice)
A car will not be bought by her. (Passive voice)
Will she buy a car? (Active voice)
Will a car be bought by her? (Passive voice)

Future Perfect Tense (Passive Voice)
Auxiliary verb in passive voice: will have been
Example: You will have started the job. (Active voice)
The job will have been started by you. (Passive voice)
You will have not started the job. (Active voice)
The job will not have been started by you. (Passive voice)
Will you have started the job? (Active voice)
Will the job have been started by you? (Passive voice)

Note:
The following tenses cannot be changed into passive voice.
(i) Present perfect continuous tense
(ii) Past perfect continuous tense
(iii) Future continuous tense
(iv) Future perfect continuous tense

Passive Voice for Present/Future Modals

Can, May, Might, Should, Must, Ought to
To change sentences having present/future modal into passive voice, auxiliary verb "be" is added after modal in sentence.
Passive voice for Present/Future Modals: Can, May, Might, Should, Must, Ought to
Auxiliary verb in passive voice: be

Can → Can be
Example: She can play a violin. (Active voice)
A violin can be played by her. (Passive voice)
She cannot play a violin. (Active voice)
A violin cannot be played by her. (Passive voice)
Can she play a violin? (Active voice)
Can a violin be played by her? (Passive voice)

May → May be
Example: I may buy a computer. (Active voice)
A computer may be bought by me. (Passive voice)
I may not buy a computer. (Active voice)
A computer may not be bought by me. (Passive voice)
May I buy a computer? (Active voice)
May a computer be bought by me? (Passive voice)

Might → Might be
Example: Guests might play chess. (Active voice)
Chess might be played by guests. (Passive voice)
Guests might not play chess. (Active voice)
Chess might not be played by guests. (Passive voice)

Should → Should be
Example: Students should study all lessons. (Active voice)
All lessons should be studied by students. (Passive voice)
Students should not study all lessons. (Active voice)
All lessons should not be studied by students. (Passive voice)
Should students study all lessons? (Active voice)
Should all lessons be studied by students? (Passive voice)

Must → Must be
Example: You must learn the test-taking strategies. (Active voice)
Test-taking strategies must be learnt by you. (Passive voice)
You must not learn the test-taking strategies. (Active voice)
Test-taking strategies must not be learnt by you. (Passive voice)

Ought to → Ought to be
Example: They ought to take the examination. (Active voice)
The examination ought to be taken by them. (Passive voice)

Passive Voice for Past Modals
To change sentences having past modal into passive voice, auxiliary verb "been" is added after modal in sentence.
"May Have, Might Have, Should Have, Must Have, Ought Have to"
Auxiliary verb in passive voice: been

May have → May have been
Example: You may have availed the opportunity. (Active voice)
The opportunity may have been availed by you. (Passive voice)
You may not have availed the opportunity. (Active voice)
The opportunity may not have been availed by you. (Passive voice)

Might have → Might have been
Example: He might have eaten meal. (Active voice)
Meal might have been eaten by him. (Passive voice)
He might not have eaten meal. (Active voice)
Meal might not have been eaten by him. (Passive voice)

Should have → Should have been
Example: You should have studied the book. (Active voice)
The book should have been studied by you. (Passive voice)
You should not have studied the book. (Active voice)
The book should have not been studied by you. (Passive voice)

Must have → Must have been
Example: He must have started job. (Active voice)
Job must have been started by him. (Passive voice)
He must not have started job. (Active voice)
Job must not have been started by him. (Passive voice)

Ought to have → Ought to have been
Example: You ought to have helped him. (Active voice)
He ought to have been helped by you. (Passive voice)

Passive Voice of Imperative Sentences (Command and Request)
A sentence which expresses command or request or advice is called imperative sentence.
Example: Open the door.
Turn off the television.
Learn your lesson.
For changing these sentences into passive voice, auxiliary verb 'be' is used. The word 'Let' is added before such sentences in passive voice. Auxiliary verb 'be' is added after object in sentences in passive voice. Main verb (base form) of imperative sentence is changed to 3rd form of verb (past participle) in passive voice.
Example: Open the door. (Active voice)
Let the door be opened. (Passive voice)
Complete the work. (Active voice)
Let the work be completed. (Passive voice)
Turn off the television. (Active voice)
Let the television be turned off. (Passive voice)
Learn your lesson. (Active voice)
Let your lesson be learnt. (Passive voice)
Kill the snake. (Active voice)
Let the snake be killed. (Passive voice)
Punish him. (Active voice)
Let him be punished. (Passive voice)
Speak the truth. (Active voice)
Let the truth be spoken. (Passive voice)
Help the poor. (Active voice)
Let the poor be helped. (Passive voice)

Revise your book. (Active voice)
Let your book be revised. (Passive voice)
Clean your room. (Active voice)
Let your room be cleaned. (Passive voice)

Sentences which cannot be changed into Passive Voice

- A verb can be either transitive or intransitive. A transitive verb needs an object (in sentence) to give complete meaning while intransitive verb does not need an object (in sentence) to give complete meaning.

  Example: He sent a letter. (Transitive verb)
  (Send is a transitive verb and it needs an object i.e. letter to express full meaning.)
  He laughs. (Intransitive verb)
  (Laugh is an intransitive verb and it does not need object for expressing full meaning.)
  Sleep, go, reach, sit, die are examples of intransitive verbs.

- Intransitive verb cannot be changed into passive voice. The sentences having intransitive verbs (belonging to any tense) cannot be changed into passive voice. The reason is that there is not any object in such sentences and without object of sentence passive voice is not possible.

- A sentence can be changed into passive voice if it has a subject and an object. Sometimes subject may not be written in passive voice but it does not mean that it has no subject. Such sentences have subject but the subject is so common or familiar or known that if even it is not written in passive voice, it gives full meaning.

  Example: Cloth is sold in yards.

Narration

Narration is the manner in which the words of speaker are expressed.

There are two ways to express the words spoken by a person to another person:
(i) Direct speech
(ii) Indirect speech
Example: John said, "I will give you a pen". (Direct speech)
John said that he would give me a pen. (Indirect speech)

- In direct speech, the original words of the speaker are narrated (no change is made) and are enclosed in quotation marks. While in indirect speech some changes are made in original words of the person because these words have been uttered in past so the tense will change accordingly and pronoun may also be changed accordingly.

- In indirect speech, the statement of the person is not enclosed in quotation marks, the word "that" may be used before the statement to show that it is indirect speech. Indirect speech is also called reported speech because reported speech refers to the second part of indirect speech in which something has been told by a person.

Reporting verb: The verb first part of sentence (i.e. he said, she said, he says, they said, she says) before the statement of a person in sentence is called reporting verb.

Example: In all of the following examples, the reporting verb is 'said':
He said, "I work in a factory". (Direct speech)
He said that he worked in a factory. (Indirect speech)
They said, "we are going to cinema". (Direct speech)
They said that they were going to cinema. (Indirect speech)

Reported Speech: The second part of indirect speech in which something has been told by a person (which is enclosed in quotation marks in direct speech) is called reported speech. For example, a sentence of indirect speech is: He said that he worked in a factory. In this sentence, the second part "he worked in a factory" is called reported speech and that is why the indirect speech as a whole can also be called reported speech.

Fundamental Rules for Indirect Speech

- Reported speech is not enclosed in quotation marks.

- The word 'that' is used as a conjunction between the reporting verb and reported speech.

- Change in pronoun: The pronoun (subject) of the reported speech is changed according to the pronoun of reporting verb or object (person) of reporting verb (first part of sentence). Sometimes the pronoun may not change. In the following example, the pronoun of reported speech is 'I' which will be changed in indirect speech into the pronoun (Subject) of reporting verb that is 'he'.

Example: He said, "I am happy" (Direct speech)
He said that he was happy. (Indirect Speech)
I said to him, "You are intelligent" (Direct speech)
I told him that he was intelligent. (Indirect speech)
('You' changed to 'he' the person of object of reporting verb)

- Change in time: Time is changed according to certain rules like
  now → then
  today → that day
  tomorrow → next day
  yesterday → previous day
  Example: He said, "I am happy today" (Direct speech)
  He said that he was happy that day. (Indirect speech)

- Change in the tense of reported speech: If the first part of sentence (reporting verb) belongs to past tense, the tense of reported speech will change. If the first part of sentence (reporting verb) belongs to present or future tense, the tense of reported speech is not changed.
  Example: He said, "I am happy" (Direct speech)
  He said that he was happy. (Indirect speech) (Tense of reported speech changed)
  He says, "I am happy" (Direct speech)
  He said that he is happy. (Indirect speech) (Tense of reported speech didn't change)
  Rules for change in tense of reported speech for all Tenses.

Change in Tense

Tense (Direct Speech)	→	Tense (Indirect Speech)
Present simple tense	→	Past simple
Present Continuous tense	→	Past continuous
Present Perfect tense	→	Past perfect
Present Perfect Continuous	→	Past perfect continuous
Past simple	→	Past Perfect
Past Continuous	→	Past Perfect Continuous
Past Perfect	→	Past Perfect
Future simple (will)	→	would
Future Continuous (will be)	→	would be
Future Perfect (will have)	→	would have

Present Simple changes into **Past Simple**
Example: She said, "He goes to school daily" (Direct speech)
He said that she went to school daily. (Indirect speech)
They said, "We love our country" (Direct speech)
They said that they loved their country. (Indirect speech)

Present Continuous changes into **Past Continuous**
Example: He said, "He is listening to the music" (Direct speech)
He said that he was listening to the music. (Indirect speech)
They said, "We are enjoying the weather" (Direct speech)
They said that they were not enjoying the weather. (Indirect speech)

Present Perfect changes into **Past Perfect**
Example: She said, "He has finished his work" (Direct speech)
She said that he had finished his work. (Indirect speech)
I said, "She has eaten the meal" (Indirect speech)
I said that she had eaten the meal. (Indirect speech)

Present Perfect Continuous changes into **Past Perfect Continuous**
Example: He said, "I have been studying since 3 O'clock" (Direct speech)

He said that he had been studying since 3 O'clock. (Indirect speech)

I said, "She has been working in this office since 2007" (Direct speech)

I said that she had been working in this office since 2007. (Indirect speech)

Past Simple changes into **Past Perfect**
Example: He said to me, "You answered correctly." (Direct speech)

He told me that I had answered correctly. (Indirect speech)

She said, "I didn't buy a car" (Direct speech)

She said that she had not bought a car. (Indirect speech)

Past Continuous changes into **Past Perfect Continuous**
Example: They said, "We were enjoying the weather" (Direct speech)

They said that they had been enjoying the weather. (Indirect speech)

He said to me, "I was waiting for you" (Direct speech)

He told me that he had been waiting for me. (Indirect speech)

Past Perfect changes into **Past Perfect (Tense does not change)**
Example: She said, "She had visited a doctor." (Direct speech)

She said that she had visited a doctor. (Indirect speech)

He said, "I had started a business." (Direct speech)

He said that he had started a business. (Indirect speech)

They said, "We had not gone to New York." (Direct speech)

They said they had not gone to New York. (Indirect speech)

Future Simple Tense
Will changes into would
Example: He said, "I will study the book." (Direct speech)

He said that he would study the book. (Indirect speech)

She said, "I will buy a computer." (Direct speech)

She said that she would buy a computer. (Indirect speech)

They said to me, "We will send you gifts." (Direct speech)

They said to me that they would send me gifts. (Indirect speech)

Future Continuous Tense
Will be changes into would be
Example: I said to him, "I will be waiting for him." (Direct speech)

I told him that I would be waiting for him. (Indirect speech)

He said, "I will be working hard." (Indirect speech)

He said that he would be working hard. (Indirect speech)

Future Perfect Tense
Will have changes into would have
Example: He said, "I will have finished the work." (Direct speech)

He said that he would have finished the work. (Indirect speech)

She said, "They will have passed the examination." (Direct speech)

She said that they would have passed the examination. (Indirect speech)

He said, "I will have gone." (Direct speech)

He said that he would have gone. (Indirect speech)

> **Note:**
> The tense of reported speech may not change if reported speech is a universal truth though its reporting verb is in past tense.

Example: He said, "Mathematics is a science." (Direct speech)

He said that mathematics is a science. (Indirect speech)

He said, "Sun rises in east." (Direct speech)

He said that sun rises in east. (Indirect speech)

Indirect Speech for Interrogative Sentence

For changing interrogative (question) sentence into indirect speech, we have to observe the nature of question and then change it into indirect speech according to the rules for indirect speech. A question can be of two types: Questions which can be answered in only yes or no and the questions which need a little bit explanation for its answer and cannot be answered in only yes or no.

Example: Do you like music? (It can be answered in yes or no)

How are you? (It cannot be answered in yes or no but it needs a little bit explanation, i.e, I am fine.)

Questions which can be answered in Yes/No

To change questions (which can be answered in yes or no) into indirect speech, word "if" or "whether" is used before the question in indirect speech. Rules for change in tense of question sentences are same as for change in normal tenses in indirect speech but sentence will not start with the auxiliary verb of the tense. The word "that" is not used between reporting verb and reported speech as conjunction in indirect speech for question sentence. Question mark is not used in indirect speech.

Example: He said to me, "Do you like music?" (Direct speech)

He asked me if I liked music. (Indirect Speech)

He asked me whether I liked music. (Indirect Speech)

She said, "Will he participate in the quiz competition?" (Direct speech)

She asked me if he would participate in the quiz competition. (Indirect Speech)

I said to him, "Are you feeling well?" (Direct speech)

I asked him if he was feeling well. (Indirect Speech)

Question which cannot be answered in Yes/No

To change such questions into indirect speech, the words "if" or "whether" is not used. The tense of the question is changed according to the rules for change in normal tenses in indirect speech but sentence will not start with the auxiliary verb of the tense. The word "that" is not used between reporting verb and reported speech as conjunction in indirect speech for question sentence. Question mark is not used in indirect speech.

Example: He said to me, "How are you?" (Direct speech)

He asked me how I was. (Indirect Speech)

She said to him, "Why did you come late?" (Direct speech)

She asked him why he had come late. (Indirect Speech)

She asked her son, "Why are you crying?" (Direct speech)

She asked her son why he was crying. (Indirect Speech)

Indirect Speech of Modals

☞ Can changes into could

Example: He said, "I can drive a car." (Direct speech)

He said that he could drive a car. (Indirect Speech)

She said, "He can play a violin." (Direct speech)

She said that he could play a violin. (Indirect Speech)

☞ May changes into might

Example: He said, "I may buy a computer." (Direct speech)

He said that he might buy a computer. (Indirect Speech)

She said, "He may visit a doctor." (Direct speech)

She said that he might visit a doctor. (Indirect Speech)

■ Must changes into had to

Example: She said, "They must carry on their work." (Direct Speech)

She said that they had to carry on their work. (Indirect Speech)

I said to him, "You must learn the test-taking strategies." (Direct Speech)

I said to him that he had to learn the test-taking strategies. (Indirect Speech)

Would → No change

Example: They said, "We would apply for a visa." (Direct Speech)

They said that they would apply for visa. (Indirect Speech)

He said, "I would start a business. (Direct Speech)

He said that he would start a business. (Indirect Speech)

She said, "I would appear in the exam." (Direct Speech)

She said that she would appear in the exam. (Indirect Speech)

Could → No change
Example: She said, "She could play a piano." (Direct Speech)

She said that she could play a piano. (Indirect Speech)

They said, "We couldn't learn the lesson." (Direct Speech)

They said they couldn't learn the lesson. (Indirect Speech)

He said, "I could run faster." (Direct Speech)

He said that he could run faster. (Indirect Speech)

Might → No change
Example: He said, "Guests might come." (Direct Speech)

He said that guest might come. (Indirect Speech)

She said, "It might rain." (Direct Speech)

She said that it might rain. (Indirect Speech)

John said, "I might meet him." (Direct Speech)

John said that he might meet him. (Indirect Speech)

Should → No change
Example: He said, "I should avail the opportunity." (Direct Speech)

He said that he should avail the opportunity. (Indirect Speech)

She said, "I should help him." (Direct Speech)

She said that she should help him. (Indirect Speech)

They said, "We should take the exam." (Direct Speech)

They said that they should take the exam. (Indirect Speech)

Ought to → No change
Example: He said to me, "You ought to wait for him." (Direct Speech)

He said to me that I ought to wait for him. (Indirect Speech)

She said, "I ought to learn method of study." (Direct Speech)

She said that she ought to learn method of study. (Indirect Speech)

They said, "We ought to attend our classes." (Direct Speech)

They said that they ought to attend their classes. (Indirect Speech)

Indirect Speech of Imperative Sentences

A sentence which expresses command, request, advice or suggestion is called imperative sentence.

Example: Open the door.

Please help me.

Learn your lesson.

- To change such sentences into indirect speech, the word "ordered" or "requested" or "advised" or "suggested" or "forbade" or "not to do" is added to reporting verb depending upon nature of imperative sentence in reported speech.

    Example: He said to me, "Please help me." (Direct Speech)

    He requested me to help him. (Indirect Speech)

    She said to him, "You should work hard for exam" (Direct Speech)

    She suggested him to work hard for exam. (Indirect Speech)

    They said to him, "Do not tell a lie" (Direct Speech)

    They said to him not to tell a lie. (Indirect Speech)

    He said, "Open the door." (Direct Speech)

    He ordered to open the door. (Indirect Speech)

    The teacher said to student, "Do not waste time." (Direct Speech)

    The teacher advised the students not to waste time. (Indirect Speech)

    He said, "Please give me a glass of water." (Direct Speech)

    He requested to give him a glass of water. (Indirect Speech)

    Doctor said to me, "Do not smoke." (Direct Speech)

    Doctor advised me not to smoke. (Indirect Speech)

The teacher said to him, "Get out." (Direct Speech)
The teacher ordered him to get out. (Indirect Speech)

Indirect Speech of Exclamatory Sentences

Sentence which expresses state of joy or sorrow or wonder is called exclamatory sentence.
Example: Hurrah! We won the match.
Alas! I failed the test.
Wow! What a nice shirt it is.

- To change such sentences, the words "exclaimed with joy" or "exclaimed with sorrow" or "exclaimed with wonder" is added in the reporting verb depending upon the nature of exclamatory sentence in indirect speech.

  Example: He said, "Hurrah! I won a prize." (Direct Speech)
  He exclaimed with joy that he had won a prize. (Indirect Speech)
  She said, "Alas! I failed in the exam." (Direct Speech)
  She exclaimed with sorrow that she failed in the exam. (Indirect Speech)
  John said, "Wow! What a nice shirt it is." (Direct Speech)
  John exclaimed with wonder that it was a nice shirt. (Indirect Speech)
  She said, "Hurrah! I am selected for the job." (Direct Speech)
  She exclaimed with joy that she was selected for the job. (Indirect Speech)
  He said, "Oh no! I missed the train." (Direct Speech)
  He exclaimed with sorrow that he had missed the train. (Indirect Speech)
  They said, "Wow! What a pleasant weather it is." (Direct Speech)
  They exclaimed with wonder that it was a pleasant weather. (Indirect Speech)

Changes in Pronoun in Indirect Speech

The pronoun (subject) of the reported speech is changed according to the pronoun of reporting verb or object (person) of reporting verb (first part of sentence). Sometimes the pronoun may not change.

- First person pronoun in reported speech i.e. I, we, me, us, mine, or our is changed according to the pronoun of reporting verb if pronoun in reporting verb is third person pronoun i.e. he, she, it, they, him, his, her, them or their.

  Example: He said, "I live in New York." (Direct Speech)
  He said that he lived in New York. (Indirect Speech)
  They said, "We love our country." (Direct Speech)
  They said that they loved their country. (Indirect Speech)

- First person pronoun in reported speech i.e. I, we, me, us, mine, or our is not changed if the pronoun (Subject) of reporting is also first person pronoun i.e. I or we.

  Example: I said, "I write a letter" (Direct Speech)
  I said that I wrote a letter. (Indirect Speech)
  We said, "We completed our work" (Direct Speech)
  We said that we completed our work. (Indirect Speech)

- Second person pronoun in reported speech i.e. you, yours is changed according to the person of object of reporting verb.

  Example: She said to him, "You are intelligent." (Direct Speech)
  She said to him that he was intelligent. (Indirect Speech)
  He said to me, "You are late for the party." (Direct Speech)
  He said to me that I was late for the party. (Indirect Speech)

- Third person pronoun in reported speech i.e. he, she, it, they, him, his, her, them or their is not changed in indirect speech.

  Example: Direct speech: They said, "He will come." (Direct Speech)
  Indirect speech: They said that he would come. (Indirect Speech)
  Direct speech: You said, "They are waiting for the bus." (Direct Speech)
  Indirect speech: You said that they were waiting for the bus. (Indirect Speech)

Changes in Time and Adverbs in Indirect Speech

- Today → that day/the same day
- Tomorrow → the next day/the following day

- Yesterday → the day before/the previous day
- Next week/month/year → the following week/month/year
- Last week/month/year → the previous week/month/year
- Now/just → then
- Ago → before
- Here → there
- This → that

Example: He said, "I will buy a book tomorrow." (Direct Speech)

He said that he would buy a book the next day. (Indirect Speech)

She said, "I am happy now." (Direct Speech)

She said that she was happy then. (Indirect Speech)

He said, "I like this book." (Direct Speech)

He said that he liked that book. (Indirect Speech)

Vocabulary

Free Time Activities

- Read books: Many people love to read both fiction and non-fiction books and magazines. If you like fiction, you can read novels, short stories, crime fiction, romance. If you like non-fiction, you can read biographies, autobiographies, or books on history, science, philosophy, religion, or any other topic you are interested in.
- Write notes: Many people like to write in their diary. Another name for a diary is a journal. You can also write poetry, novels, letters, short stories.
- Go to the park: You can go to the park alone, with family or with friends. You can take a picnic rug and a picnic basket and have a picnic. You can read, sleep, kick a football around, play on the children's playground.
- Go to cultural locations and events: You can go to the museum, to an art gallery or to the zoo to see animals from around the world. You can go to concerts, plays, musicals, dance recitals and opera performances.
- Go shopping: Many people like to go to shopping malls and the areas known for shopping to buy clothes or items for their houses and gardens.
- Cook the food: Many people like to cook different types of food. You can make meals for breakfast, lunch and dinner. You can bake cakes, cookies, slices and pastries in the oven.
- Learn a skill: You can study a language; such as cooking or making furniture.
- Make art and crafts: You can paint, draw, sew, crochet, knit, sculpt, engrave, make furniture, make jewelry, or you can even create your own new art form.
- Do gardening: You can plant trees and grow vegetables or herbs and pull the weeds and feed the plants with fertilizer.
- Exercise and play a sport: To stay fit and healthy, you can do exercise such as swimming or working out at a gym, or you can play a team sport such as football or basketball.
- Go to the cinema: You can watch Hollywood blockbuster movies, Bollywood movies (from India), art films, animated films. Some categories of film are: Comedy, Drama, Horror, Thriller, Action, Science Fiction (Sci-Fi), Fantasy, Documentary, Musical.
- Watch TV: Different types of television programs are: The News, Soap Operas, Criminal Investigation Dramas, Medical Dramas, Reality TV, Situation Comedies (Sit-Coms), Talk Shows, Documentaries, Cartoons, Game Shows, Sports programs, Movies, Political programs, Religious programs.
- Spend time with family: You can spend time with your family. Usually, the fact that you are together is more important than any activity.
- Go out with afriends: You can go out to a bar, go to a dancing club, have dinner at a restaurant, play a sport, sit down and talk, go out for a coffee, have a barbeque, or any other activity that you all enjoy.
- Surf the internet: On the internet, you can research a topic you are interested in using a search engine, visit your favourite websites, watch music videos, create your own video and upload it for other people to see, maintain contact with your friends using a social networking site, write your

thoughts in a blog, learn what is happening in the world by reading news websites, etc.
- Play video games: You can play games on your computer or on game consoles, like Play Station, X-Box, Wii, PSP, Gameboy. You can play on your own or with your friends or family.
- Play a musical instrument: Learn to play the piano, guitar, violin, cello, flute, piano accordion, mouth organ, panpipes, clarinet, saxophone, trumpet. You can play on your own or with a group, such as a band or an orchestra.
- Listen to music: Turn up the volume and listen to your favourite type of music such as, pop, rock, hip hop, rhythm and blues, jazz, classical, soul, heavy metal.

Furniture and Household Items
Furniture
armchair
Bed
Bedside table
Bookcase
Bookshelf
Chair
Chest of drawers
Clock
Coat stand
Coffee table
Cupboard
Desk
Double bed
Dressing table
Drinks cabinet
Filing cabinet
Mirror
Piano
Sideboard
Single bed
Sofa
Sofa-bed
Stool
Table
Wardrobe

Household Appliances
Alarm clock
Bathroom scales
Blu-ray player
CD player
DVD player
Electric fire
Games console
Gas fire
Hoover or vacuum cleaner
Iron
Lamp
Radiator
Radio
Record player
Spin dryer
Stereo
Telephone
TV (abbreviation for television)
Washing machine

Soft Furnishings
Blanket
Blinds
Carpet
Curtains
Cushion
Duvet
Mattress
Pillow
Pillowcase
Rug
Sheet
Tablecloth
Towel
Wallpaper

Household Things
Bath
Bin
Broom
Bucket
Coat hanger
Cold tap
Door handle
Door knob
Doormat
Dustbin

Voices and Narration

Dustpan and brush
Flannel
Fuse box
Hot tap
Houseplant
Ironing board
Lampshade
Light switch
Mop
Ornament
Painting
Picture
Plug
Plug socket or power socket
Plughole
Poster
Sponge
Tap
Torch
Vase
Waste paper basket

Places

The words below are the most important words used when talking about different places and areas such as shops, towns and the countryside.

Buildings
- Apartment
- Block
- Apartment block
- Block of flats (British English)
- Bungalow
- Cottage
- Duplex (American English)
- Flat (British English)
- Floor on the ground / first / top floor
- House
- Detached house (British English)
- Semi-detached house (British English)
- Terraced house
- Story - ten / multi-story building (British English storey)

Common Buildings
- Bar (American English)
- Car park
- Castle
- Cathedral
- Church
- Office
- Office block
- Park
- Post office
- Pub
- Restaurant
- Skyscraper
- Station
- Bus station
- Fire station
- Police station
- Railway station
- Town hall

Stores and Shops
- Baker's
- Butcher's
- Department store
- Dry cleaner's
- Fishmonger's (British English)
- Fish-shop
- Greengrocer's
- Grocer's
- Ironmonger's (British English)
- Hardware store (American English)
- Shop
- Shopping mall (American English)
- Stationer's
- Sweetshop (British English)
- Tobacconist's (British English)

Communities
- City
- Capital city
- Port
- Resort
- Holiday resort
- Seaside resort
- Ski resort
- Town
- Village

Parts and Areas of Communities
- Area
- Country area
- Residential area
- Rural area
- Urban area
- Center
- City center
- Town center
- District
- Outskirts
- Region
- Suburb

Geographical Features
- Bay
- Beach
- Cliff
- Coast
- On the coast
- Countryside
- Flat (adj)
- Forest
- Hill
- Hilly (adj)
- Lake
- Mountain
- Mountainous (adj)
- Plain (n)
- River
- Sea
- Seaside
- Shore
- Stream (n)
- Valley
- Wood
- Woody/wooded (adj)

Sports
Common Sports
- Archery
- Badminton
- Cricket
- Cycling
- Darts
- Football
- Golf
- Horse Racing
- Snooker
- Squash
- Table
- Tennis

Contact Sports
- Boxing
- Judo
- Rugby
- Wrestling
- Water Sports

Water Sports
- Angling/Fishing
- Canoeing
- Kayaking
- Rowing
- Sailing
- Water Skiing

Ice Sports
- Curling
- Ice Skating
- Skiing

Less Usual Sports
- Croquet
- Fencing
- Hockey
- Lacrosse
- Polo
- Hunting/Skeet/Shooting

How to play sports?

Badminton
A racquet sport played by either two players (singles) or two pairs (doubles). Played on a court divided by a net with racquets and a shuttlecock.

Cricket
A teamgame, usually played outdoors, on a cricket pitch, with a bat, a cricket ball, and stumps. There are 11 players in each team. Gloves, Thigh pads and helmet are also required.

Darts
Darts is a game played by two players. Darts are thrown at a dart board. You earn points based on where dart lands.

Voices and Narration

Football (Footy)
A team sport, usually played outdoors, on a football pitch, with a round football, a goal, with two teams of 11 players, and a goal keeper (goalie). Lionel Messi, Sunil Chettri and Christiano Ronaldo are some footballers. Americans insist on calling it soccer.

Golf
Usually played by individuals, golf is played on a golf course, using several types of golf clubs and a golf ball. You play a round of golf.

Rugby
A team sport, played outdoors, on a rugby pitch, with an oval rugby ball, and two teams of 15 players. You play a rugby match.

Tennis
A racquet sport played by either two players (singles) or two pairs (doubles). Played on a court divided by a net with racquets and a tennis ball. Serena Williams and Sania Mirza are popular tennis players.

Word Bank
A
Airfare
Airplane
Airport
Amusement park
Automobile
B
Backpack
Baggage
Bags
Bathing suit
Beach
Bicycle
Bike
Binoculars
Boat
Bus
C
Cab
Cabin
Camera
Campground
Camping
Car
Carry-on
Chart
Coast
Cruise
Cruise ship
Currency
Customs
D
Depart
Departure
Destination
Downtime
Drive
E
Embark
Excursion
Expedition
Explore
F
Ferry
Flew
Flight
Fly
Foreign
Foreigner
G
Garment bag
Getaway
Go
Guide
Guided tour
H
Hiatus
Highway
Hike
Holiday
Hostel
Hotel
I
Inn
Island
Itinerary
J
Jet
Journey
K
Keepsake
Knapsack
L
Lake
Landing
Leave
Leisure
Lodge

Lodging
Luggage
M
Map
Motel
Mountains
Museum
N
National park
O
Ocean liner
Outdoors
Overnight bag
P
Pack
Passage
Passport
Photos
Photographs
Pictures
Plane
Port
Postcard
R
Recreation
Red-eye
Relax
Relaxation
Reservations
Resort
Rest
Restaurant
Return
Room
S
Sack
Safari
Sail
Scenery
Schedule
Sea
Seashore
Ship
Shore
Sights
Sight-seeing
Ski lodge
Souvenir
Stand-by
State park
Station

Stay
Subway
Suitcase
Sunscreen
Swim
Swimsuit
T
Takeoff
Taxi
Tent
Ticket
Tip
Tote
Tour
Tour bus
Tour guide
Tourist
Tourist trap
Trail
Train
Train station
Tram
Tramway
Translate
Transportation
Travel
Travel agent
Travel bag
Trip
Trunk
U
Umbrella
Unpack
V
Vacation
Vehicle
Video
Video camera
Visa
Visit
Voyage
W
Walk
Wander
Waterfall
Waterpark
Weekend
Y
Yacht
Z
Zoo

Voices and Narration

MUST REMEMBER

- Voice is the form of verb which expresses whether the person or thing denoted by the subject does something or something is done to it.
- In 'active voice,' subject acts upon object, while in 'passive voice' object is acted upon by subject.
- The real meaning of a sentence does not change if the sentence is expressed either by active voice or by passive voice.
- Subject of sentence can be omitted in passive voice, if without subject it can give enough meaning in passive voice.
- To change sentences having past modal into passive voice, auxiliary verb "been" is added after modal in sentence.
- A transitive verb needs an object (in sentence) to give complete meaning while intransitive verb does not need an object (in sentence) to give complete meaning.
- Intransitive verb cannot be changed into passive voice.
- A sentence can be changed into passive voice if it has a subject and an object.
- Narration is the manner in which the words of speaker are expressed.
- Indirect speech is also called reported speech because reported speech refers to the second part of indirect speech in which something has been told by a person.
- The verb first part of sentence before the statement of a person in sentence is called reporting verb.
- The second part of indirect speech in which something has been told by a person is called reported speech.
- A sentence which expresses command, request, advice or suggestion is called imperative sentence.
- Sentence which expresses state of joy or sorrow or wonder is called exclamatory sentence.
- The pronoun (subject) of the reported speech is changed according to the pronoun of reporting verb or object (person) of reporting verb (first part of sentence).

PRACTICE EXERCISE

I. Fill in the blanks with suitable active and passive form of verb.

1. This house _____ in 1970 by my grandfather.
   (a) built
   (b) was built
   (c) was build
   (d) has built

2. The robbers _____ by the police.
   (a) have arrested
   (b) have been arrested
   (c) was arrested
   (d) had arrested

3. We _____ for the examination.
   (a) have preparing
   (b) are preparing
   (c) had preparing
   (d) have been prepared

4. It _____ since yesterday.
   (a) is raining
   (b) has been raining
   (c) have been raining
   (d) was raining

5. I _____ for five hours.
   (a) have been working
   (b) has been working
   (c) was working
   (d) am working

6. The students _____ to submit their reports by the end of this week.
   (a) have asked
   (b) are asked
   (c) has asked
   (d) are asking

7. She _____ for a while.
   (a) are ailing
   (b) is ailing
   (c) has been ailing
   (d) have been ailing

8. The teacher _____ the student for lying.
   (a) has been punished
   (b) punished
   (c) is punished
   (d) was punished

9. I _____ to become a successful writer.
   (a) have always wanted
   (b) am always wanted
   (c) was always wanted
   (d) am always wanting

10. The inmates of the juvenile home _____ well by their caretakers.
    (a) were not being treated
    (b) were not treating
    (c) have not being treated
    (d) was not being treated

II. From the given alternatives, choose the one which best expresses the given sentence in Passive/Active voice.

1. They have built a perfect dam across the river.
   (a) Across the river a perfect dam was built.
   (b) A perfect dam has been built across the river by them.
   (c) A perfect dam should have been built by them.
   (d) Across the river was a perfect dam.

2. Do you imitate others?
   (a) Are others being imitated by you?
   (b) Are others imitated by you?
   (c) Have others being imitated by you?
   (d) Were others being imitated by you?

3. You need to clean your shoes properly.
   (a) Your shoes are needed to clean properly.
   (b) You are needed to clean your shoes properly.
   (c) Your shoes need to be cleaned properly by you.
   (d) Your shoes are needed by you to clean properly.

Voices and Narration

4. He is said to be very rich.
   (a) He said he is very rich.
   (b) People say he is very rich.
   (c) He said it is very rich.
   (d) People say it is very rich.
5. The invigilator was reading out the instructions.
   (a) The instructions were read by the invigilator.
   (b) The instructions were being read out by the invigilator.
   (c) The instructions had been read out by the invigilator.
   (d) The instructions had been read by the invigilator.

III. Choose the correct option to fill in the blanks.

1. Over a million dollars in cash _____ from the Bank of East Asia in Central.
   (a) have stolen
   (b) have been stolen
   (c) had stolen
   (d) been stolen
2. Thieves _____ over a million dollars in cash from the Bank of East Asia in Central.
   (a) stolen
   (b) were stolen
   (c) have stolen
   (d) was been stolen
3. I'll have to come by bus as my car _____ .
   (a) is repairing
   (b) is being repaired
   (c) repaired
   (d) been repaired
4. The gold _____ in a cave near the top of the mountain.
   (a) was discovered
   (b) discovered
   (c) been discovered
   (b) had discovered
5. Archaeologists _____ the gold in a cave near the top of the mountain.
   (a) were discovered
   (b) was discovered
   (c) discovered
   (d) none of these
6. The meeting _____ until the end of the month.
   (a) has postponed
   (b) has been postponed
   (c) is been postponed
   (d) none of these
7. We have _____ the meeting until the end of the month.
   (a) been postponed
   (b) postponed
   (c) had postponed
   (d) being postponed
8. VW cars _____ in Germany and the Czech Republic.
   (a) making
   (b) made
   (c) are made
   (d) make
9. In Hong Kong, many shops _____ at around nine in the morning.
   (a) open
   (b) are opened
   (c) opened
   (d) being opened
10. Your letter _____ yesterday morning.
    (a) was arrived
    (b) has arrived
    (c) arrived
    (d) none of these
11. Helmets must _____ past this point.
    (a) wear
    (b) are worn
    (c) be worn
    (d) none of these
12. Any vehicles found parked in front of these gates will _____ .
    (a) removing
    (b) remove
    (c) be removed
    (d) are removed
13. We will _____ any vehicles found parked in front of these gates.
    (a) removing
    (b) be removed
    (c) remove
    (d) have removed

14. A number of people _____ following a demonstration in the Serbian capital, Belgrade.
    (a) have arrested
    (b) have been arrested
    (c) arrested
    (d) being arrested

15. Police _____ a number of people following a demonstration in the Serbian capital, Belgrade.
    (a) have arrested
    (b) have been arrested
    (c) arresting
    (d) been arrested

16. It _____ that the painting is fake.
    (a) is now believed   (b) believed now
    (c) is believing   (d) none of these

17. Experts _____ that the painting is fake.
    (a) now believe   (b) is now believed

18. It _____ if you could reply as soon as possible.
    (a) appreciate
    (b) is appreciated
    (c) would be appreciated
    (d) noneo of these

19. I would very much _____ it if you could reply as soon as possible.
    (a) be appreciated   (b) appreciate
    (c) being appreciate (d) been appreciate

20. All bills must _____ promptly.
    (a) settle   (b) be settled
    (c) settled   (d) being settled

IV. **Choose the correct option from the choices given below.**

1. Mary "I love chocolate."
   Jill: "Mary said (that) she ___ chocolate."
   (a) loved
   (b) loves
   (c) loving
   (d) none of these

2. Mary: "I went skiing."
   Jill: "Mary said (that) she ___ skiing."
   (a) went   (b) had gone
   (c) have gone   (d) none of these

3. Mary: "I will eat steak for dinner."
   Jill: "Mary said (that) she ___ eat steak for dinner."
   (a) willing   (b) will
   (c) would   (d) none of these

4. Mary: "I have been to Sydney."
   Jill: "Mary said (that) she ___ to Sydney."
   (a) had been   (b) has been
   (c) was being   (d) none of these

5. Mary: "I have had three cars."
   Jill: "Mary said (that) she ___ three cars."
   (a) has   (b) has had
   (c) had had   (d) none of these

6. Mary: "I'm going to go to Long Beach."
   Jill: "Mary said (that) she ___ going to go to Long Beach."
   (a) is   (b) was
   (c) went   (d) none of these

7. Mary: "I don't like spinach."
   Jill: "Mary said (that) she ___ like spinach."
   (a) doesn't   (b) don't
   (c) didn't   (d) none of these

8. Mary: "I have never been to London."
   Jill: "Mary said (that) she ___ never been to London."
   (a) had   (b) has
   (c) have   (d) none of these

9. Mary: "I was swimming."
   Jill: "Mary said (that) she ___ swimming."
   (a) has been   (b) had been
   (c) have been   (d) none of these

10. Mary: "I had a cat."
    Jill: "Mary said (that) she had ___ a cat."
    (a) have
    (b) has
    (c) had
    (d) none of these

Voices and Narration

V. Select the most appropriate option to fill in the blanks.

1. I told him ____ do it.
   (a) to not
   (b) to don't
   (c) not to
   (d) don't

2. He asked us ____ show our passports.
   (a) if
   (b) to
   (c) for
   (d) that

3. She asked us if we ____ finished the work on Monday.
   (a) have
   (b) had
   (c) either could be used here
   (d) none of these

4. She asked us ____ on time.
   (a) to be
   (b) for being
   (c) been
   (d) being

5. She asked if she ____ leave early.
   (a) can
   (b) could
   (c) may
   (d) must

6. They asked me ____ going to the party.
   (a) that I was
   (b) if I was
   (c) that they were
   (d) if I had

7. He told me ____ my father.
   (a) phone
   (b) to phone
   (c) phoned
   (d) to be phoned

8. She said that no one ____ to the meeting last week.
   (a) has come
   (b) had come
   (c) have come
   (d) had been come

9. She told me ____ she wasn't going to come.
   (a) that
   (b) if
   (c) either could be used here
   (d) none of these

10. He asked me what I ____ if I failed to get the job.
    (a) would do
    (b) would have done
    (c) done
    (d) would done

11. He told me he ____ be here by three o'clock at the latest and it's half past already.
    (a) will
    (b) would
    (c) either could be used here
    (d) None of these

12. She promised she ____ do it by the end of the week and then let me down.
    (a) will
    (b) would
    (c) either could be used here
    (d) None of these

13. She said it ____ raining when she got here.
    (a) already started
    (b) had already started
    (c) either could be used here
    (d) None of these

14. She explained how ____ do it.
    (a) to
    (b) I should
    (c) either (a) or (b)
    (d) none of these

15. He said he ____ her before.
    (a) didn't meet
    (b) hadn't met
    (c) either (a) or (b)
    (d) none of these

HOTS

I. **Choose the option which best expresses the given sentence in Indirect/Direct speech.**

1. The boy said, "Who dare call you a thief?"
    (a) The boy enquired who dared call him a thief.
    (b) The boy asked who called him a thief.
    (c) The boy told that who dared call him a thief.
    (d) The boy wondered who dared call a thief.

2. She exclaimed with sorrow that it was a very miserable plight.
    (a) She said with sorrow, "What a pity it is."
    (b) She said, "What a mystery it is."
    (c) She said, "What a miserable sight it is."
    (d) She said, "What a miserable plight it is."

3. Dhruv said that he was sick and tired of working for that company.
    (a) Dhruv said, "I am sick and tired of working for this company."
    (b) Dhruv said, "He was tired of that company."
    (c) Dhruv said to me, "I am sick and tired of working for this company."
    (d) Dhruv said, "I will be tired of working for that company."

4. "Are you alone, my son?" asked a soft voice close behind me.
    (a) A soft voice asked that what I was doing there alone.
    (b) A soft voice said to me are you alone son.
    (c) A soft voice from my back asked if I was alone.
    (d) A soft voice behind me asked if I was alone.

5. She said to him, "Why don't you go today?"
    (a) She asked him why he did not go that day.
    (b) She said to him why he don't go that day.
    (c) She asked him not to go that day.
    (d) She asked him why he did not go today.

6. He exclaimed with joy that India had won the Sahara Cup.
    (a) He said, "India has won the Sahara Cup"
    (b) He said, "India won the Sahara Cup"
    (c) He said, "How! India will win the Sahara Cup"
    (d) He said, "Hurrah! India has won the Sahara Cup"

7. The little girl said to her mother, "Did the sun rise in the East?"
    (a) The little girl said to her mother that the sun rose in the East.
    (b) The little girl asked her mother if the sun rose in the East.
    (c) The little girl said to her mother if the sun rises in the East.
    (d) The little girl asked her mother if the sun is in the East.

8. The man said, "No, I refuse to confess guilt."
    (a) The man emphatically refused to confess guilt.
    (b) The man refused to confess his guilt.
    (c) The man told that he did not confess guilt.
    (d) The man was stubborn enough to confess guilt.

9. Nita ordered her servant to bring her a cup of tea.
    (a) Nita told her servant, "Bring a cup of tea."
    (b) Nita said, "Bring me a cup of tea."
    (c) Nita said to her servant, "Bring me a cup of tea."
    (d) Nita told her servant, "Bring her that cup of tea."

10. My cousin said, "My room-mate had snored throughout the night."

Voices and Narration

(a) My cousin said that her room-mate had snored throughout the night.
(b) My cousin told me that her room-mate snored throughout the night.
(c) My cousin complained to me that her room-mate is snoring throughout the night.
(d) My cousin felt that her room-mate may be snoring throughout the night.

11. "Please don't go away", she said.
(a) She said to please her and not go away.
(b) She told me to go away.
(c) She requested me not to go away.
(d) She begged that I not go away.

12. She said to her friend, "I know where is everyone"
(a) She told that she knew where was everyone.
(b) She told her friend that she knew where everyone was.
(c) She told her friend that she knew where is everyone.
(d) She told her friend that she knows where was everyone.

II. Select the best option to fill in the blanks.

1. Carla: "I have to do my laundry."
George: "Carla said (that) she _____ to do her laundry."
(a) had   (b) has
(c) have   (d) none of these

2. The girl said, 'It gives me great pleasure to be here this evening.'
The girl said that it _____ her great pleasure to be there that evening.
(a) gave   (b) gives
(c) has given   (d) none of these

3. The man said, 'I must go as soon as possible.'
The man said that he _____ go as soon as possible.
(a) should   (b) will
(c) must   (d) none of these

III. Change the following active voice sentences into passive voice.

1. They have informed him of his mother's death.
2. They took all the necessary precautions.
3. Have you finished your job?
4. Help him.
5. I will finish the job by the end of this week.

IV. In the following questions, arrange P, Q, R, S in order to describe the completeness of process.

1. P: The mode of conveyance is decided. Then, the expenses are worked out and contributions are made.

Q: Some friends get together and decide to arrange a picnic. First of all, the day is fixed, according to their convenience.

R: Then, the picnic spot is chosen. It is usually in the lap of nature, far away from the noise and away from the city. After that duties are assigned.

S: Time and place of departure are also settled. On the appointed day they assemble at the fixed place and set out for the picnic.
(a) QRPS   (b) QPRS
(c) QRSP   (d) PQRS

2. P: Every year hundreds of people are killed in road accidents because they do not observe rules of the road.

Q: Most of them are pedestrians who are crushed under some vehicle while crossing a busy street.

R: While crossing a busy road, one should look for the traffic signal, and cross the road only when the sign says 'Go'.

S: If there is no arrangement of signed lights on the road, one should look to the right, then to the left, and again to the right before crossing the road. In case the road is not clear one should wait.
(a) QRPS   (b) QPRS
(c) QRSP   (d) PQRS

3. P: Now, look at the column of mercury to make sure that it stands a few degrees below the normal mark. If it is not, shake the thermometer to bring the column of mercury down.

Q: To use a clinical thermometer, first remove the thermometer carefully from its case.

R: Thereafter, place the bulb of the thermometer inside the patient's mouth below the tongue. Take care that the patient keeps his mouth shut. After about three minutes, remove the thermometer from his mouth and read the temperature.

S: Before you put the thermometer back in its case, don't forget to shake down the column of mercury and clean the thermometer with methylated spirit. If there is no methylated spirit simply wash the thermometer with water and wipe it.

(a) QRPS (b) QPRS
(c) QRSP (d) PQRS

4. P: He will issue you a receipt for the amount received with the post office date-stamp.

Q: To send a money order you should first get a money order form from the post-office. It costs ten paise only. Now you should fill it up very carefully.

R: You should write the amount to be sent in words as well as in figures on the lines provided for it. The address of the payee and your own address should be written very carefully. There is a little space for writing the message and you can use it if you wish.

S: You should also put your signature and date at the place meant for it. Now you should give the completed form and the money, including M.O. commission to the M.O. clerk at the post office.

(a) QRPS (b) QPRS
(c) QRSP (d) PQRS

5. P: The woman thought about God holding us in such a hot spot, then she thought again about the verse that says: "He will sit as a refiner and purifier of silver." She asked the silversmith if it was true that he had to sit there in front of the fire the whole time the silver was being refined.

Q: The man answered that yes, he not only had to sit there holding the silver, but he had to keep his eyes on the silver the entire time it was in the fire. If the silver was left a moment too long in the flames, it would be destroyed. The woman was silent for a moment. Then she asked the silversmith, "How do you know when the silver is fully refined?" He smiled at her and answered, "Oh, that's easy - when I see my image in it."

R: As they were studying chapter three, they came across verse three, which says: "He will sit as a refiner and purifier of silver." This verse puzzled the women and they wondered what this statement meant about the character and nature of God. One of the women offered to find out the process of refining silver and get back to the group at their next Bible Study. That week, this woman called up a silversmith and made an appointment to watch him at work She didn't mention anything about the reason for her interest, beyond her curiosity about the process of refining silver.

S: As she watched the silversmith, he held a piece of silver- over the fire and let it heat up. He explained that in refining silver, one needed to hold the silver in the middle of the fire where the flames were hottest as to burn away all the impurities.

Select your answer from the given choices:

(a) PRSQ (b) RQPS
(c) RSPQ (d) SRQP

Voices and Narration

SECTION 2
READING COMPREHENSION

Reading Comprehension

Reading comprehension is the ability to read a text, process it and understand its meaning. An individual's ability to comprehend text is influenced by their traits and skills, one of which is the ability to make inferences. If word recognition is difficult, students use too much of their processing capacity to read individual words, which interferes with their ability to comprehend what is read. There are a number of approaches to improve reading comprehension, including improving one's vocabulary and reading strategies.

Comprehension is the act of or capacity of grasping with the intellect. It is the last step of the reading process taught to children, after they've learned phonics, fluency, and vocabulary. The term is most often used in connection with tests of reading skills and language abilities, though other abilities (e.g. mathematical reasoning) may also be examined.

Types of Reading Comprehension

There are five types of reading comprehension:

(i) Lexical Comprehension
(ii) Literal Comprehension
(iii) Interpretive Comprehension
(iv) Applied Comprehension
(v) Affective Comprehension

To really understand these different levels, let's take a familiar text and see how different types of questions probe different understandings of the same story.

The fairy tale Cinderella tells the story of a young girl, whose evil stepmother won't let her go to the ball. Cinderella's fairy godmother, however, magically whisks her off for the night and Cinderella eventually marries her Prince Charming.

5 Types of Reading Comprehension

Lexical Comprehension
Understand key vocabulary in the text

> Preview vocabulary before reading the story or text.
> Review new vocabulary during or after the text.
> **Example: Lexical Compression Question:**
> What does 'enchanted' mean?
> What words are most like 'enchanted': Magical of funny? Scary or special?

Literal Comprehension
Answer Who, What, When, and Where questions

> Look in the text to find the answers in the story.
> Ask questions from the beginning, middle, and end of the story.
> **Example: Literal Comprehension Questions:**
> Who was the girl who lost the glass slipper?
> Where did Cinderella go to live at the end of the story?

Interpretive Comprehension
Answer What if, Why, and How questions

> Understand 'facts' that are not explicitly stated in the story.
> Illustrations may help to infer meaning.
> **Example: Interpretive Comprehension Questions:**
> How did the pumpkin turn into a carriage?
> What would have happened to Cinderella if she hadn't lost her slipper?

Applied Comprehension
Relate story to existing knowledge or opinion

> Not a simple question that can be marked right or wrong.
> Challenge children to support their answer with logic or reason.
> **Example: Applied Comprehension Question:**
> Do you think Cinderella was wrong for going to the ball after her stepmother told her she couldn't go?

Affective Comprehension
Understand social and emotional aspect

> Preview social scripts to ensure understanding of plot development.
> Connect motive to plot and character development.
> **Example: Applied Comprehension Question:**
> What do you do when you're disappointed because you cannot do something fun? Is that how Cinderella reacted?

Comprehension Strategies

⇒ **Make Connections:** Readers connect the topic or information to what they already know about themselves, about other texts, and about the world.

⇒ **Ask Questions:** Readers ask themselves questions about the text, their reactions to it, and the author's purpose for writing it.

⇒ **Visualize:** Readers make the printed word real and concrete by creating a 'movie' of the text in their minds.

⇒ **Determine Text Importance:** Readers
  (a) distinguish between what's essential versus what's interesting
  (b) distinguish between fact and opinion
  (c) determine cause-and-effect relationship
  (d) compare and contrast ideas or information
  (e) discern themes, opinions, or perspectives
  (f) pinpoint problems and solutions
  (g) name steps in a process
  (h) locate information that answers specific questions
  (i) summarize

⇒ **Make Inferences:** Readers merge text clues with their prior knowledge and determine answers to questions that lead to conclusions about underlying themes or ideas.

⇒ **Synthesize:** Readers combine new information with existing knowledge to form original ideas, new lines of thinking, or new creations.

Note:
Students quickly grasp how to make connections, ask questions, and visualize. However, they often struggle with the way to identify what is most important in the text, identify clues and evidence to make inferences, and combine information into new thoughts. All these strategies should be modelled in isolation many times so that students get a firm grasp of what the strategy is and how it helps them comprehend text.

However, students must understand that good readers use a variety of these strategies every time they read. Simply knowing the individual strategies is not enough, nor is it enough to know them in isolation. Students must know when and how to collectively use these strategies.

Tips to Improve Reading Comprehension Skills

There are many ways to conduct think-alouds:
- The teacher models the think-aloud while she reads aloud, and the students listen.
- The teacher thinks aloud during shared reading, and the students help out.
- Students think aloud during shared reading, and the teacher and other students monitor and help.
- The teacher or students think aloud during shared reading while writing on an overhead, on self-stick notes, or in a journal.
- Students think aloud in small-group reading, and the teacher monitors and helps.
- Students individually think aloud during independent reading using self-stick notes or a journal. Then students compare their thoughts with others.

When you introduce a new comprehension strategy, model during read-aloud and shared reading:

- Decide on a strategy to model.
- Choose a short text or section of text.
- Read the text ahead of time. Mark locations where you will stop and model the strategy.
- State your purpose—name the strategy and explain the focus of your think-alouds.
- Read the text aloud to students and think aloud at the designated points.
- If you conduct a shared reading experience, have students highlight words and phrases that show evidence of your thinking by placing self-stick notes in the book.
- Reinforce the think-alouds with follow-up lessons in the same text or with others.

SOLVED PASSAGE–1

I. Read the passage below and answer the following questions.

If the 1950s was a sparse period for Black poetry, the 1960s more than compensated for it; during the 1960s, Black poets appeared all over the United States. By the end of the decade not only had poetic giants such as Melvin Tolson, LeRoi Jones, Gwendolyn Brooks, Robert Hayden, and Langston Hughes reappeared with new volumes of poetry, but also at least five anthologies of Black poetry were published. Some of the new Black poets made their debuts in the anthologies. Others were first published in Harlem's new avant-garde literary publication, Umbra. As the decade drew to a close, the "Broadside Press" poets appeared through Dudley Randall's series of Broadside Press editions and in Hoyt Fuller's Negro Digest, which was later known as Black World. These poets brought with them new poetic concepts, a new aesthetic, and a strong awareness of the Black ghetto experience.

Like the spirituals and the secular songs of slavery, the new Black poetry burst forth out of a time of racial turmoil. The catalyst for creativity was a series of events beginning with the Montgomery bus boycott and encompassing the nonviolent sit-in demonstrations of the early 1960's and big-city riots of the mid-1960s. Behind the poets and their songs of bitter protest against racism in America, were the bombings, the assassinations, the burning ghettos, the screaming sirens, the violent confrontations, and the cruel awareness of spreading Black poverty amid white affluence.

The most forthrightly militant representatives of the new Black mood in poetry were the Broadside Press poets so called because their poems are social, political, and moral broadsides protesting against the body politic and the establishment. Before the Broadside Press poets emerged as a definable literary group, other poets had written protest poetry in the early 1960s, which was caustic, bitter, and at times mordantly cynical. But the poetry became more than bitter militant protest. Under the leadership of LeRoi Jones and others, there developed a Black aesthetic that, in one measure, prescribed the guidelines for Black poetic militancy. Under the racial pressures of the late 1950's and early 1960's Jones himself had undergone a metamorphosis, moving from an avant-garde aestheticism to a Black nationalism-activism.

In the process, he abandoned his 'slave' name and became Imamu Amiri Baraka. He also moved out of the deep melancholy and pessimism that permeate many of his earlier poems. His 'Black Art' indicates that his pessimism was replaced by a vigilant and militant activism. Indeed, 'Black Art' announces the credo of the new Black aesthetic - that the direct objective of all Black artistic expression is to achieve social change and moral and political revolution. Poems, Jones asserts, should be "fists and daggers and pistols to clean up the sordid Black world for virtue and love".

1. It can be inferred from the passage that the Broadside Press poets believed that poetry should be primarily
   (a) Entertaining   (b) Descriptive
   (c) Aesthetic   (d) Escapist
   (e) Remonstrative

2. The author mentions all of the following as indications of the new importance of Black poetry in the 1960's except
   (a) The appearance of several anthologies of Black poetry.
   (b) The appearance of new literary journals for Black literature.
   (c) Courses in Black literature at most colleges and universities.
   (d) New volumes of poetry by established Black writers.
   (e) The emergence of a committed Black literary group.

3. The primary purpose of the passage is to
   (a) Discuss the strengths and weaknesses of a new literary group.
   (b) Compare contrasting literary movements.
   (c) Analyze the impact of a literary movement on American social structure.
   (d) Describe a literary movement and the factors that influenced it.
   (e) Outline the history of a literary genre.

4. It is most likely that immediately preceding this passage the author had discussed
   (a) Black poetry of the 1950's
   (b) Black prose of the 1960's
   (c) Some minor Black poets of the 1960's
   (d) The racial atmosphere of America in the 1960's
   (e) The new periodicals devoted to Black literature

5. According to the passage, the new Black poetry was characterized by
   (a) Individual introspection
   (b) Profound despair
   (c) Moral pessimism
   (d) Psychological detachment
   (e) Social protest

6. According to the passage, the flourishing of Black poetry during the 1960's was chiefly a reflection of
   (a) An increased awareness of Black cultural heritage.
   (b) A renewed interest in the work of older Black poets.
   (c) The feeling that poetry is more expressive than prose.
   (d) The racial trouble in the United States at the time.
   (e) New goals the older Black writers had set for themselves.

7. The passage implies that LeRoi Jones' main contribution to the new Black poetry was to
   (a) Make other Black writers more aware of social conditions.
   (b) Attract the attention of Whites to Black literature.
   (c) Provide a link between the older and the younger generations of Black writers.
   (d) Provide the philosophy of the new Black literature.
   (e) Serve as a personal example of what the artist's role should be.

8. In which of the following ways is the passage organized?
   (a) A phenomenon is discussed and then further explained by its appearances in history
   (b) A trend is described, followed by an example of a group which exemplified that trend.
   (c) A hypothesis is stated and then proven through historical examples
   (d) A group is praised for its historical merits and then shown to be part of a larger movement
   (e) A perspective is analyzed and then called into question

EXPLANATIONS

1. **(e) Inference**
   Reading through the passage, the key word mentioned about the poetry of the Broadside Press poets is protest. Remonstrate means to protest or to argue forcibly. Hence (e) is the right choice. If you don't know what "remonstrate" means, you can still solve this question by eliminating all of the other answer choices when they do not fit your understanding of poetry's purpose in the passage. All other choices use words from the passage but none are relevant to the Broadside press. This question requires you to understand the basic purpose of poetry for the Broadside Press poets and translate that purpose into a single, descriptive word. (500)

2. **(c) Detail of the passage**
   All except (c) are mentioned as indication of the new importance of Black poetry in the 1960s. This is a clear and straightforward question that can be answered simply by referring back to the details contained in paragraph 1. You can rule out the other answer choices when you see them in the passage.

3. **(d) Purpose of the passage**
   The primary purpose of the passage is to describe the Black literary movement and factors like the awareness of spreading Black poverty amid white affluence that led to the literary movement. Hence (d) covers this well and comprehensively. The other choices either hint at only partial objectives of the passage or relate to unsupported arguments. (a) is incorrect because there are no weaknesses discussed; (b) because there is no comparison; (c) because no impact on social structure is discussed, and (e) because, although a history is discussed, this isn't a historical outline.

4. **(a) Inference**
   The author begins by comparing the sparse collection of Black poetry in the 1950s to the wealth of poetry from Blacks in the 1960s. The author then goes on to describe the explosion of Black poetry in the 1960s. Hence the proceeding passage would discuss (a). For this question one needs to just read the beginning of the passage; paragraph 1 provides all the evidence.

5. **(e) Detail of the passage**
   Evidence from paragraphs 1 and 2 highlight that the new Black poetry was characterized by bitter protest against racism in America. Hence choice (e).

6. **(d) Inference**
   Paragraph 2 sums the influencing factor behind the 1960s backlash of Black poetry in the United States.

The question is partially evidence supported and partially based on your ability to translate what you read into a summary of the paragraph.

7. **(d) Inference**

   Paragraph 3 says that under the leadership of LeRoi Jones there developed a Black aesthetic that in some measure prescribed the guidelines for Black poetic militancy. This is clearly captured by Choice (d) The question is partially evidence supported and partially based on your ability to translate what you read into a summary of the paragraph. (a) may have been true, but there was nothing specific about him doing this. (b) and (c) are not mentioned and can be immediately ruled out. (e) is close, but the essay describes LeRoi's leadership and ideas rather than specifically what he did as an example. This is a subtle distinction that makes (d) the better answer.

8. **(b) Organization of the passage**

   The passage runs from general to specific, describing the trend of black poetry in the 60s and ending with the Broadside Poets, a highly respected group of black writers working during this time. Therefore, (b) is correct. This passage is about a specific time in history, namely the 1960s, so (a) is incorrect as it refers to many appearances of a phenomenon through time. There is no hypothesis contained in the passage, since the author simply discusses writers and their activism. Therefore (c) is incorrect. (d) is tricky because it presents (b) backwards. In truth, the group is praised after the larger movement is described, not before it. (e) is wrong because, as stated earlier, the passage simply discusses writers and their activism and does not call into question his/her or anyone's perspective.

SOLVED PASSAGE – 2

II. **Read the passage below and answer the following questions.**

Although the twentieth century saw the rise of women as professional musicians, the majority of composers and performers were, and still are, men. The music industry in the U.S. and Britain overwhelmingly reflects the values of a patriarchal society; the success or failure of a female artist is based largely on her physical appearance and gendered performance style. Blues, rock, and pop began as genres dominated by men, and thus included styles of dress, lyrics, and sound born of a male perspective. The history of these genres, then, is also a history of women seeking to locate their space within a predominately masculine musical environment.

Women are always judged, in part, on their image, and it is through the manipulation of this image that some women artists have been able to push the boundaries of gender identity. Women have been able to enter popular genres of music either by playing with the aesthetics of masculinity, or by playing into a male expectation of femininity. Sexuality, therefore, is a tool women continue to use to shape and reshape their place within popular music.

Pushing boundaries is a balancing act, however, and a contradictory process. In order to gain access to the world of popular music, a female artist must at once be pleasing her audience, and, at the same time, remain true to herself as a woman. A desire to be too much "one of the guys" can lead to identity problems and ultimately to self-destruction. An artist's use of irony or parody may run the risk of being mistaken for genuineness, causing her to be objectified. Working within the limits of popular music has proven difficult and dangerous for women. But due to the professionalism and inventiveness of many female performers, the space for women in popular music is being expanded and redefined.

1. According to the passage, successful women in popular music
   I. parody their gender
   II. are under constant scrutiny by audiences
   III. use sexuality to their advantage
   (a) I only
   (b) III only
   (c) I and III
   (d) II and III
   (e) I, II, and III

2. The passage suggests which of the following about the 20th century?
   (a) Female musicians were tolerated because of their physical appearance.
   (b) Professional male musicians did not respect women.
   (c) Song lyrics changed over time to fit the most current female perspective.
   (d) Rapid technological advancements helped women achieve notoriety in music.
   (e) Women's musical progress happened slowly and with much struggle.

3. Which of the following best describes summarizes the main idea of the last paragraph?
   (a) Entering the music world is not easy for women but they are making progress.
   (b) Parody and irony are the only ways in which women can hope to achieve success in music.
   (c) Women in popular music cannot escape being judged on their appearance.
   (d) Women assume stereotypically female appearances in order to attract audiences.
   (e) Popular music has space for women if only they would seek it out.

4. The author is likely to have which of the following attitudes when advising women about the music business?
   (a) persuasive
   (b) cautionary
   (c) ambivalence
   (d) discouraging
   (e) hostile

5. From which of the following sources was the passage most likely excerpted?
   (a) A newspaper editorial
   (b) An American history textbook
   (c) A book on gender studies
   (d) A teaching manual
   (e) A music magazine

EXPLANATIONS

1. **(d) Detail of the passage**
   The passage states "In order to gain access to the world of popular music, a female artist must at once be pleasing her audience, and, at the same time, remain true to herself as a woman," indicating that audience opinion is central to a woman's success in music, so II is correct. III is also correct because the passage states: "Sexuality, therefore, is a tool women continue to use to shape and reshape their place within popular music." However, I is not stated in the passage. The passage states that parody can often lead to objectification. While it can be useful at times, it does not guarantee success and therefore is incorrect.

2. **(e) Inference**
   Only (e) is an inference based on actual information contained in the passage. (a) is partly true but the passage doesn't really mention tolerance; its focus is on acceptance of women in the music world. (b), (c) and (d) are never mentioned in the passage. (e) gets to the author's main point, and is backed up by several parts of the passage, which discuss the role of women in music and how it has changed over the century, with much trouble.

3. **(a) Main Idea**
   (c) brings up an idea from the first paragraph and therefore missed the main idea of the last. (b) misconstrues an issue in the last paragraph, while (d) brings up a detail from the last paragraph but misses the main idea. (e) is never stated anywhere in the paragraph and very much goes against the author's tone in the passage as a whole.

4. **(b) Tone**
   The author states in the last paragraph that popular music careers for women are "a balancing act" and

that "Working within the limits of popular music has proven difficult and dangerous for women." Clearly the author does not view popular music as welcoming towards women. The author is also not particularly positive in his or her description of the music world. Therefore the author is unlikely to be "persuasive" toward women seeking entrance into a music career. The author's knowledge of the subject and subsequent remarks about women show him or her to have a real opinion, and not be ambivalent. Hostile is too extreme for this author; just take a look at her subdued descriptions. If this essay were hostile, it would be very different in its writing style. Though the authors somewhat negative assessment of the music industry may cause you to think the answer is "discouraging," the author does however, explain that some women have been able to make real progress when he or she says "But due to the professionalism and inventiveness of many female performers, the space for women in popular music is being expanded and redefined." Therefore the closest attitude would be "cautionary." The author believes some women can be successful, but would likely warn any she met to be careful in the business.

5. (c) Category of Writing

The passage is most likely to come from a book on gender studies because it describes the challenges women face in a particular arena. It is not likely to be a newspaper editorial (it contains historical information and has little to do with events in the news) nor is it likely to come from a teaching manual (it does not contain directions or lessons) nor an American history textbook (the passage contains British, as well as U.S. history). A music magazine will contain articles on current trends in music, reviews, interviews, etc. This passage is too general and the language is a bit too sophisticated for a music magazine.

PRACTICE EXERCISE

I. Read the passage and answer the questions that follow.

The name of Florence Nightingale lives in the memory of the world by virtue of the heroic adventure of the Crimea. Had she died - as she nearly did - upon her return to England, her reputation would hardly have been different; her legend would have come down to us almost as we know it today - that gentle vision of female virtue which first took shape before the adoring eyes of the sick soldiers at Scutari. Yet, as a matter of fact, she lived for more than half a century after the Crimean War; and during the greater part of that long period all the energy and all the devotion of her extraordinary nature were working at their highest pitch. What she accomplished in those years of unknown labor could, indeed, hardly have been more glorious than her Crimean triumphs; but it was certainly more important. The true history was far stranger even than the myth. In Miss Nightingale's own eyes the adventure of the Crimea was a mere incident - scarcely more than a useful stepping-stone in her career. It was the fulcrum with which she hoped to move the world; but it was only the fulcrum. For more than a generation she was to sit in secret, working her lever: and her real life began at the very moment when, in popular imagination, it had ended.

She arrived in England in a shattered state of health. The hardships and the ceaseless efforts of the last two years had undermined her nervous system; her heart was affected; she suffered constantly from fainting-fits and terrible attacks of utter physical prostration. The doctors declared that one thing alone would save her - a complete and prolonged rest. But that was also the one thing with which she would have nothing to do. She had never been in the habit of resting; why should she begin now? Now, when her opportunity had come at last; now, when the iron was hot, and it was time to strike? No; she had work to do; and, come what might, she would do it. The doctors protested in vain; in vain her family lamented and entreated, in vain her friends pointed out to her the madness of such a course. Madness? Mad - possessed - perhaps she was. A frenzy had seized upon her. As she lay upon her sofa, gasping, she devoured blue-books, dictated letters, and, in the intervals of her palpitations, cracked jokes. For months at a stretch she never left her bed. But she would not rest. At this rate, the doctors assured her, even if she did not die, she would become an invalid for life. She could not help that; there was work to be done; and, as for rest, very likely she might rest ... when she had done it.

Wherever she went, to London or in the country, in the hills of Derbyshire, or among the rhododendrons at Embley, she was haunted by a ghost. It was the specter of Scutari - the hideous vision of the organization of a military hospital. She would lay that phantom, or she would perish. The whole system of the Army Medical Department, the education of the Medical Officer, the regulations of hospital procedure ... rest? How could she rest while these things were as they were, while, if the like necessity were to arise again, the like results would follow? And, even in peace and at home, what was the sanitary condition of the Army? The mortality in the barracks, was, she found, nearly double the mortality in civil life. 'You might as well take 1,100 men every year out upon Salisbury Plain and shoot them,' she said. After inspecting the hospitals at

Chatham, she smiled grimly. 'Yes, this is one more symptom of the system which, in the Crimea, put to death 16,000 men.' Scutari had given her knowledge; and it had given her power too: her enormous reputation was at her back - an incalculable force. Other work, other duties, might lie before her; but the most urgent, the most obvious, of all was to look to the health of the Army.

Adapted from: Eminent Victorians, Lytton Strachey (1918)

1. According to the author, the work done during the last fifty years of Florence Nightingale's life was, when compared with her work in the Crimea, all of the following except
   (a) less dramatic
   (b) less demanding
   (c) less well-known to the public
   (d) more important
   (e) more rewarding to Miss Nightingale herself.

2. The 'fulcrum' (para 1) refers to her
   (a) reputation
   (b) mental energy
   (c) physical energy
   (d) overseas contacts
   (e) commitment to a cause

3. Paragraph 2 paints a picture of a woman who is.
   (a) an incapacitated invalid
   (b) mentally shattered
   (c) stubborn and querulous
   (d) physically weak but mentally indomitable
   (e) purposeful yet tiresome

4. The primary purpose of paragraph 3 is to.
   (a) account for conditions in the army
   (b) show the need for hospital reform
   (c) explain Miss Nightingale's main concerns
   (d) argue that peacetime conditions were worse than wartime conditions
   (e) delineate Miss Nightingale's plan for reform

5. The series of questions in paragraphs 2 and 3 are.
   (a) the author's attempt to show the thoughts running through Miss Nightingale's mind
   (b) Miss Nightingale questioning her own conscience
   (c) Miss Nightingale's response to an actual questioner
   (d) Responses to the doctors who advised rest
   (e) The author's device to highlight the reactions to Miss Nightingale's plans

6. The author's attitude to his material is.
   (a) disinterested reporting of biographical details
   (b) over-inflation of a reputation
   (c) debunking a myth
   (d) uncritical presentation of facts
   (e) interpretation as well as narration

7. In her statement, Miss Nightingale intended to.
   (a) criticize the conditions in hospitals
   (b) highlight the unhealthy conditions under which ordinary soldiers were living
   (c) prove that conditions in the barracks were as bad as those in a military hospital
   (d) ridicule the dangers of army life
   (e) quote important statistics

II. **Read the passage and answer the questions that follow.**

14-lane, 7500 Crore Delhi-Meerut Expressway Launched By PM Modi December 31, 2015 14:33 IST NOIDA: Prime Minister Narendra Modi on Thursday launched a Rs. 7500 Crore project to widen the Delhi-

Meerut highway and replace it with an expressway to decongest Delhi. He described it as the "road to freedom from pollution." The road connecting Meerut to Delhi is the busiest highway in the region, Union minister Nitin Gadkari said minutes before the prime minister spoke. The expressway will do away with 31 traffic signals on the road and make it "signal free", reducing travel time between Meerut and Delhi from two and a half hours to around 40 minutes, he said. "This highway will show the path to tackle pollution," PM Modi said. Delhi is the most polluted capital in the world." In the changing times, pace will not slacken. It will only get faster," he said. Mr Modi said his government will take forward the programmes started by the Atal Bihari Vajpayee government. "Vajpayee ji had two projects - the Golden quadrilateral connecting four corners of the country and he started a programme to give connectivity to villages," he said referring to the Prime Minister Rural Roads Programme. Even the villagers now are not satisfied with single lane roads. They want double lane and four lane roads. Every villager understands that if his village has to be connected to the path of development, his village must be connected to the highway," PM Modi said.

1. Which project has been launched by PM Modi?
2. In how many phases the project will be launched?
3. How much time will the new road save after it is ready to use?
4. How many projects did Mr Atal Bihari Vajpayee ji launch?
5. What is the total cost of the project?

HOTS

Read the passage and answer the questions accordingly.

SEAT BELTS

"Click!" That's the sound of safety. That's the sound of survival. That's the sound of a seat belt locking in place. Seat belts save lives and that's a fact. That's why I don't drive anywhere until mine is on tight. Choosing to wear your seat belt is a simple as choosing between life and death. Which one do you choose?

Think about it. When you're driving in a car, you may be going 60 MPH or faster. That car is zipping down the road. Then somebody ahead of you locks up his or her brakes. Your driver doesn't have time to stop. The car that you are in crashes. Your car was going 60 miles per hour. Now, it has suddenly stopped. Your body, however, is still going 60 MPH. What's going to stop your body? Will it be the windshield or your seat belt? Every time that you get into a car you make that choice. I choose the seat belt.

Some people think that seat belts are uncool. They think that seat belts cramp their style, or that seat belts are uncomfortable. To them I say, what's more uncomfortable? Wearing a seat belt or flying through a car windshield? What's more uncool? Being safely anchored to a car, or skidding across the road in your jean shorts? Wearing a seat belt is both cooler and more comfortable than the alternatives.

Let's just take a closer look at your choices. If you are not wearing your seat belt, you can hop around the car and slide in and out of your seat easily. That sounds like a lot of fun. But, you are also more likely to die or suffer serious injuries. If you are wearing a seat belt, you have to stay in your seat. That's no fun. But, you are much more likely to walk away unharmed from a car accident. Hmmm... A small pleasure for a serious pain. That's a tough choice. I think that I'll avoid the serious pain.

How about giving money away? Do you like to give your money away? Probably not. And when you don't wear your seat belt, you are begging to give your money away. That's because kids are required to wear seat belts in every state in America. If you're riding in a car, and you don't have a seat belt on, the police can give you or your driver a ticket. Then you will have to give money to the city. I'd rather keep my money, but you can spend yours how you want.

Wearing a seat belt does not make you invincible. You can still get hurt or killed while wearing your seat belt. But wearing them has proven to be safer than driving without them. You are much less likely to be killed in a car wreck if you are wearing a seat belt. You are much less likely to get seriously injured if you are wearing one. So why not take the safer way? Why not go the way that has been proven to result in fewer deaths? You do want to live, don't you?

1. Which title best expresses the main idea of this text?
    (a) Car Accidents: Ways That We Can Prevent Them
    (b) Slow Down: Save Lives By Driving Slower
    (c) Seat Belts: Wear Them to Survive Any Wreck
    (d) Why Not? Improve Your Odds with Seat Belts

2. Which best expresses the author's main purpose in writing this text?
    (a) To inform readers about seat belt laws
    (b) To persuade readers to wear seat belts
    (c) To entertain readers with stories and jokes about seat belts
    (d) To describe what car accidents are like without seat belts

3. Which best defines the word alternatives as it is used in the third paragraph?
    (a) Being safe   (b) Being unsafe
    (c) Other choices   (d) Driving fast

4. Which statement would the author most likely agree with?
    (a) Being safe is more important than being cool.
    (b) Moving freely around a car is worth the risks.
    (c) Seat belts will keep you safe in any car accident.
    (d) You should be most concerned with your comfort.

5. Which argument is not made by the author?
    (a) Not wearing a seat belt can be expensive.
    (b) Penalties for not wearing a seat belt should increase.
    (c) Seat belts keep you from flying through the windshield.
    (d) Wearing a seat belt is cooler than suffering an injury.

SECTION 3
SPOKEN AND WRITTEN EXPRESSIONS

Spoken and Written Expression

Conversation is the spontaneous exchange of words, ideas and thoughts between two or more people. It is an important tool of socialization. The kind of choices with words or expressionswe make decides the flow and tone of our conversation. Our fluency and knowledge of words and phrases determine our ability to engage in and understand conversations based on different situations, like requesting, giving information, expressing surprise, pronunciation, etc.

Requesting

We use polite language when we make a request. Requests can range from asking for something like help, directions, permission, action, an object, food.

Example: Could you please close the box?

Can you please come here once?

Would you mind if I ask your help?

I request you to grant me leave.

Kindly allow me to talk.

I am sorry to trouble you but, I need your help.

I was wondering if I could borrow your pen for a minute.

Is there any chance you could call me back at three?

Pass me the salt, please.

When we make a request, the language we use should be polite and formal. We can use the modal verbs of request like 'can,' 'could,' 'would,' and 'will.' There are a variety of expressions in English language that can be used to sound polite while making a request. Some of them have been used in the above examples like, 'kindly allow me,' 'Do you mind,' and 'sorry to trouble you'.

Remember if you are not using polite language while making a request, you may sound rude or your language may sound commanding or ordering.

Giving Information

When you are giving information, it is important that you are clear, precise and effective. Too much of information articulated in lengthy and complex sentences may confuse the listener and the purpose of the conversation (i.e., giving information) may become futile. A clear, precise and effective delivery of information ensures you hold the attention of the listener; otherwise, they may get distracted or fail to understand you.

To be able to use language for giving information to someone else, you should first understand the following things yourself.

Example: What is the important information I am trying to convey?

What is the most important piece of information you want to give?

What is your relationship with the person you are talking to?

What is their background of the information you want to convey to them? (For eg. Do they already know some part of it? Do they have absolutely no idea about the information you are giving them?)

The language you use in your communication will depend on all these factors mentioned above.

You might have to give information in various contexts. A few examples are discussed below.

If somebody asks you for direction, you may say, "Take the right and then turn to the second left. The last house on that lane is Mina's house."

If you are updating someone about a certain notice or circular that they have not read yet but you are aware of, you may deliver the information in the following way, "There's going to be a drawing competition next Sunday at the Parade Ground at 10 am. Please carry your own stationery; drawing sheets will be provided by the organizers."

Expressing Surprise

Surprise is expressed in English not only through our tone of speaking but also through the language we use or, more precisely, through our choice of words in speaking. In speaking, it is important to make your voice go up at the end, so there is a rising intonation in your voice when you are expressing surprise. In writing, you can use exclamation marks (What a surprise!), question marks (Really?) or interjections (Wow!) to express surprise.

Example: I don't believe it!
You're kidding!
Wow! That's great!
Are you sure?

Pronunciation

Pronunciation is the way a word or a language is spoken, or the manner in which someone utters a word. Pronunciation of a word may vary from region to region, native vs. non-native speakers, duration of exposure to a language, education levels, social class, ethnic group, or speech/voice disorders. In spite of all the variations brought about by these influences, it is important to pronounce a word as close as possible to what is universally accepted. For example, the only difference in the sounds of the two words 'sit' and 'seat' is the sound of the vowel in between the consonants 's' and 't.' While there is a short vowel sound between 's' and 't' in the word 'sit,' there is a long vowel sound in between 's' and 't' in the word 'seat.' The difference is minor (only the length of the vowel sound) but in case of a wrong pronunciation, it may be difficult for the listener to understand exactly what is being said.

Pronunciations in English do not always follow a specific rule and there are many exceptions. Therefore, the best ways you can improve your pronunciation are by listening to native speakers of English and referring to dictionaries.

PRACTICE EXERCISE

I. Fill in the blanks below to complete the conversation.

Mishka: Hey Rene! I heard you got into IIT.

Rene: Yes, I did.

Mishka: (1) _____

Rene: It is, isn't it? But I studied real hard for my JEE.

Mishka: (2) _____

Rene: I guess next week. I've already submitted my fees there.

Mishka: (3) _____

Rene: Yup! I've been saving for this for a long time.

II. Fill in the blanks to complete the conversation.

Pete: Good Morning, Ma'am.

Mrs. Dixit: (1) _____

Pete: I'm fine, thank you. How are you?

Mrs. Dixit: I am fine too. This is my husband Ravi. Ravi, this is Pete, my student in the Art school.

Pete: (2) _____

Mr. Dixit: Same here, Pete.

Pete: I'll take your leave now. It was nice meeting you both, goodbye.

Mrs. Dixit: (3) _____

HOTS

Find the missing sentence to complete the paragraph.

In questions 1, 2, and 3, sentences 1 and 3 are given. Sentence 2 is missing. Find the right sentence for sentence 2 from the given options.

1. Dora: Anne, I notice you hardly practise tennis these days?

   Anne: _____

   Dora: I hope to see you at the tennis court next week.

   (a) I don't play tennis anymore.
   (b) I have got tennis elbow.
   (c) I am busy with my exams this week.
   (d) I practise football now.

2. Nancy: I have to buy a dress for my best friend.

   Lara: _____

   Nancy: She is visiting me this weekend.

   (a) You shouldn't waste money on your friends.
   (b) She lives abroad, doesn't she?
   (c) Where does she live?
   (d) Why don't you gift her shoes instead?

3. Sentence 1: Public speaking is the process of communicating information to an audience.

   Sentence 2: _____
   _____
   _____

   Sentence 3: The benefits of knowing how to communicate to an audience include sharpening critical thinking and verbal/non-verbal communication skills.

   (a) It involves communicating information before a large audience.
   (b) Public speaking dates back centuries
   (c) It is usually done before a large audience, like in school, the workplace and even in our personal lives.
   (d) There are so many reasons why everyone should learn how to speak in a public forum.

   In questions 4 and 5, sentences 1 and 4 are given. Sentences 2 and 3 are missing. Select two sentences that will complete the paragraph.

4. Sentence I: After the invention of PC and the internet, smart phones and tablet PC are the common gadgets that can be easily found among people in Indonesia.

   Sentence II: _____
   _____
   _____

Sentence III: _____

Sentence IV: In writing for example, many young students today tend to write using the keyboard rather than handwriting
   (a) Preliminary observation suggests that students who used IT or communication gadgets have developed a different attitude compared to those who are not.
   (b) Besides its advantages, these instruments change the way users communicating to the others.
   (c) From the writer's point of view, it is believed that the characteristic of these communication gadgets has influenced the way most young teenagers act, talk, and behave.
      (a) A, B   (b) C, B
      (c) A, C   (d) B, A

5. Sentence I: Gastronomy is becoming an important attribute in the development of niche travel and niche destinations.

Sentence II: _____

Sentence III: _____

Sentence IV: Does a destination's gastronomy contribute to the tourists' quality of experiences while visiting the destination?
   (A) For example, is there a gastronomy-tourism market segment?
   (B) The results of the study provide evidence suggesting that motivation to travel for gastronomy reasons is a valid construct.
   (C) Although the literature supports the view that there is a connection between tourism and gastronomy, little is known about gastronomy tourists.
      (a) A, B   (b) C, B
      (c) C, A   (d) B, A

SECTION 4
ACHIEVERS' SECTION

Some Thoughtful Questions

1. **In groups discuss whether wars are a good way to end conflicts between countries. Then present your arguments to your friends.**

   Answer:

   War brings in a lot of hatred and devastation with it. It exhibits the unseen and unfair side of humans. Nations fight a war sometimes for petty reasons like sharing or conquering a piece of land or due to religion. Soldiers who fight the war leave their families behind, their children become orphaned, and wives become widows when they lay down their lives for their respective countries. Therefore, wars are definitely not an ideal way to end conflicts and cause huge destruction to life and property.

   (**Note:** Students may depict their views in front of the whole class as per their own thinking).

2. **What kind of presents do you like and why? What are the things you keep in mind when you buy presents for others? Discuss with your friend.**

   Answer:

   On the personal front, I do not like the practice of exchanging costly gifts. However, if we really want to thank someone with a present, we can buy some flowers as a token of affection for the respective person. Due to this reason, we notice that on formal occasions, many guests bring flower bouquets as gifts to express their warm feelings.

   (**Note:** Students may depict their own views and discuss it with their friend as per their convenience).

3. **It is likely that someone who is original and intelligent does not do very well at school. Should such a learner be called a failure? If not, why not?**

   Answer:

   A learner who is original and intelligent, but does not do very well at school cannot be called a failure in life. This is because every student has their own set of strengths and weaknesses. People should try to nurture their natural talent and polish it in order to stand out in a crowd. One might not be academically bright, but might have hidden talent of painting, dancing etc. individual's talent is not always visible in their academic records. Hence, such people should be encouraged to showcase their hidden talent and be appreciated for it, instead of considering them to be an utter failure.

4. **Who, in your view, is an 'unusual' learner? What can schools do to draw out the best in unusual learners? Suggest whatever seems reasonable to you.**

   Answer:

   In my opinion, an unusual learner is one who is a genius in his/her own right. This means that a person who is bright and intelligent and has a hidden talent or skill needs to polish it from every angle.

   One of the best options for schools to draw out the best in unusual learners is to stop comparing or categorizing every child on the basis of their academic performance. They should stop measuring children by simply following mechanical methods of teaching. They should appreciate the hidden talent or skill of the learners and encourage them to polish their abilities in every aspect.

5. **Is fighting the only way of resolving differences of opinion? What else can be done to reach a mutually acceptable settlement?**

Answer:

No, fighting is never the only way to resolve differences of opinion. Any differences between two parties or people can be resolved in a coolheaded manner through discussion. Even if the difference of opinion continues, a middleman should try to resolve the conflict between the two parties peacefully.

6. **Have you ever been in a serious fight only to realize that it was unnecessary and futile? Share your experience/views with others frankly and honestly.**

   Answer:

   Yes, it is in human nature to pick a fight on minor issues sometimes. However, such fights or arguments can be resolved through discussion and respecting each other's point of view. Once both parties agree to resolve the conflict, they can do it peacefully without hurting each other's emotions and sentiments.

7. **Why do some of us find it necessary to prove that we are better than others? Will you be amused or annoyed to read the following sign at the back of the car in front of you?**

   "I may be going slow, but I am ahead of you."

   Answer:

   It is common in human nature when one person tries to pull down another by exhibiting one's superiority over the other person. We should avoid ego clashes and misunderstandings from creeping into our relationships with other people.

   In my opinion, I would be amused to read the sign "I may be going slow, but I am ahead of you." and take it on a lighter note and laugh it off.

8. **Given below is the outline of a story. Construct the story using the outline.**

   A young, newly married doctor .... freedom fighter .... exiled to the Andaman and Nicobar Islands by the British .... infamous Cellular Jail .... prisoners tortured .... revolt by inmates .... doctor hanged .... wife waits for his return .... becomes old .... continues to wait with hope and faith.

   Answer:

   In the year 1929, when India was under the British Raj, the English education system enlightened the minds of a few people. Gradually people started thinking progressively and were fighting hard to free the country from British rule. At that time, a young, newly-married doctor was framed in a conspiracy case and sent to Andaman and Nicobar Islands, which was located in the Bay of Bengal. He was a freedom fighter who was exiled to the infamous Cellular Jail for a few years. He, along with other prisoners in this jail, was subjected to inhuman torture due to the revolt made by the inmates. One day, he was hanged. But his wife kept waiting for his return until she grew old. However, she never lost her hope and faith and continues to wait for her husband to return someday.

9. **Here are some words. Arrange them in the order in which they would appear in the dictionary. Write down some idioms and phrasal verbs connected to these words. Use the dictionary for more idioms and phrasal verbs.**

   | close | draw | make | wonder | scrawny |
   | parted | clearing | sweet | light | pick |

   Answer:

   The words would appear in the following sequential order when arranged properly:

   | clearing | close | draw | light | make |
   | parted | pick | scrawny | sweet | wonder |

   Some idioms and phrasal verbs connected to these words are listed below:

   Clearing: clearing out, clearing the air, clearing off.

Close: a close shave, a close thing, a close call.

Draw: draw a blank, draw a line, draw interest.

Light: a light heart, bring to light, a guiding light.

Make: make a last-ditch effort, make a pass, make up your mind.

Parted: part with, parting of the ways, part and parcel.

Pick: pick out, pick at, take your pick.

Scrawny: scrawny thin, scrawny neck, scrawny persona.

Sweet: sweet tooth, sweet sixteen, sweet-speaking.

Wonder: little wonder, a nine days' wonder, do wonders.

10. Look at the following words.

    like – likeness

    punctual – punctuality

    The words on the left are adjectives and those on the right are their noun forms.

    Write the noun forms of the following words by adding -ness or -ity to them appropriately. Check the spelling of the new words.

    (i) lofty _____
    (ii) able _____
    (iii) happy _____
    (iv) near _____
    (v) noble _____
    (vi) enormous _____
    (vii) pleasant _____
    (viii) dense _____
    (ix) great _____
    (x) stable _____

    Answer:
    (i) lofty *loftiness*
    (ii) able *ability*
    (iii) happy *happiness*
    (iv) near *nearness*
    (v) noble *nobility*
    (vi) enormous *enormity*
    (vii) pleasant *pleasantness*
    (viii) dense *density*
    (ix) great *greatness*
    (x) stable *stability*

Subjective Section

1. **Punctuate the following lines correctly.**

   To become fluent readers students must read outside school hours Moreover students are expected to read at least one English classic every six weeks. They can also join book clubs reading groups and literature circles Finally I believe that all teachers in every content area should be responsible for teaching reading

   Answer:
   To become fluent readers, students must read outside school hours. Moreover, students are expected to read at least one English classic every six weeks. They can also join book clubs, reading groups and literature circles. Finally, I believe that all teachers, in every content area, should be responsible for teaching-reading.

2. **Use the following homonyms in sentences of your own to bring out the differences in meaning.**
   - (a) (i) sole (ii) soul
   - (b) (i) witch (ii) which
   - (c) (i) principal (ii) principle
   - (d) (i) role (ii) roll
   - (e) (i) pray (ii) prey

   Answer:
   - (a) (i) Sole: The sole of my shoe has torn.
     - (ii) Soul: Meditation provides peace to your soul.
   - (b) (i) Witch: She is playing role of a witch in the play.
     - (ii) Which: Which are your books?
   - (c) (i) Principal: I have written an application to the Principal.
     - (ii) Principle: My sports coach is a man of principles.
   - (d) (i) Role: I want the main role in the play.
     - (ii) Roll: Can you roll the sheet?
   - (e) (i) Pray: Please pray for me.
     - (ii) Prey: The tigress is very hungry and is hunting for a prey.

3. **List down all the different types of nouns along with examples of each.**

   Answer:
   There are different types of nouns namely:

   Proper nouns always start with a capital letter and refer to specific names of persons, places, or things. Examples: Volkswagen Beetle, Shakespeare.

   Common nouns are generic names of persons, things, or places. Examples: car, pizza.

   Concrete nouns refer to nouns, which you can perceive through your five senses. Examples: folder, sand, board.

   Abstract nouns unlike concrete nouns, are those, which you can't perceive through your five senses. Examples: happiness, grudge, bravery.

   Countable nouns refer to nouns that are countable and have a singular and plural form. Examples: kitten, video, ball.

   Mass nouns are the opposites of count nouns. Therefore, they are also called non-countable nouns, and they need to have 'counters' to quantify them like kilo, cup, meter, etc. Examples of Mass Nouns: rice, flour, garter.

   Collective nouns refer to a group of persons, animals, or things. Example: faculty (group of teachers), class (group of students), pride (group of lions).

4. **What are the different types of Adjectives of Number? Explain with examples.**

   Answer:
   The **Adjectives of Number** are used to show the number of nouns and their place in an order. There are three different sections within adjectives of number; they are:

Definite Numeral Adjective: Those adjectives, which clearly denote an exact number of nouns or the order of the noun. For eg., One, Two, Twenty, Thirty-Three etc. also known as Cardinals. First, Second, Third, Seventh etc. also known as Ordinals.

Indefinite Numeral Adjective: Those adjectives that do not give an exact numerical amount but just give a general idea of the amount. For e.g., Some, Many, Few, Any, Several, All. There were 'many' people present at the meeting.

Distributive Numeral Adjective: Those adjectives that are used to refer to individual nouns within the whole amount. For example; Either, Neither, Each, Another, Other, etc.

5. **Write the following sentence in all the 12 kinds of tenses:**

   'Jack plays in the park.'

   Answer:
   Jack plays in the park (Present simple). Jack played in the park (Past simple). Jack will play in the park (Future simple). Jack is playing in the park (Present progressive). Jack was playing in the park (Past progressive). Jack will be playing in the park (Future progressive). Jack has played in the park (Present perfect). Jack had played in the park (Past perfect). Jack will have played in the park (Future perfect). Jack has been playing in the park (Present perfect continuous). Jack had been playing in the park (Past perfect continuous). Jack will have been playing in the park (Future perfect continuous).

6. **Tick the correct option.**

   In direct/indirect speech, the original words of the speaker are narrated (no/some change is made) and are/are not enclosed in quotation marks. On the other hand, in indirect/direct speech, no/some changes are made in original words of the person because these words have been uttered in present/past/future so the tense will/will not change accordingly and pronoun may also be changed accordingly. In direct/indirect speech, the statement of the person is/is not enclosed in quotation marks, the word "that" may be used before/after the statement to show that it is direct/indirect speech. Direct/Indirect speech is also called reported speech because reported speech refers to the first/second part of direct/indirect speech in which something has been told by a person.

   Answer:
   In direct speech, the original words of the speaker are narrated (no change is made) and are enclosed in quotation marks. On the other hand, in indirect speech, some changes are made in original words of the person because these words have been uttered in past so the tense will change accordingly and pronoun may also be changed accordingly. In indirect speech, the statement of the person is not enclosed in quotation marks, the word "that" may be used before the statement to show that it is indirect speech. Indirect speech is also called reported speech because reported speech refers to the second part of indirect speech in which something has been told by a person.

7. **To make question tags, do you add negative tags to negative sentences or positive tags to positive sentences? Explain with examples.**

   Answer:
   No, to make question tags, we add positive tags to negative statements, as in, 'They aren't funny, are they?' and negative tags to positive statements, as in, 'They will come, won't they?'

8. **Identify the misspellings and re-write the passage with correct spellings.**

   In the anceint days, people used to spend their liesure time watching courageuos acts of deuls between human biengs and animals. It was quiet common in the Roman countryes. The fighters had to put there lives at stake for the amuzement of the spectators.

Answer:

In the ancient days, people used to spend their leisure time watching courageous acts of duels between human beings and animals. It was quite common in the Roman countries. The fighters had to put their lives at stake for the amusement of the spectators.

9. **Write the meanings of the following idioms and use them in sentences of your own.**
   (a) A boon in disguise
   (b) Break the ice
   (c) An eye for an eye
   (d) From cradle to grave
   (e) In black and white

   Answer:
   (a) A boon in disguise: a benefit in loss: His accident was a blessing in disguise because it gave him lots of time to think about his life while he was recovering.
   (b) Break the ice: to become more relaxed with a person whom you have not met earlier, to break the silence: A nice smile does a lot to break the ice.
   (c) An eye for an eye: This is an expression for retributive justice, where the punishment equals the crime: In some countries, justice operates on the principle of an eye for an eye, that is, if you kill someone, you deserve to die.
   (d) From cradle to grave: during the whole span of your life: The government promised to take care of us from the cradle to the grave.
   (e) In black and white: to give in writing: Your offer sounds good, but I want you to put it in black and white.

10. **Write the meaning of the following one words:**
    (a) Clarify   (b) Dermatologist
    (c) Ellipsis   (d) Fragile
    (e) Iconography

Answer:
(a) Clarify: Make clear
(b) Dermatologist: One who treates skin diseases
(c) Ellipsis: The ommission from a sentence of a work or words that would complete the construction
(d) Fragile: That which can be easily broken
(e) Iconography: Teaching by pictures and models

11. **The table below contains a list of nouns and some adjectives. Use as many adjectives as you can to describe each noun. You might come up with some funny descriptions!**

Nouns	Adjectives
Elephant	circular, striped, enormous, multi-coloured, round, cheerful, wild, blue, red, chubby, large, medium-sized, cold
Face	
Building	
Water	

Answer:

Nouns	Adjectives
Elephant	enormous, large, cheerful, wild, medium-sized
Face	round, cheerful, chubby,
Building	multi-coloured, blue, red, medium-sized
Water	blue, cold

12. **Fill in the blanks in the sentences below (the verbs given in brackets will give you a clue).**
    (i) The earth trembled, but not many people felt the _____. (tremble)
    (ii) When the zoo was flooded, there was a lot of _____ and many animals escaped into the countryside. (confuse)
    (iii) We heard with _____ that the lion had been recaptured. (relieve)
    (iv) The zookeeper was stuck in a tree and his _____ was filmed by the TV crew. (rescue)

(v) There was much _____ in the village when the snake charmer came visiting. (excite)

Answer:
(i) The earth trembled, but not many people felt the *trembling*.
(ii) When the zoo was flooded, there was a lot of *confusion* and many animals escaped into the countryside.
(iii) We heard with *relief* that the lion had been recaptured.
(iv) The zookeeper was stuck in a tree and his *rescue* was filmed by the TV crew.
(v) There was much *excitement* in the village when the snake charmer came visiting.

13. **Say whether the following sentences are in the Active or the Passive voice. Write A or P after each sentence.**
    (i) Someone stole my bicycle.
    (ii) The tyres were deflated by the traffic police. _____
    (iii) I found it last night in a ditch near my house. _____
    (iv) It had been thrown there. _____
    (v) My father gave it to the mechanic. _____
    (vi) The mechanic repaired it for me. _____

Answer:
(i) Someone stole my bicycle. ___A___
(ii) The tyres were deflated by the traffic police. ___P___
(iii) I found it last night in a ditch near my house. ___A___
(iv) It had been thrown there. ___P___
(v) My father gave it to the mechanic. ___A___
(vi) The mechanic repaired it for me. ___A___

14. **Change the following sentences into indirect speech.**
    (i) First man: We must educate our brothers.
    Second man: And try to improve their material conditions.
    Third man: For that, we must convey our grievances to the British Parliament.
    (a) The first man said that _____
    (b) The second man added that _____
    (c) The third man suggested that _____

    (ii) First soldier: The white soldier gets huge pay, mansions and servants.
    Second soldier: We get a pittance and slow promotions.
    Third soldier: Who are the British to abolish our customs?
    (a) The first soldier said that _____
    (b) The second soldier remarked that _____
    (c) The third soldier asked _____

Answer:
(i)
(a) The first man said that *they must educate their brothers.*
(b) The second man added that *they must try to improve their material conditions.*
(c) The third man suggested that *they must convey their grievances to the British Parliament.*

(ii)
(a) The first soldier said that *the white soldier got huge pay, mansions and servants.*
(b) The second soldier remarked that *they got a pittance and slow promotions.*
(c) The third soldier asked *who the British were to abolish their customs.*

15. Look at the italicised phrases and their meanings given in brackets.

    Mountains are nature (nature's best form and appearance) at its *best*.

    Your life is at *risk*. (in danger; you run the risk of losing your life.)

    He was *at his* (it was his best/worst performance.) *best/worst* in the last meeting.

    Fill in the blanks in the following dialogues choosing suitable phrases from those given in the box.

at hand	at once	at all	at a low ebb
at first sight			

    (i) Teacher: You were away from school without permission. Go to the principal _____ and submit your explanation.
    Pupil: Yes, Madam. But would you help me write it first?
    (ii) Arun: Are you unwell?
    Ila: No, not _____ Why do you ask?
    Arun: If you were unwell, I would send you to my uncle. He is a doctor.
    (iii) Mary: Almost every Indian film has an episode of love _____.
    David: Is that what makes them so popular in foreign countries?
    (iv) Asif: You look depressed. Why are your spirits _____ today? (Use such in the phrase)
    Ashok: I have to write ten sentences using words that I never heard before.
    (v) Shieba: Your big moment is close _____.
    Jyoti: How should I welcome it?
    Shieba: Get up and receive the trophy.

Answer:
(i) Teacher: You were away from school without permission. Go to the principal *at once* and submit your explanation.
Pupil: Yes, Madam. But would you help me write it first?
(ii) Arun: Are you unwell?
Ila: No, not *at all* Why do you ask?
Arun: If you were unwell, I would send you to my uncle. He is a doctor.
(iii) Mary: Almost every Indian film has an episode of love *at first sight*.
David: Is that what makes them so popular in foreign countries?
(iv) Asif: You look depressed. Why are your spirits *at a low ebb* today? (Use such in the phrase)
Ashok: I have to write ten sentences using words that I never heard before.
(v) Shieba: Your big moment is close *at hand*.
Jyoti: How should I welcome it?
Shieba: Get up and receive the trophy.

16. Write the noun forms of the following words adding -ance or -ence to each.
    (i) endure _____
    (ii) persist _____
    (iii) signify _____
    (iv) confide _____
    (v) maintain _____
    (vi) abhor _____

Answer:
(i) endure *endurance*
(ii) persist *persistence*
(iii) signify *significance*
(iv) confide *confidence*
(v) maintain *maintenance*
(vi) abhor *abhorrence*

17.
(i) Match words under A with their meanings under B.

A	B
Remote	difficult to overcome
Means	most prominent

Dominant	be overcome/ overpowered
formidable	method(s)
overwhelmed	far away from

(ii) Fill in the blanks in the sentences below with appropriate words from under A.

(a) There were _____ obstacles on the way, but we reached our destination safely.

(b) We have no _____ of finding out what happened there.

(c) Why he lives in a house _____ from any town or village is more than I can tell.

(d) _____ by gratitude, we bowed to the speaker for his valuable advice.

(e) The old castle stands in a _____ position above the sleepy town.

Answer:
(i)

A	B
Remote	far away from
Means	method(s)
Dominant	most prominent
formidable	difficult to overcome
overwhelmed	be overcome/ overpowered

(ii)

(a) There were *formidable* obstacles on the way, but we reached our destination safely.

(b) We have no *means* of finding out what happened there.

(c) Why he lives in a house *remote* from any town or village is more than I can tell.

(d) *Overwhelmed* by gratitude, we bowed to the speaker for his valuable advice.

(e) The old castle stands *dominant* above the sleepy town.

18. Look at these pairs of sentences.

Penny said to Jody, "*Will* you be back before dinner?"

Penny asked Jody if *he would* be back before dinner.

"How *are you* feeling, *Pa*?" asked Jody.

Jody asked *his father* how *he was* feeling.

Here are some questions in direct speech. Put them into reported speech.

(i) Penny said, "Do you really want it son?"

(ii) Mill-wheel said, "Will he ride back with me?"

(iii) He said to Mill-wheel, "Do you think the fawn is still there?"

(iv) He asked Mill-wheel, "Will you help me find him?"

(v) He said, "Was it up here that Pa got bitten by the snake?"

Answer:

(i) Penny asked his son if he really wanted the fawn.

(ii) Mill-wheel asked if Jody would ride back with him.

(iii) Jody asked Mill-wheel if he thought the fawn was still there.

(iv) Jody asked Mill-wheel if he would help him find the fawn.

(v) Jody asked Mill-wheel if it was up there that Pa got bitten by the snake.

19. Look at these two sentences.

He *tumbled* backward.

It *turned* its head.

The first sentence has an *intransitive verb*, a verb without an *object*.

The second sentence has a *transitive* verb. It has a direct object. We can ask: "What did it turn?" You can answer: "Its head. It turned its head."

Say whether the verb in each sentence below is transitive or intransitive. Ask yourself a 'what' question about the verb, as in the example above. (For some verbs, the object is a person, so ask the question 'who' instead of 'what').

(i) Jody then *went* to the kitchen.

(ii) The fawn *wobbled* after him.

(iii) You *found* him.

(iv) He *picked* it up.

(v) He *dipped* his fingers in the milk.

(vi) It *bleated* frantically and *butted* him.
(vii) The fawn *sucked* his fingers.
(viii) He *lowered* his fingers slowly into the milk.
(ix) It *stamped* its small hoofs impatiently.
(x) He *held* his fingers below the level of the milk.
(xi) The fawn *followed* him.
(xii) He *walked* all day.
(xiii) He *stroked* its sides.
(xiv) The fawn *lifted* its nose.
(xv) Its legs *hung* limply.

Answer:
(i) Jody then *went* to the kitchen. – **Intransitive**
(ii) The fawn *wobbled* after him. – **Intransitive**
(iii) You *found* him. – **Transitive**
(iv) He *picked* it up. – **Transitive**
(v) He *dipped* his fingers in the milk. – **Transitive**
(vi) It *bleated* frantically and *butted* him. – **Intransitive, Transitive**
(vii) The fawn *sucked* his fingers. – **Transitive**
(viii) He *lowered* his fingers slowly into the milk. – **Transitive**
(ix) It *stamped* its small hoofs impatiently. – **Transitive**
(x) He *held* his fingers below the level of the milk. – **Transitive**
(xi) The fawn *followed* him. – **Transitive**
(xii) He *walked* all day. – **Intransitive**
(xiii) He *stroked* its sides. – **Transitive**
(xiv) The fawn *lifted* its nose. – **Transitive**
(xv) Its legs *hung* limply. – **Intransitive**

20. **Identify the correct form of pronoun in the following sentences.**
    (i) Many of them came, but few stayed long.
    (ii) Give everybody something to eat before they leave.
    (iii) What did you bring?
    (iv) Did they teach themselves how to speak French?
    (v) After he cut himself, he went for a tetanus shot.
    (vi) All of those are expensive.
    (vii) I know the girl whose name is Jane.
    (viii) She walked downstairs.
    (ix) The boy ate his dinner.
    (x) Mia and Jones love each other.

Answer:
(i) Many (**Indefinite**), them (**Personal**), few (**Indefinite**)
(ii) Everybody, something (**Indefinite**), they (**Personal**)
(iii) What (**Interrogative**), you (**Personal**)
(iv) They (**Personal**), themselves (**Reflexive**)
(v) He (**Personal**), himself (**Reflexive**)
(vi) All (**Indefinite**), those (**Demonstrative**)
(vii) I (**Personal**), whose (**Relative**)
(viii) She (**Personal**)
(ix) His (**Pronominal possessive**)
(x) Each other (**Reciprocal**)

21. **Rearrange the following words / phrases so as to make meaningful sentences.**
    (i) all / have been eaten / mangoes / the
    (ii) school / rooms / our / forty / has
    (iii) cricket ball / leather / a / made of / is
    (iv) Italy / a young boy / to / art / study / went to
    (v) the boy / did / was / everything / very clever
    (vi) that boy / in Florence / grew up / to be / painter / the greatest

Answers:
(i) All the mangoes have been eaten.
(ii) Our school has forty rooms.
(iii) A cricket ball is made of leather.
(iv) A young boy went to Italy to study art.
(v) Everything the boy did was veiy clever.
(vi) That boy grew up to be the greatest painter in Florence.

22. **Give the past and past participle forms of the following verbs.**
    (i) Worry   (ii) Send
    (ii) Remove   (iv) Shake
    (v) Survive   (vi) Walk
    (vii) Dwell   (viii) Certify
    (ix) Fly   (x) Drink

Answer:

Main Verb	Past Tense	Past Participle
1. Worry	Worried	Worried
2. Send	Sent	Sent
3. Remove	Removed	Removed
4. Shake	Shook	Shaken
5. Survive	Survived	Survived
6. Walk	Walked	Walked
7. Dwell	Dwelled	Dwelled
8. Certify	Certified	Certified
9. Fly	Flew	Flown
10. Drink	Drank	Drunk

23. **In the following sentences underline each adjective.**
    (i) That programme is a good comedy.
    (ii) Two people can set up camp in a short time.
    (iii) James is popular with both young and old people.
    (iv) Those long questions were hard for me.
    (v) The melon was large and sweet.
    (vi) The window of the store was full of new, attractive clothes.
    (vii) Little work can be done on the project now.
    (viii) A thousand people turned up for the first conference.
    (ix) Many students study foreign languages.
    (x) Much rain fell during the month of June.

Answer:
(i) That programme is a <u>good</u> comedy.
(ii) <u>Two</u> people can set up camp in a <u>short</u> time.
(iii) James is <u>popular</u> with both <u>young</u> and <u>old</u> people.
(iv) Those <u>long</u> questions were hard for me.
(v) The melon was <u>large</u> and <u>sweet</u>.
(vi) The window of the store was <u>full</u> of <u>new</u>, <u>attractive</u> clothes.
(vii) <u>Little</u> work can be done on the project now.
(viii) A <u>thousand</u> people turned up for the <u>first</u> conference.
(xi) <u>Many</u> students study foreign languages.
(x) <u>Much</u> rain fell during the month of June.

24. **Use the following conjunctions to make sentences.**
    (i) Yet
    (ii) As if
    (iii) Though
    (iv) Nonetheless
    (v) Now that
    (vi) Because

Answer:
(i) Though he is poor <u>yet</u> he is honest.
(ii) Akash always talked in a haughty way <u>as if</u> he had conquered the world.
(iii) This place is comfortable <u>though</u> not so spacious.
(iv) It was a prohibited area. <u>Nonetheless</u>, the officer allowed us to see the peacock from near the gate. '
(v) <u>Now that</u> Kejriwal has become the CM, let's see what New Delhi gets to see.
(vi) The project cannot be approved <u>because</u> it lacks in many aspects.

25. **Change the following sentences to passive voice.**
    (i) She sings a song.
    (ii) Help Suhani.
    (iii) Are you writing a letter?
    (iv) I will finish the task before the evening.
    (v) The boy killed the ant.
    (vi) They took all the necessary precautions.
    (vii) They have informed him of his mother's death.
    (viii) The students did some research on the topic.

Subjective Section

(ix) The car hit the dog.
(x) The dolphins have learned many tricks.

Answer:
(i) A song is sung by her.
(ii) Let Suhani be helped.
(iii) Is a letter being written by you?
(iv) The task will be finished by me before the evening.
(v) The ant was killed by the boy.
(vi) All the necessary precautions were taken by them.
(vii) He has been informed of his mother's death,
(viii) Some research on the topic has been done by the students.
(ix) The dog was hit by the car.
(x) Many tricks have been learnt by the dolphins.

26. **Change the following sentences to active voice.**
(i) The guitar was played by Lisa.
(ii) The book is being read by Mary.
(iii) The rat is eaten by the cat.
(iv) A washing machine has been bought by him.
(v) The lucky draw will be won by him.
(vi) A stone was being thrown by the man.
(vii) The door had been locked by someone.
(viii) A seat was offered to them by her.
(ix) Some trees have been planted by the gardener.
(x) Some advice will be given to you by the doctor.

Answer:
(i) Lisa played the guitar.
(ii) Mary is reading the book.
(iii) The cat eats the rat.
(iv) He has bought a washing machine.
(v) He will win the lucky draw.
(vi) The man was throwing a stone.
(vii) Someone had locked the door.
(viii) She offered them a seat.
(ix) The gardener has planted some trees.
(x) Doctor will give you some advice.

27. **Change the following into indirect speech.**
(i) I said to Prerana, "How do you travel to office everyday?".
(ii) Shivam said to his mother, "Where does the rain come from?"
(iii) "Do you know the way to the paradise?" A crazy man asked me.
(iv) Maria said to her daughter, "At what time will you come back?"
(v) The man said to the mechanic, "By what time will you have fixed the tyre of my bike?"
(vi) Varun says to Tarun, "Where did you go yesterday?"
(vii) "Is there anything special in it?" She asked.
(viii) "Hark! I can smell something here" said Mr. Naik to his colleagues.
(ix) "Alas! we have lost the game." said Shishir to his friend.
(x) "How intelligent you are!" Manjiri said to her grandfather.

Answer:
(i) I asked Prerana how she travel to office everyday.
(ii) Shivam asked his mother where the rain comes from.
(iii) A crazy man asked me whether I knew the way to Paradise.
(iv) Maria asked her daughter at what time she would come back.
(v) The man asked the mechanic by what time he would have fixed the tyre of his bike.
(vi) Varun asks Tarun where he went yesterday.
(vii) She asked whether there was anything special in it.
(viii) Mr. Naik exclaimed with fear and said to his colleagues that he could smell something there.
(ix) Shishir exclaimed with sorrow and told his friend that they have lost the game.
(x) Manjiri told her grandfather that he was very intelligent.

28. Rewrite the sentences into direct speech from indirect speech.
  (i) Miara said that she wrote a letter.
  (ii) Kiran said that she was going to the temple.
  (iii) The teacher said that the Sun rises in the East.
  (iv) He said that he had been reading a novel.
  (v) Nelson said that he had been playing badminton.
  (vi) He ordered her to be careful.
  (vii) Raman exclaimed joyfully that she was very beautiful.
  (viii) He asked where she was going.
  (ix) He said that he didn't know the way and asked her if she did.
  (x) The Science teacher told the class that ice floats on water.

Answer:
  (i) Miara said, "I write a letter."
  (ii) Kiran said, "I am going to the temple."
  (iii) The teacher said, "The Sun rises in the East."
  (iv) He said, "I have been reading a novel."
  (v) Nelson said, "I have been playing badminton."
  (vi) "Be careful", he said to her.
  (vii) "How beautiful she is!" said Raman.
  (viii) He said, "Where is she going?"
  (ix) "I don't know the way. Do you?" he asked.
  (x) The science teacher told the class, "Ice floats on water."

Model Test Paper 1

For questions 1 and 2, identify the misspelt word.

1.
   (a) Throw (b) Through
   (c) Thorogh (d) Tough

2.
   (a) Ambivalent (b) Equavalent
   (c) Insolvent (d) Malevolent

Choose the word with same or similar meaning to the underlined word.

3. 'There is no <u>dearth</u> of talent in our country All we need is a TV programme to tap it.'
   (a) Absence (b) Abundance
   (c) Visibility (d) Shortage

For questions 4 and 5, choose the word with the opposite meaning to the underlined word.

4. 'This has been made possible with <u>persistent</u> efforts by everyone on the team.'
   (a) Constant (b) Tireless
   (c) Relentless (d) Sporadic

5. 'This cream <u>counteracts</u> the excessive loss of moisture in the skin.'
   (a) Blocks (b) Allows
   (c) Prevents (d) Checks

For questions 6 to 14, choose the best option.

6. A group of fish is called a _____.
   (a) gang (b) posse
   (c) shoal (d) army

7. 'The movie must be very good. It's got _____ reviews in the media.'
   (a) wordy (b) lopsided
   (c) meagre (d) rave

8. 'I look forward to _____ you.'
   (a) meet (b) meets
   (c) have met (d) meeting

9. 'How come you don't know, what _____ these days?'
   (a) she will be doing
   (b) will she be doing
   (c) is she doing
   (d) she is doing

10. 'Oh, Kate is such a darling, _____?'
    (a) is she (b) isn't she
    (c) wasn't she (d) isn't it

11. It has been raining incessantly _____ morning.
    (a) since (b) for
    (c) from (d) in

12. If something does not allow the light to pass through it, it is _____.
    (a) transparent (b) opaque
    (c) luminous (d) radiant

13. A 'knock on' effect, it is _____ effect.
    (a) straight (b) indirect
    (c) deep (d) superficial

14. The police are looking — the matter.
    (a) into (b) up
    (c) for (d) after

For questions 15 to 19, choose the part of the sentence that has an error.

15.
    (a) By the age of 13,
    (b) Maureen was able to walk normally,
    (c) but by then
    (d) she has learnt to curse her condition.

16.
    (a) The other day,
    (b) my son insisted on
    (c) go to a movie that
    (d) has been dubbed the worst movie of the year.

17.
    (a) 'I've told you
    (b) many a times
    (c) not to ride your bike
    (d) on the pavement.'

18.
    (a) Will you rather (b) he came
    (c) with us (d) to the museum?

19.
    (a) I believe that
    (b) the harder I work
    (c) the lucky
    (d) I would get.

For questions 20 to 23, read the story and answer the questions that follow.

Oliver Twist

by Charles Dickens

Introduced by : Garth Nix

Puffin: Puffin Classics 2008 Relaunch

Hardback Library Edition: £14.99

Paperback: £7.99

Audio Book: £5.99

E-book: £3.99

Special 15% discount for school students on any edition of their choice.

Age Group: 9 - 11 years

With an inspirational and light-hearted introduction by author Garth Nix, Oliver Twist by Charles Dickens is one of the twelve wonderful classic stories beingre published in Puffin Classics.

It is the classic story of an orphan boy who flees from a work house and comes to London to seek fortune, but gets involved in crimes there. It all begins after Oliver Twist asks nasty Mr. Bumble, in-charge of the workhouse,for more food, but is refused. On reaching London, Oliver runs into the Artful Dodger, a young pick pocket, who leads him to Faginand his gang of pickpockets.

Oliver narrowly escapes prison when a thieving mission goes wrong. Fortunately for him, he is adopted by a kind gentleman, Mr. Brownlow. Meanwhile, Fagin and the brutal Bill Sikes go in search of the young boy, determined to drag him back ......

Puffin: Publishing the most innovative and imaginative children's literature for generations at affordable prices!

20. For a student, the cheapest option is to buy_____ edition of Oliver Twist.
    (a) hardback (b) paperback
    (c) e-book (d) audio book
21. Apart from Oliver Twist, how many other'wonderful classic' stories has Puffin republished, according to the write-up?
    (a) 7 (b) 9
    (c) 11 (d) 12
22. The brief story line given here says nothing about which of the following?
    (a) Why Oliver Twist fled from the workhouse?
    (b) How Oliver meets the Artful Dodger and Fagin?
    (c) How Oliver's life changes for the better?
    (d) Whether Fagin and company find Oliver again?
23. How many characters of the story are mentioned in this write-up?
    (a) 4 (b) 6
    (c) 8 (d) 10

For questions 24 to 29, read the passage and answer the questions that follow.

Methane Leaks from Seabeds

You know that methane (CH_4) is a greenhouse gas that is emitted during the production and transport of coal, natural gas, and oil. Its emissions also results from livestock and other agricultural practices, and by the decay of organic wastes in municipal solid wastes landfills. But, did you know that the gas also leaks from seabeds, too? Yes, atleast in some areas on the Atlantic coast of the USA.

Scientists believe that methane stored under the seabed is one of the largest reserves on the planet. They have identified hundreds of 'seeps' along the American Atlantic coast — places where gas bubbles out of the sea floor — and believe that "tens of thousands"more seeps to be lying undiscovered. You would be surprised that seabed methane 'seeps' are not a new phenomenon. Scientists claim that they have continued for over 1000 years!

Some experts believe that climate change could cause huge quantities of methane to be released from the Arctic seabed and the others who believe that evidence, that suggest these underwater emissions have increased. While, it is likely that as global temperatures rise, more methane will be emitted from such seafloor reservoirs, most of the scientists doubt the amount released will be big, when compared to other natural sources.

This research has two important implications. First, it leads scientists to wonder where else suchleaks maybe going on or may occur in future. In case, these seafloor emissions are significantly high, they could radically change calculations of natural carbon emissions, scientists fear.

Secondly, undersea methane seeps could have serious implications for marine life. Since, methane increases the acidity of seawater and reduces its oxygen content of seawater; even small changes in acidity can interfere with the shell formation in small marine creatures, the foundation of ocean food webs. So, any impact on them will, in turn, have indirect effect on other things.

So, while the research doesn't suggest a huge increase in methane emissions to the atmosphere, the wider impacts of these findings may have significant implications for the world's oceans nonetheless. For example, the gas originating from these reservoirs could trigger a rat race among oil companies to determine whether they can be tapped for oil and natural gas.

24. The largest reserves of methane on the planet are believed to be located _____.
    (a) on the East Coast of the U. S. of America
    (b) in farmlands, organic and solid waste
    (c) at several locations under the seabeds
    (d) at sites where oil and natural gas are produced

25. Scientists have the evidence that such seepage of methane has been going on for_____ years, if not more.
    (a) one hundred   (b) one thousand
    (c) one million   (d) one billion

26. Scientists doubt that methane emissions _____.
    (a) will rise significantly with every rise in global temperatures
    (b) from seabeds will be huge in comparison to other sources
    (c) due to agriculture, waste decays, oil and gas production
    (d) from other natural sources will higher than any other sources

27. One of the two implications of research on methane leaks from seabed is that it could adversely affect the marine life. The other implication is that these leaks _____.
    (a) have left scientists in awe and fear of nature
    (b) have been slowly going on for ages now
    (c) can alter the estimates of natural carbon release
    (d) are significantly high and a cause of Alarm

28. 'So any impact on them'. Here, 'them' refers to _____.
    (a) undersea methane seeps
    (b) acidity and oxygen of seawater
    (c) small undersea organisms
    (d) ocean food webs

29. In the expression, 'whether they can be tapped for oil and natural gas'. The word, 'tapped' means _____.
    (a) discovered   (b) preserved
    (c) monitored   (d) exploited

SPOKEN AND WRITTEN EXPRESSION

For questions 30 to 34, choose the best option.

30. Which of the following expressions best expresses 'a doubt'?
    (a) It's obvious…
    (b) I'm not too sure…
    (c) I reckon…
    (d) It's beyond any doubt…

31. If someone says, 'It's yours for the taking.' He/she is _____.
    (a) offering something
    (b) asking for something
    (c) enquiring about something
    (d) refusing to lend something

32. Which of the following expressions is the most suitable for politely suggesting that' you have a different opinion'?
    (a) I refuse to agree…
    (b) I hate to disagree…
    (c) I would insist that …
    (d) I cannot but agree…

33. Which of the following is the most polite way of making a request?
    (a) Please, shut the door.
    (b) Can you shut the door, please?
    (c) Will you shut the door, please?
    (d) Would you mind shutting the door, please?

34. The expression 'make no mistake about it,'means the same as _____.
    (a) don't make a mistake
    (b) have no doubt
    (c) be careful
    (d) don't be distracted

For questions 35 to 43, choose the best option to fill in the blanks.

Sharon Draper — America's 1997 Teacher of the Year

Sharon Draper, a teacher of English at a school in Cincinnati, U.S.A., was worried when one of her eighth standard students, Richard _____(35)_____ neglected to do his homework. _____(36)_____ America's 1997 National Teacher of the year, Draper, finally resorted to, _____(37)_____ Richard, "If you don't start doing your work, I'm coming to your house for dinner." With several of his older siblings _____(38)_____ by Draper, Richard knew his teacher had _____(39)_____ formed a strong bond with his mother, Ruth Cissel. He immediately _____(40)_____ his homework! Ruth explains, "He knew that if he didn't, I was going to hear about it." Draper encourages parents to establish direct contact with their child's teachers _____(41)_____ in the year. "Then the parents understand the teacher's expectations and the child sees a _____(42)_____ front", she says.

"It is not important for parents to just tell their children that school is important; they need to show that learning doesn't stop with a grade or a diploma— _____(43)_____ ", she adds.

35.
    (a) hardly   (b) rarely
    (c) occasionally   (d) regularly

36.
    (a) Being named   (b) Named
    (c) Naming   (d) To name

37.
    (a) to tell   (b) tell
    (c) told   (d) teasing

38.
    (a) having taught
    (b) have been taught
    (c) having been taught
    (d) have been teaching

39.
    (a) before   (b) already
    (c) afterwards   (d) subsequently

40.
    (a) starts doing
    (b) had started doing
    (c) started doing
    (d) was to start doing

41.
    (a) early   (b) later
    (c) during   (d) throughout

42.
    (a) union   (b) unionist
    (c) united   (d) unifying

43.
    (a) it's the way to live
    (b) it's a way to life
    (c) its a way of life
    (d) it's the way of living

For questions 44 and 45, choose the correct stress pattern for the underlined words.

44. He took a <u>photograph</u> of me.
    (a) PHOtograph   (b) phoTOgraph
    (c) photoGRAph   (d) photograPH

45. 'Serena Williams is a picture of <u>concentration</u> in the court.'
    (a) CONcentration   (b) conCENtration
    (c) concenTRAtion   (d) concentration

ACHIEVERS SECTION

46. Choose the word with same or similar meaning to the underlined word.
'How can you be so <u>naive</u>, John?'
    (a) Shrewd   (b) Innocent
    (c) Careless   (d) Dishonest

Choose the part of the sentence THAT HAS AN ERROR.

47.
    (a) No sooner had
    (b) the police leave the scene
    (c) than the trouble
    (d) started brewing again.

For questions 48 to 50, choose the best option.

48. As a government official, he is _____ to a lot of classified information, which he must never disclose to anyone.
    (a) entitled   (b) privy
    (c) exposed   (d) party

49. '_____, I would think twice before making such a promise.'
    (a) If I am you
    (b) If I had been you
    (c) If I were you
    (d) If I would be you

50. Which of the following is the most formal way of making a request or seeking permission?
    (a) Is it okay, if I leave early today?
    (b) Can I leave early today, please?
    (c) Would you mind if I left early today?
    (d) I'm leaving early today, can I?

Model Test Paper 2

1. Identify the misspelt word.
   - (a) Remand
   - (b) Command
   - (c) Reccomend
   - (d) Commend

For questions 2 and 3, choose the word with same or similar meaning to the underlined word.

2. The <u>zealous</u> politician made promises that he knew he could not possibly keep.
   - (a) Jealous
   - (b) Enthusiastic
   - (c) Fantastic
   - (d) Callous

3. She is suffering from a <u>chronic</u> chest infection.
   - (a) Fatal
   - (b) Genetic
   - (c) Prolonged
   - (d) Untreatable

For questions 4 and 5, choose the word with opposite meaning to the underlined word.

4. Socrates was <u>profound</u> and eloquent and spoke straight from the depths of his heart.
   - (a) Unimpressive
   - (b) Superficial
   - (c) Artificial
   - (d) Controversial

5. The women were singing in <u>melancholy</u> tones.
   - (a) Amused
   - (b) Dismal
   - (c) Cheerful
   - (d) Hoarse

For questions 6 to 14, choose the best option.

6. Somebody who is respected because of age or some distinction, called.
   - (a) eminent
   - (b) illustrious
   - (c) prominent
   - (d) venerable

7. Mr. Watson, my new neighbour, is such a pain in the —
   - (a) neck
   - (b) mind
   - (c) heart
   - (d) head

8. Someone who watches too much TV, sitting or lying down, is called:
   - (a) a mouse potato
   - (b) a hot potato
   - (c) a small potato
   - (d) a couch potato

9. The fiftieth anniversary of any event is called .
   - (a) Silver Jubilee
   - (b) Golden Jubilee
   - (c) Diamond Jubilee
   - (d) Platinum Jubilee

10. After his father's death, Tim had to look — the family business.
    - (a) after
    - (b) into
    - (c) at
    - (d) up

11. Mr. Wilson is — old to take the stairs to his fifth floor apartment.
    - (a) much
    - (b) very
    - (c) so
    - (d) too

12. The musician was playing the final piece when we — the auditorium.
    - (a) were to enter
    - (b) had entered
    - (c) have entered
    - (d) entered

13. 'Maria, can you find out the baby is crying? Does she need a change?'
    - (a) where
    - (b) when
    - (c) why
    - (d) how

14. It's definitely something to aspire .
    - (a) of
    - (b) to
    - (c) by
    - (d) with

For questions 15 to 19, choose the part of the sentence that has an error.

15.
    - (a) Yesterday,
    - (b) Bryan bought a new car
    - (c) and drives it
    - (d) to his home in Hong Kong.

16.
    - (a) I'll visit you
    - (b) when I will come
    - (c) to Chennai
    - (d) next week.

17.
    - (a) She has
    - (b) a
    - (c) good news
    - (d) for you.

214   International English Olympiad – 8

18.
   - (a) Vibhor
   - (b) is married
   - (c) with
   - (d) a dentist.

19.
   - (a) I have been
   - (b) waiting for you
   - (c) since
   - (d) more than two hours.

For questions 20 to 24, read the passage and answer the questions that follow.

Volunteers Set the Mood of the Games

Olympic Gold Medallist Rower Katherine Grainger was born and bred in Glasgow and strongly believes that people have got a great sense of humour. Speaking of the importance of volunteers in the forthcoming Commonwealth Games, she says, "I think that a sense of humour is really a huge requirement for a lot of the volunteer roles, especially in sports festivals. I reckon, it is more important than any previous experience of volunteering." She is very confident that the organisers will get plenty of right people for volunteering that everyone will get a chance to savour Scottish humour.

The volunteers she remembers most from London Olympics 2012 were those individuals with their own personalities. "You could never say that the Games Makers were a production line of certain people. They were different ages and from different backgrounds, and they'd all welcome you in a different way," she says.

An interesting incident, she recalls her encounter with a volunteer boy in the London Olympics 2012. When she turned up on the morning of her rowing final, a volunteer welcomed her and other team members and pointing to the chocolate medal in his neck, jokingly commented, 'Hey everyone, I bet you're jealous of my gold medal!' She and her team members could not help smiling.

Another thing about the London Olympics 2012 that left her particularly impressed were the long chains of volunteers on the way to and from the stadiums. The way they were high-fiving people, dancing and singing was the most amazing sight. They enhanced the excitement and gaiety of the extravaganza and painted a very positive picture of their country, she recalls. Commenting on the general notion that volunteering may be a thankless job, she says, "Some of the volunteering roles could perhaps have been seen as mundane or not particularly glamorous, but I believe volunteering is a crucial job and that volunteers should be made to feel admired, respected and loved. That would make them even happier to be doing those roles and rub off the feel-good spirit on everyone else."

"Volunteers can really set the mood of the Games. If you get it right, people arrive and leave happy," she says.

20. What kind of people, according to Katherine, are just right for volunteering?
   - (a) People who were born in Glasgow.
   - (b) People who can make others laugh.
   - (c) People who have experience of volunteering.
   - (d) People who understand Scottish humour.

21. A quality of the volunteers of London Olympics 2012 does Katherine remember most is the.
   - (a) similarities in their personalities and behaviour
   - (b) uniformity in their ages and backgrounds
   - (c) distinct character and conduct of each member
   - (d) common way in which they welcomed guests

22. The volunteer boy with a chocolate medal in his neck was trying to—Katherine and her teammates.
   - (a) Please
   - (b) taunt
   - (c) incite
   - (d) flatter

23. According to paragraph 4, Katherine was most impressed with the:
   - (a) extraordinary atmosphere of celebration that prevailed in the games
   - (b) way volunteers added to the charm and enthusiasm of the games
   - (c) amount of respect and affection that volunteers get from one and all
   - (d) extraordinarily large crowds of spectators that thronged the stadiums

24. The general view about most jobs of volunteering is that they are very .
    (a) stylish and very beautiful
    (b) ordinary and unrewarding
    (c) crucial jobs few can do well
    (d) interesting and happy jobs

For questions 25 to 29, read the passage and answer the questions that follow.

16-Feet Waves-Where There Was Once Only Ice!

i. National Geographic correspondent Jane J. Lee in a recent article describes how reduced sea ice has allowed the build-up of huge waves in the Beaufort Sea. She talks of sea waves as high as 16-feet in the Arctic Ocean where there was once only ice. Her fear is that because wave action breaks up sea ice, allowing more sunlight to warm the ocean, can trigger a cycle that leads to even less ice, more wind, and higher waves.

ii. According to Jane, scientists had hitherto never measured waves in the Beaufort Sea, an area north of Alaska because of the perpetual sheet of ice that prevented their formation. But, much of the region, she says, is now ice-free by September, and researchers have, as a result, been able to anchor a sensor to measure wave heights in the central Beaufort Sea in 2012.

iii. An alarming point that Jane raises is that if winds are free to blow for a longer distance over the open ocean, they can produce higher and higher waves. Sea ice restricts how far winds can blow, thus limits the formation of waves. The loss of this cover is, therefore, a cause of great concern.

iv. Jane talks of how scientists predict that in future larger waves may be rising, if the seasonal ice cover in the Arctic, continues to diminish.

v. If that happens, it will have serious implications for the world — shorelines may be getting hit with larger and larger waves, and could erode rapidly. Moreover, reduced ice cover could also alter the amount of carbon dioxide being exchanged between the atmosphere and the ocean. As a result, the Arctic may be releasing more greenhouse gas into the atmosphere.

vi. The amount of open water, Jane says, varies annually in the Beaufort. There is virtually no open water in April, when sea ice is at its maximum, but during sea ice minimums in September, it spreads over an area of 621 miles (1,000 kilometres). Although, the Arctic has been steadily losing its sea ice cover since the late 1970s that loss was particularly quick in 2002. The 16-feet waves the scientists' instrument picked up occurred during a powerful storm on September 18, 2012.

25. What gave rise to waves in the Beaufort Sea?
    (a) Scientific studies going on there.
    (b) Presence of gentle winds in the area.
    (c) Less sea ice due to warmer climate.
    (d) A shorter summer season.

26. Until recently scientists had not measured the sea waves in the Beaufort Sea because of .
    (a) its ice-free summers
    (b) its permanent ice-cover
    (c) their failure to deploy sensors there
    (d) the particularly bad weather there

27. In third paragraph of the passage suggests that the formation of waves can be limited if somehow.
    (a) the ice cover on the sea is further reduced
    (b) scientists carry out more studies in the area
    (c) winds can travel longer distance over the open sea
    (d) winds are not allowed to travel long distances

28. Larger waves in the Arctic, in future, may result in .
    (a) reduced CO_2 exchange between the ocean and the atmosphere
    (b) no open water in the Arctic in summer season
    (c) wider, thicker ice cover in winters in the Arctic
    (d) discharge of more greenhouse gases in the atmosphere

29. The year saw an increase in the speed at which the loss of the Arctic ice-cover occurred.
   (a) 1970 (b) 1972
   (c) 2002 (d) 2012

For questions 30 to 34, choose the best option.

30. You say 'You've got to be kidding me' when you doubt that someone is .
   (a) pretending to be a kid
   (b) worrying too much
   (c) not speaking the truth
   (d) trying to be extra polite

31. If you want someone else to go ahead of you or pass through ahead of you, which of the following expressions would you use?
   (a) You first, please.
   (b) After you, please.
   (c) First you, please.
   (d) Go before me, please.

32. If someone says, 'No worries', he/she wants to say ' '.
   (a) I'm a carefree person
   (b) there is nothing to lose
   (c) that's all right
   (d) what will happen, will happen

33. If you don't hear something properly, you can politely request the speaker to repeat what they said, by using the expression?
   (a) What?
   (b) Repeat.
   (c) Come again, please.
   (d) Once again.

34. After hours of struggle, when Bob finally succeeded in starting the car, Mary shouted in great excitement, ' !'
   (a) What the hell
   (b) Way to go
   (c) Oh, no
   (d) What the Dickens

For questions 35 to 43, choose the best option to fill in the blanks.

Delhi's Latest Tourist Attraction: Delhi Eye

Years after its construction, New Delhi's (35) tourist attraction, Delhi Eye is (36) open to public. Constructed (37) the famous flyers in London and Singapore, it has been created by the same Dutch company that made the Singapore Flyer. (38) an 18-storey building (45 metres or 200 feet), this Ferris wheel has cost approximately £7 million and has a total capacity of 288 people. Its 36 air-conditioned cabins offer a (39) view of the popular sites in the vicinity – (40) Akshardham Temple, Humayun's Tom and Lotus Temple, all in (41) of 20 minutes.

On a (42) day, one can even see Connaught Place from a distance. Its observatory-style experience would be special for the visitors, since the (43) view over Delhi is spectacular.

35.
   (a) lost (b) last
   (c) later (d) latest

36.
   (a) newly (b) partially
   (c) initially (d) finally

137.
   (a) along the lines of
   (b) in line with
   (c) out of line with
   (d) on the right lines

38.
   (a) So tall as
   (b) As tall as
   (c) More tall than
   (d) Much taller than

39.
   (a) naked eye (b) worm's eye
   (c) bird's eye (d) satellite's

40.
   (a) include (b) includes
   (c) included (d) including

41.
   (a) an interval (b) an area
   (c) a span (d) a section

42.
   (a) hazy (b) cloudy
   (c) clear (d) rainy

43.
   (a) overreaching (b) far reaching
   (c) within reach (d) beyond reach

For questions 44 and 45, choose the correct stress pattern for the underlined words.

44. Annual <u>examinations</u> are held in the month of June every year.
    (a) EXaminations (b) exaMInations
    (c) examiNAtions (d) examinaTIons

45. That's an interesting *activity*.
    (a) ACTivity (b) acTIvity
    (c) actiVIty (d) activiTY

46. Identify the misspelt word.
    (a) Dyeing (b) Fungi
    (c) Sking   (d) Taxing

47. Choose the part of the sentence that has an error.
    (a) She wants
    (b) to know
    (c) why
    (d) is the baby crying.

48. Choose the correct stress pattern for the underlined word.

    She is a well-known <u>choreographer</u> of the film industry.
    (a) CHOreographer
    (b) choreOgrapher
    (c) choreoGRAPHer
    (d) choreographER

For questions 49 and 50, choose the best option.

49. Someone who can speak many languages is called a/an .
    (a) orator   (b) linguistics
    (c) polyglot   (d) ventriloquist

50. If at a restaurant your friends say, 'Let's go Dutch', they mean to say that .
    (a) only one of the members will pay for all
    (b) they wish to try some Dutch dishes
    (c) they wish to eat in the way, the Dutch eat
    (d) everyone will pay for himself or herself

Answer Keys

Scan the QR Code to see the Hints and Solutions

Access Content Online on Dropbox: https://www.dropbox.com/scl/fi/x1il8nzpuzwm1qyz8yycu/NSO-01-Science-Olympiad-Hints-and-Solutions.pdf?rlkey=kzkx1753ie7dfs4rlkt3yo4pa&dl=0

SECTION 1: WORD AND STRUCTURE KNOWLEDGE

1. SPELLINGS AND COLLOCATIONS

Answer Key									
I									
1. (a)	2. (a)	3. (a)	4. (c)	5. (d)	6. (a)	7. (b)	8. (c)	9. (d)	10. (c)
11. (d)	12. (a)	13. (d)	14. (a)	15. (b)	16. (c)	17. (a)	18. (a)	19. (d)	20. (a)
21. (c)	22. (c)	23. (a)	24. (c)	25. (a)	26. (b)	27. (b)	28. (a)	29. (c)	30. (b)
31. (d)	32. (d)	33. (a)	34. (a)	35. (b)	36. (c)	37. (d)	38. (a)	39. (d)	40. (c)
41. (a)	42. (c)	43. (d)	44. (b)	45. (c)	46. (a)	47. (b)	48. (a)	49. (c)	50. (d)
51. (a)	52. (d)	53. (a)	54. (a)	55. (c)					
II									
1. (b)	2. (b)	3. (c)	4. (b)	5. (c)	6. (b)	7. (c)	8. (b)	9. (a)	10. (b)
III									
1. (a)	2. (b)	3. (c)	4. (d)	5. (d)	6. (a)	7. (b)	8. (c)	9. (d)	10. (d)
11. (a)	12. (b)	13. (c)	14. (d)	15. (d)	16. (a)	17. (b)	18. (c)	19. (d)	20. (d)

HOTS				
1. (c)	2. (a)	3. (d)	4. (b)	5. (a)

2. SYNONYMS, ANTONYMS, HOMONYMS AND HOMOPHONES

Answer Key

I

1. (d)	2. (c)	3. (b)	4. (a)	5. (a)	6. (c)	7. (d)	8. (c)	9. (c)	10. (c)
11. (b)	12. (a)	13. (a)	14. (d)	15. (b)	16. (c)	17. (a)	18. (b)	19. (d)	20. (c)
21. (c)	22. (d)	23. (a)	24. (c)	25. (d)	26. (d)	27. (b)	28. (b)	29. (d)	30. (c)
31. (a)	32. (c)	33. (d)	34. (b)	35. (a)	36. (d)	37. (d)	38. (b)	39. (b)	40. (b)

II

1. (c)	2. (d)	3. (a)	4. (b)	5. (b)	6. (c)	7. (b)	8. (a)	9. (c)	10. (d)
11. (d)	12. (b)	13. (c)	14. (c)	15. (d)	16. (c)	17. (c)	18. (b)	19. (d)	20. (a)
21. (a)	22. (d)	23. (b)	24. (c)	25. (b)	26. (c)	27. (a)	28. (d)	29. (c)	30. (c)
31. (c)	32. (d)	33. (a)	34. (a)	35. (c)	36. (d)	37. (a)	38. (d)	39. (b)	40. (c)

III

1. (a)	2. (b)	3. (b)	4. (b)	5. (c)	6. (b)	7. (b)	8. (a)	9. (b)	10. (a)
11. (b)	12. (b)	13. (a)	14. (b)	15. (a)	16. (b)	17. (b)	18. (b)	19. (a)	20. (b)
21. (b)	22. (b)	23. (a)	24. (b)	25. (b)	26. (a)	27. (b)	28. (b)	29. (a)	30. (a)
31. (b)	32. (b)	33. (b)	34. (b)	35. (b)	36. (c)	37. (b)	38. (a)	39. (b)	40. (b)

HOTS

| 1. (b) | 2. (d) | 3. (b) | 4. (a) | 5. (c) |

3. ANALOGIES AND ONE WORD

Answer Key

I

| 1. (d) | 2. (b) | 3. (b) | 4. (c) | 5. (d) | 6. (d) | 7. (d) | 8. (d) | 9. (b) | 10. (d) |
| 11. (c) | 12. (a) | 13. (c) | 14. (d) | 15. (d) | 16. (b) | 17. (d) | 18. (b) | 19. (d) | 20. (a) |

II

| 1. (d) | 2. (c) | 3. (d) | 4. (c) | 5. (c) | 6. (b) | 7. (b) | 8. (b) | 9. (d) | 10. (a) |

11. (d)	12. (c)	13. (a)	14. (c)	15. (c)	16. (d)	17. (a)	18. (c)	19. (d)	20. (a)
21. (c)	22. (c)	23. (d)	24. (c)	25. (d)					

III

1. (c)	2. (d)	3. (b)	4. (b)	5. (b)	6. (b)	7. (a)	8. (d)	9. (a)	10. (c)
11. (a)	12. (a)	13. (c)	14. (d)	15. (c)	16. (b)	17. (c)	18. (b)	19. (b)	20. (a)
21. (d)	22. (c)	23. (b)	24. (c)	25. (b)	26. (a)	27. (a)	28. (c)	29. (d)	30. (b)
31. (c)	32. (b)	33. (b)	34. (c)	35. (a)	36. (a)	37. (a)	38. (c)	39. (b)	40. (d)
41. (b)	42. (b)	43. (a)	44. (b)	45. (a)					

HOTS

1. (c)	2. (b)	3. (b)	4. (a)	5. (d)

4. PHRASAL VERBS, IDIOMS AND PROVERBS

Answer Key

I

1. (b)	2. (a)	3. (d)	4. (c)	5. (a)	6. (c)	7. (d)	8. (a)	9. (b)	10. (d)
11. (c)	12. (a)	13. (a)	14. (a)	15. (c)	16. (d)	17. (d)	18. (a)	19. (a)	20. (b)
21. (d)	22. (c)	23. (b)	24. (c)	25. (d)	26. (a)	27. (c)	28. (d)	29. (b)	30. (c)

II

1. (c)	2. (b)	3. (b)	4. (d)	5. (a)	6. (b)	7. (b)	8. (b)	9. (b)	10. (c)
11. (d)	12. (c)	13. (b)	14. (d)	15. (a)	16. (c)	17. (a)			

III

1. (b)	2. (c)	3. (c)	4. (a)	5. (d)	6. (c)	7. (a)	8. (c)	9. (c)	10. (d)
11. (a)	12. (c)	13. (a)	14. (d)	15. (c)	16. (b)	17. (b)	18. (d)		

HOTS

1. (c)	2. (c)	3. (d)	4. (c)	5. (b)

5. NOUNS AND PRONOUNS

Answer Key

I

1. (c)	2. (b)	3. (a)	4. (c)	5. (b)	6. (b)	7. (a)	8. (a)	9. (c)	10. (a)
11. (c)	12. (c)	13. (b)	14. (a)	15. (a)	16. (a)	17. (b)	18. (c)	19. (a)	20. (a)

II

1. (b)	2. (b)	3. (a)	4. (a)	5. (b)

III

1. (b)	2. (b)	3. (a)	4. (c)	5. (a)

IV

1. (a)	2. (a)	3. (a)	4. (b)	5. (a)	6. (a)	7. (a)	8. (a)	9. (a)	10. (a)

HOTS

I

1. (b)	2. (b)	3. (b)	4. (c)	5. (c)

II

1. (b)	2. (d)	3. (c)	4. (b)	5. (a)	6. (d)	7. (a)	8. (d)	9. (c)	10. (b)

III

1. (e)	2. (b)	3. (a)	4. (d)	5. (c)	6. (e)	7. (d)	8. (b)	9. (d)	10. (c)

6. VERBS AND ADVERBS

Answer Key

I

1. (d)	2. (a)	3. (b)	4. (d)	5. (b)	6. (c)	7. (c)	8. (a)	9. (d)	10. (a)

II

1. (b)	2. (c)	3. (d)	4. (a)	5. (b)	6. (b)	7. (d)	8. (b)	9. (a)	10. (b)

11. (d)	12. (c)	13. (a)	14. (d)	15. (a)	16. (d)	17. (d)	18. (c)	19. (c)	20. (a)
III									
1. (a)	2. (c)	3. (b)	4. (a)	5. (c)	6. (c)	7. (a)	8. (a)	9. (c)	
IV									
1. (a)	2. (c)	3. (a)	4. (c)	5. (c)	6. (c)	7. (b)	8. (b)	9. (a)	10. (a)
V									
1. (a)	2. (d)	3. (d)	4. (a)	5. (c)	6. (c)	7. (d)	8. (c)	9. (a)	10. (c)

HOTS				
I				
1. (b)	2. (c)	3. (a)	4. (d)	5. (a)
II				
1. usually	2. never	3. once	4. always	5. often

7. ADJECTIVES

Answer Key									
I									
1. (b)	2. (a)	3. (a)	4. (c)	5. (c)	6. (c)	7. (a)	8. (a)	9. (c)	10. (c)
II									
1. (b)	2. (c)	3. (a)	4. (c)	5. (a)	6. (a)	7. (b)	8. (b)	9. (a)	10. (b)

HOTS									
1. (c)	2. (a)	3. (d)	4. (c)	5. (c)	6. (b)	7. (d)	8. (b)	9. (d)	10. (b)

8. ARTICLES AND PREPOSITIONS

Answer Key

I

| 1. (a) | 2. (c) | 3. (b) | 4. (a) | 5. (c) | 6. (b) | 7. (a) | 8. (a) | 9. (a) | 10. (c) |

II

| 1. (a) | 2. (d) | 3. (b) | 4. (b) | 5. (c) | 6. (a) | 7. (a) | 8. (a) | 9. (c) | 10. (d) |

III

| 1. (b) | 2. (b) | 3. (a) | 4. (c) | 5. (d) | 6. (d) | 7. (b) | 8. (b) | 9. (d) | 10. (a) |
| 11. (d) | 12. (c) | 13. (d) | 14. (a) | 15. (c) | 16. (a) | 17. (c) | 18. (d) | 19. (d) | 20. (a) |

IV

1. (b)	2. (c)	3. (b)	4. (b)	5. (a)	6. (b)	7. (d)	8. (a)	9. (c)	10. (b)
11. (c)	12. (a)	13. (a)	14. (b)	15. (c)	16. (c)	17. (a)	18. (a)	19. (b)	20. (c)
21. (a)	22. (b)	23. (a)	24. (c)	25. (b)	26. (b)	27. (c)	28. (b)	29. (a)	30. (a)
31. (c)	32. (a)	33. (b)	34. (c)	35. (b)	36. (c)	37. (c)	38. (c)	39. (b)	40. (a)
41. (a)	42. (c)	43. (a)	44. (c)	45. (c)	46. (c)	47. (c)	48. (a)	49. (d)	50. (b)

HOTS

| 1. (d) | 2. (c) | 3. (b) | 4. (a) | 5. (c) | 6. (b) | 7. (e) | 8. (a) | 9. (a) | 10. (c) |

9. CONJUNCTIONS AND PUNCTUATIONS

Answer Key

I

1. (c)	2. (c)	3. (a)	4. (b)	5. (b)	6. (d)	7. (c)	8. (a)	9. (c)	10. (d)
11. (a)	12. (a)	13. (c)	14. (b)	15. (d)	16. (a)	17. (a)	18. (d)	19. (b)	20. (c)
21. (b)	22. (b)	23. (d)	24. (c)	25. (a)	26. (c)	27. (d)	28. (b)	29. (d)	30. (b)
31. (c)	32. (a)	33. (c)	34. (a)	35. (a)	36. (b)	37. (b)	38. (a)	39. (a)	40. (a)

II									
1. (d)	2. (a)	3. (a)	4. (b)	5. (d)	6. (c)	7. (c)	8. (b)	9. (c)	10. (a)
11. (a)	12. (d)	13. (d)	14. (c)	15. (d)					

III									
1. (d)	2. (a)	3. (b)	4. (d)	5. (d)					

HOTS

I									
1. (b)	2. (b)	3. (b)	4. (d)	5. (a)	6. (a)	7. (c)	8. (d)	9. (b)	10. (b)

II									
1. (d)	2. (a)	3. (d)	4. (d)	5. (c)	6. (d)	7. (c)	8. (d)	9. (b)	10. (a)

10. QUESTION TAGS

Answer Key

I									
1. (a)	2. (b)	3. (c)	4. (b)	5. (c)	6. (b)	7. (b)	8. (c)	9. (a)	10. (b)
11. (a)	12. (a)	13. (c)	14. (b)	15. (a)	16. (a)	17. (b)	18. (b)	19. (c)	20. (c)

II									
1. (a)	2. (d)	3. (b)	4. (d)	5. (a)	6. (a)	7. (d)	8. (d)	9. (b)	10. (a)
11. (b)	12. (c)	13. (d)	14. (c)	15. (b)	16. (c)	17. (b)	18. (b)	19. (d)	20. (d)

III									
1. (b)	2. (c)	3. (c)	4. (d)	5. (b)	6. (a)	7. (d)	8. (b)	9. (b)	10. (d)
11. (c)	12. (a)	13. (a)	14. (b)	15. (a)	16. (b)	17. (a)	18. (c)	19. (c)	20. (b)
21. (b)	22. (c)	23. (c)	24. (b)	25. (a)					

HOTS

1. (b)	2. (c)	3. (c)	4. (a)	5. (b)

11. TENSES

Answer Key

I

1. (c)	2. (a)	3. (c)	4. (c)	5. (a)	6. (a)	7. (b)	8. (a)	9. (b)	10. (b)
11. (b)	12. (a)	13. (c)	14. (a)	15. (a)					

II

1. (a)	2. (b)	3. (b)	4. (c)	5. (d)	6. (a)	7. (b)	8. (c)	9. (a)	10. (d)

III

1. (a)	2. (c)	3. (b)	4. (c)	5. (c)	6. (b)	7. (a)	8. (d)	9. (b)	10. (b)
11. (d)	12. (a)	13. (a)	14. (c)	15. (d)	16. (d)	17. (d)	18. (a)	19. (b)	20. (b)

HOTS

1. have had	2. have loved	3. have been thinking, have become	4. has been working, has enjoyed	5. have you been

12. VOICE AND NARRATION

Answer Key

I

1. (b)	2. (b)	3. (b)	4. (b)	5. (a)	6. (b)	7. (c)	8. (b)	9. (a)	10. (a)

II

1. (b)	2. (b)	3. (c)	4. (b)	5. (b)					

III

1. (b)	2. (c)	3. (b)	4. (a)	5. (c)	6. (b)	7. (b)	8. (c)	9. (a)	10. (c)
11. (c)	12. (c)	13. (c)	14. (b)	15. (a)	16. (a)	17. (a)	18. (c)	19. (b)	20. (a)

IV

1. (a)	2. (a)	3. (c)	4. (a)	5. (c)	6. (b)	7. (a)	8. (a)	9. (b)	10. (c)

V									
1. (c)	2. (b)	3. (b)	4. (a)	5. (b)	6. (b)	7. (b)	8. (b)	9. (a)	10. (a)
11. (b)	12. (b)	13. (b)	14. (c)	15. (b)					

HOTS

I									
1. (a)	2. (d)	3. (a)	4. (d)	5. (a)	6. (d)	7. (b)	8. (a)	9. (c)	10. (a)
11. (c)	12. (b)								

II		
1. (a)	2. (a)	3. (c)

III

1. He has been informed of his mother's death. (Active verb – has/have informed; passive verb – has/have been informed)
2. All the necessary precautions were taken by them. (Active verb – took; passive verb – was/were taken)
3. Has your job been finished by you? (Active verb – has/have finished; passive verb – has/have been finished)
4. Let him be helped. (Imperative sentences in the passive voice begin with let.)
5. The job will be finished (by me) by the end of this week. (Active verb – will finish; passive verb – will be finished)

IV				
1. (a)	2. (d)	3. (b)	4. (c)	5. (c)

Answer Keys

SECTION 2: READING COMPREHENSION

READING COMPREHENSION

Answer Key

I

| 1. (b) | 2. (a) | 3. (d) | 4. (c) | 5. (a) | 6. (e) | 7. (b) | | |

II

1. The project called 'road to freedom from pollution' has been launched by PM Modi.
2. The expressway will do away with 31 traffic signals.
3. The new road will save 1 hour 50 minutes after it is ready to use.
4. Mr. Atal Bihari Bajpayee ji launched two projects.
5. The total cost of the project is Rs. 7500 crores.

HOTS

| 1. (d) | 2. (b) | 3. (c) | 4. (a) | 5. (b) |

SECTION 3: SPOKEN AND WRITTEN EXPRESSION

SPOKEN AND WRITTEN EXPRESSION

Answer Key

I

1. Wow! That's awesome!	2. So when are you leaving?
3. Wow! That's great! All by yourself?	

II

1. Good morning, Pete. How are you?	2. Pleased to meet you, sir.
3. Bye Pete. See you tomorrow at the school.	

HOTS

| 1. (c) | 2. (b) | 3. (c) | 4. (d) | 5. (c) |

MODEL TEST PAPER – 1

Answer Key

1. (c)	2. (b)	3. (d)	4. (d)	5. (b)	6. (c)	7. (d)	8. (d)	9. (d)	10. (b)
11. (a)	12. (b)	13. (b)	14. (a)	15. (d)	16. (c)	17. (b)	18. (a)	19. (c)	20. (c)
21. (c)	22. (d)	23. (b)	24. (c)	25. (b)	26. (b)	27. (c)	28. (c)	29. (d)	30. (b)
31. (a)	32. (b)	33. (d)	34. (b)	35. (d)	36. (b)	37. (d)	38. (c)	39. (b)	40. (c)
41. (a)	42. (c)	43. (c)	44. (a)	45. (c)	46. (b)	47. (b)	48. (b)	49. (c)	50. (c)

MODEL TEST PAPER – 2

Answer Key

1. (c)	2. (b)	3. (c)	4. (b)	5. (c)	6. (d)	7. (a)	8. (d)	9. (b)	10. (a)
11. (d)	12. (d)	13. (c)	14. (b)	15. (c)	16. (b)	17. (b)	18. (c)	19. (c)	20. (b)
21. (c)	22. (a)	23. (b)	24. (b)	25. (c)	26. (b)	27. (d)	28. (d)	29. (c)	30. (c)
31. (b)	32. (c)	33. (c)	34. (b)	35. (d)	36. (d)	37. (a)	38. (b)	39. (c)	40. (d)
41. (c)	42. (c)	43. (b)	44. (c)	45. (b)	46. (c)	47. (d)	48. (b)	49. (c)	50. (d)

Appendix

There are different organizations that conduct these examinations and covering all of them is not needed as the focus should be to understand the main type of exams conducted. They are similar for these organizations with the difference being the change in name of the exam.

\multicolumn{3}{c}{Science Olympiad Foundation (SOF)}
S. No.	Name of Exam	Grade
1.	National Science Olympiad (NSO)	Class 1-10
2.	National Cyber Olympiad (NCO)	Class 1-10
3.	International Mathematics Olympiad (IMO)	Class 1-10
4.	International English Olympiad (IEO)	Class 1-10
5.	International Commerce Olympiad (ICO)	Class 1-10
6.	International General Knowledge Olympiad (IGKO)	Class 1-10
7.	International Social Studies Olympiad (ISSO)	Class 1-10

\multicolumn{3}{c}{Indian Talent Olympiad (ITO)}
S. No.	Name of Exam	Grade
1.	International Science Olympiad (ISO)	Class 1-12
2.	International Math Olympiad (IMO)	Class 1-12
3.	English International Olympiad (EIO)	Class 1-12
4.	General Knowledge International Olympiad (GKIO)	Class 1-12
5.	International Computer Olympiad (ICO)	Class 1-12
6.	International Drawing Olympiad (IDO)	Class 1-12
7.	National Essay Olympiad (NESO)	Class 1-12
8.	National Social Studies Olympiad (NSSO)	Class 1-12

\multicolumn{3}{c}{EduHeal Foundation}
S. No.	Name of Exam	Grade
1.	Eduheal International Cyber Olympiad (ICO)	Class 1-12
2.	Eduheal International English Olympiad (IEO)	Class 1-12
3.	National Interactive Math Olympiad (NIMO)	Class 1-12
4.	National Interactive Science Olympiad (NISO)	Class 1-12
5.	International General Knowledge Olympiad (IGO)	Class 1-12
6.	National Space Science Olympiad (NSSO)	Class 1-12

Humming Bird Education

S. No.	Name of Exam	Grade
1.	Humming Bird Commerce Competency Olympiad (HCC)	Class 1-12
2.	Humming Bird Cyber Olympiad (HCO)	Class 1-12
3.	Humming Bird English Olympiad (HEO)	Class 1-12
4.	Humming Bird General Knowledge Olympiad (HGO)	Class 1-12
5.	Humming Bird Hindi Olympiad (HHO)	Class 1-12
6.	Humming Bird Mathematics Olympiad (HMO)	Class 1-12
7.	Humming Bird Science Olympiad (HSO)	Class 1-12
8.	Humming Bird Aptitude and Reasoning Olympiad (ARO)	Class 1-12
9.	Humming Bird Spelling Competition (Spell BEE)	Class 1-12
10.	Humming Bird Language Olympiad	Class 1-12

International Assessments for Indian Schools (IAIS) (MacMillan and EEA Collaboration)

S. No.	Name of Exam	Grade
1.	IAIS Maths Olympiad	Class 3-12
2.	IAIS ScienceOlympiad	Class 3-12
3.	IAIS English Olympiad	Class 3-12
4.	IAIS Digital Technologies Olympiad	Class 3-12

SilverZone Foundation

S. No.	Name of Exam	Grade
1.	International Informatics Olympiad	Class 1-12
2.	International Olympiad of Mathematics	Class 1-12
3.	International Olympiad of Science	Class 1-12

Unified Council

S. No.	Name of Exam	Grade
1.	Unified Council Cyber Exam	Class 1-12
2.	Unified International English Olympiad.	Class 1-12
3.	Unified International Mathematics Olympiad (UIMO)	Class 1-12

Unicus

S. No.	Name of Exam	Grade
1.	Unicus Non-Routine Mathematics Olympiad (UNRMO)	Class 1-11
2.	Unicus Mathematics Olympiad (UMO)	Class 1-11

3.	Unicus Science Olympiad (USO)	Class 1-11
4.	Unicus English Olympiad (UEO)	Class 1-11
5.	Unicus Cyber Olympiad (UCO)	Class 1-11
6.	Unicus General knowledge Olympiad (UGKO)	Class 1-11
7.	Unicus Critical Thinking Olympiad (UCTO)	Class 1-11
CREST (Online Mode)		
S. No.	Name of Exam	Grade
1.	Mathematics (CMO)	Classes KG-10
2.	Science (CSO)	Classes KG-10
3.	English (CEO)	Classes KG-10
4.	Computer (CCO)	Classes 1-10
5.	Reasoning (CRO)	Classes 1-10
6.	Spell Bee Summer (CSB)	Classes 1-8
7.	Spell Bee Winter (CSBW)	Classes 1-8
8.	Mental Maths (MMO)	Classes 1-12
9.	Green Warrior Olympiad (GWO)	Classes 1-12

How To Apply?

Anyone willing to participate in the Olympiad exam can follow these steps to apply for the exam:

- ☞ Log in to the official website of the conducting organization.
- ☞ Find the Registration Option to register
- ☞ Fill up the details such as Student Name, Parent Name, School Name, Class, Postal Address, E-mail Address, Password, etc.
- ☞ Select the subjects you want to apply for. Pay the necessary registration fees and you are done.
- ☞ You will receive necessary details on your email id.

There are no minimum marks required by the Olympiad conducting organizations to apply for the exam.

Awards

Based on the organization rules, students as well as schools participating in these exams are awarded with several recognitions based on the marks they score.

www.ingramcontent.com/pod-product-compliance
Lightning Source LLC
Chambersburg PA
CBHW081220170426
43198CB00017B/2674